SPEECH
IN THE
WESTERN STATES

Volume 1: The Coastal States

SPEECH
IN THE
WESTERN STATES

Volume 1: The Coastal States

Edited by

VALERIE FRIDLAND

TYLER KENDALL

BETSY E. EVANS

ALICIA BECKFORD WASSINK

Publication of the American Dialect Society 101

Supplement to *American Speech*, Volume 91

PUBLICATION OF THE AMERICAN DIALECT SOCIETY

Editor: ROBERT BAYLEY, *University of California, Davis*
Managing Editor: CHARLES E. CARSON, *Duke University Press*

Number 101

ISBN: 978-0-8223-7007-9

Library of Congress Cataloging-in-Publication Data

Names: Fridland, Valerie, editor. | Kendall, Tyler, 1976– editor. | Evans, Betsy, 1966– editor. | Wassink, Alicia, 1966– editor.
Title: Speech in the Western states / edited by Valerie Fridland, Tyler Kendall, Betsy Evans, and Alicia Beckford Wassink.
Other titles: Publication of the American Dialect Society ; no. 101.
Description: Durham : Duke University Press, 2016. | Series: Publication of the American Dialect Society ; Number 101 | "Supplement to *American Speech*, Volume 91." | Includes bibliographical references and index.
Contents: v. 1. The coastal states. Contents: The low vowels in California's central valley / Annette D'Onofrio, Penelope Eckert, Robert J. Podesva, Teresa Pratt, and Janneke Van Hofwegen — Between California and the Pacific Northwest: The front lax vowels in San Francisco English / Amanda Cardoso, Lauren Hall-Lew, Yova Kementchedjhieva, and Ruaridh Purse — "Do I sound like a valley girl to you?" Perceptual dialectology and language attitudes in California / Dan Villarreal — The vowels of Washington State / Alicia Beckford Wassink — Variation in West Coast English: The case of Oregon / Kara Becker, Anna Aden, Katelyn Best, and Haley Jacobson — Investigating the development of the contemporary Oregonian English vowel system / Jason Mclarty, Tyler Kendall, and Charlie Farrington — The coastal West and beyond: Looking forward.
Identifiers: LCCN 2016053086 | ISBN 9780822370079 (pbk. : alk. paper)
Subjects: LCSH: English language—Dialects–Pacific Coast (U.S.) | English language—Pacific Coast (U.S.)—Pronunciation. | English language–Spoken English—Pacific Coast (U.S.) | Pacific Coast (U.S.)—Languages.
Classification: LCC PE2970.W4 S644 2016 | DDC 472/.978–dc23
LC record available at https://lccn.loc.gov/2016053086

British Library Cataloguing-in-Publication Data available

CONTENTS

PREFACE

PENELOPE ECKERT

The development of dialect differentiation requires, at the very least, time and a significant mass of speakers. The East Coast has had plenty of both: almost 400 years and the highest population density in the continental United States. The West has had a little over 150 years for today's English dialects to form. And covering almost half the land mass of the United States, it has less than a quarter of its population. So what has this century and a half brought to English in the West? This volume is a start, focusing on the dialects of the three coastal states of the continental United States, Washington, Oregon, and California. Combining production and perception studies, it establishes that a century and a half has been ample time for the West Coast to become a distinctive, coherent, and diverse dialect area, with plenty of attitude to go with it.

The West has always been conscious of its separateness from the rest of the United States, and this is perhaps most intense on the coast. In the early years of the fur trade, it was not at all clear that the Northwest would become part of the United States rather than Russia or Great Britain. And similarities of urban coastal life have thrown the East and West Coasts into continued rivalry and competition, with robust discourses of cultural difference. But the West itself has its own differences, based in vastly distinct ecosystems yielding economic and sociocultural differences. While Washington, Oregon, and California are all coastal states, the coast is set off by mountain ranges from the more arid lands to the east, which are, in turn, diverse among themselves. And the 1,400 mile coastal stretch from San Diego to the Canadian border ranges from desert to rainland. Important independence movements, such as Cascadia (ranging from British Columbia to northern California), the state of Lincoln (combining eastern Washington with Idaho's panhandle), and the state of Jefferson (combining northern California and southern Oregon), are based in shared ecosystems and highlight divisions along the West Coast that transcend state lines. And there have been continuous proposals within California, from early settle-

Publication of the American Dialect Society 101 DOI 10.1215/00031283-3772846

ment times to the present, to partition the state in a variety of ways, along both north-south and east-west axes.

Current suggestions about partitioning California are based as much on cultural differences as on the environmental differences from which they've arisen. Hostility in the Northwest toward California has intensified in recent decades, becoming almost institutionalized in places like Seattle. But while differences along the coast are commonly expressed in terms of states and major cities, these discourses transcend political boundaries. Just as people in Seattle resent the intrusion of Californians with their money and attitudes, people in the far north of California express the same resentment of the "equity pioneers" who settle there from Los Angeles and the San Francisco Bay area. And people's placement of the north-south boundary in California creeps gradually southward from Shasta County in the extreme north, where people place the boundary just north of Chico, to Merced in the center of the state, where the boundary is placed just north of Bakersfield (Voices of California 2013). In other words, the West Coast is not just a set of three states, but an ecological and cultural continuum, hence most likely a linguistic one as well. As the chapters in this volume show, a century and a half has been sufficient time for the West Coast to become a coherent dialect area, with linguistic diversity matching the ecological diversity along the north-south axis.

According to *The Atlas of North American English* (Labov, Ash, and Boberg 2006), the West is a vast homogeneous dialect area stretching from the hundredth meridian to the Pacific. It shares with Canada what Labov (1991) has called the "Third Dialect," characterized by a low back merger (BOT and BOUGHT) and the nonraising of the low front vowel (BAT). But the atlas, which focuses on large urban areas, has thin coverage of the sparsely populated West, and because it focuses on sound changes that distinguish Eastern dialect areas, it has defined the West primarily in negative terms. Now that the West has accumulated enough dialectologists to cover the region more closely, we are moving toward a detailed Western dialectology, exploring not only urban areas, but also the rural areas that make up most of the region.

Just as it takes time to develop regional differences, it takes time to develop attitudes about them. And with cultural attitudes come language attitudes. Labov once (1966, 499) famously referred to New York as a "great sink of negative prestige." Other dialects of the East Coast don't have uniformly nice reputations either. The long years of economic and sociocultural conflict, even war, have yielded an array of highly distinctive dialects ranging up and down the East Coast, each robustly socially stratified and associated with sociocultural stereotypes. But speakers in the younger and less varied Midwest do not take the same notice of their dialects and certainly don't view them negatively. And at the other extreme from the East is the belief on the West Coast, perhaps particularly in the Northwest, that its English is the standard. More recently, the association of the California Shift with the highly stylized "valley girl" speech may well be the beginning of negative evaluation of a Western dialect, mirroring the distinction between the materialistic Surfer South and the crunchy Hippie North.

Early writings on West Coast dialects (e.g., DeCamp 1958–59) focused on the original migration from the East and the influence of Eastern dialects. But any such influence is long since buried under the West's early diversity and its more recent migrations. The dialectology of the United States has been a white Anglo dialectology, and interest in other groups has centered on the extent to which they conform to the narrowly defined regional patterns. But English in California was laid down on Spanish roots, and the Anglo dialect in much of California coexists with a quite distinct Chicano variety. With equal numbers of Latinos and white Anglos, which is California's regional dialect? What determines whether and how Asian Americans, African Americans, Native Americans, and other nonwhite populations participate in the vowel shifts we're finding? Diversity itself varies along the north-south axis, as the percentage of white Anglos increases gradually from southern California through northern Oregon, peaking in southern Oregon and decreasing somewhat in Washington State. Will there be regional differences in this participation and in these groups' contribution to the more general repertoire of the region? In other words, what will count as a dialectology of the West?

REFERENCES

DeCamp, David. 1958–59. "The Pronunciation of English in San Francisco." *Orbis* 7: 372–91; 8: 54–77.

Labov, William. 1966. *The Social Stratification of English in New York City*. Washington, D.C.: Center for Applied Linguistics.

———. 1991. "The Three Dialects of English." In *New Ways of Analyzing Sound Change*, edited by Penelope Eckert, 1–44. New York: Academic Press.

Labov, William, Sharon Ash, and Charles Boberg. 2006. *The Atlas of North American English: Phonetics, Phonology, and Sound Change*. New York: Mouton de Gruyter.

Voices of California. 2013. "Why Explore Dialectology?" Stanford University. http://web.stanford.edu/dept/linguistics/VoCal/dialectology.html.

ACKNOWLEDGMENTS

The editors would like to thank Penny Eckert and the research group at Stanford University for initiating the conversation about research on speech in the Western states that led to this volume. We are grateful for the willingness of our contributors to share their work to make this collection possible. This volume was built on a foundation tirelessly assembled by Bill Labov and his students, who planted the seed for subsequent systematic explorations of speech patterns, and so we would be remiss to not mention his important contributions to the field. We offer many thanks to Bob Bayley, Charles Carson, and the anonymous reviewer for their guidance and feedback. We also want to acknowledge the financial support provided by a variety of funding bodies for the research reported here. Lastly, we thank the speakers who gave their time so that they could be interviewed and without whom this volume would not have been possible.

Publication of the American Dialect Society 101 DOI 10.1215/00031283-3772857

1. INTRODUCTION

In 2012, a group of Western U.S. sociolinguists came together for an informal meeting at Stanford University to discuss current research on Western U.S. English dialects. The initiative was an attempt to find ways to align our research interests and encourage more work on the vastly understudied English dialects of this American region. As a result of this meeting, several participants began discussing how to synthesize our work on Western speech and organized a panel at the 2015 meeting of the American Dialect Society in Portland, Oregon. This book and the anticipated second volume to follow are a direct result of this initiative and the research presented at the ADS panel.

Our goal here is not only to examine more closely contemporary Western English dialects, but, more importantly, to build on the groundwork laid by Labov, Ash, and Boberg in their impressive *Atlas of North American English* (2006). The picture so far developed for the Western U.S. consists of both similarities and differences across the region. Simultaneously, however, it is a picture that is still only partially fleshed out, particularly in terms of how the vowel features relevant to a number of U.S. dialects are realized by Western speakers from a variety of ecologically and socially diverse backgrounds.

The chapters that follow focus on how a number of regionally defining differences in vowel positions are instantiated in parts of the West with very different migratory histories and, in modern times, with very different senses of place and practice. Owing to a dearth of concentrated sociolinguistic research in this region, knowledge of how extensive and how similar these vowel systems are across the U.S. West has been limited to broad overviews, such as that provided by Labov, Ash, and Boberg (2006), or in isolated studies of different aspects of phonology in a few Western states (Terrell 1976; Hinton et al. 1987; Luthin 1987; Moonwomon 1987; Di Paolo and Faber 1990; Faber and Di Paolo 1995; Hagiwara 1997; Fought 1999; Hall-Lew 2005, 2010; Conn 2006; Bowie 2008; Fridland and Macrae 2008; Fridland and Kendall 2012; Kendall and Fridland 2012; Kennedy and Grama 2012). This volume aims to serve as a point of departure for descriptions of the ways that American English vowels are phonetically variable within the West by examining the same key vowels in several different locales across the region. In this volume, we focus on the continental West

Publication of the American Dialect Society 101 DOI 10.1215/00031283-3772868

Coast states of California, Oregon, and Washington, with an anticipated volume still to come focusing on the Inland West.

The chapters in this volume address several of the most salient features associated with contemporary U.S. Western vowels—the low back vowel merger, short front vowel retraction, back vowel fronting, and, where relevant, the raising and fronting of /æ/ and /ɛ/ before /g/ (also called prevelar raising). A number of these features have been noted in other regions, for example, back vowel fronting in the South and Midwest, and short vowel retraction and low back merger in Canada (Labov, Ash, and Boberg 2006). We do not treat these vowel changes as a necessarily interconnected series of changes as has sometimes been done elsewhere or assume there is a relationship among the Western features and those found in other dialects. Instead, with this volume we attempt to clarify the types of phonetic variation found across the West and how they pattern in similar or distinct ways among speakers within the region and to note features that also appear in other regions of the United States. While previous research has often referred to changes in vowel systems in the U.S. West as a "vowel shift"—namely, the Canadian Vowel Shift or the California Vowel Shift—we employ caution when using this terminology to frame the work undertaken in the following chapters for two reasons. First, some scholars may use the term "shift" to refer to unrelated changes in a system, while others wish to suggest changes in a system that are systematically related, such as that described by Labov (1994). Avoiding the term "shift" limits such ambiguity. Second, it seems that the linguistic and chronological relationship among vowel changes in the U.S. West has not yet been firmly established. Therefore, referring to these changes as a chain shift (in the sense of Labov 1994) seems premature. A number of the salient features described in these chapters do appear to be recent variants and therefore might be considered changes in U.S. Western speech appearing this century. However, we hope the present research invites questions about and study of where these features began, are going, and how they are connected to similar features in Western vowel systems (or elsewhere) rather than seeking to make definitive claims about a "shift" pattern. As a reviewer so aptly put it, our goal here is to fill in the "there be dragons" areas of the map, areas that until now have simply fallen under the umbrella of the larger Western U.S. region.

It is important to note that authors of the chapters in this volume have used different elicitation materials and methodological approaches. Each author notes what procedures and measurement techniques were used in the data collection and analysis. This should be borne in mind when comparing across studies. For the purpose of clarity and continuity, authors use the conventions of the International Phonetic Alphabet throughout the chapters, though, in many cases, keywords in a B–T frame are used to highlight particular word classes and subclasses, following other recent PADS volumes (Yaeger-Dror and Thomas 2009). These frames are based upon those made for comparative study of English dialects by Wells (1982) but have been adapted to allow representation of the particular vowel changes and conditioning environments of interest to the present study of the U.S. West. Table 1.1 overviews this adopted Wellsian convention system, presenting lax vowels first, then tense, followed by diphthongs and (r)-colored vowels.

To help orient the reader with the areas under study in the chapters that follow, figure 1.1 presents a map depicting the Western portion of the United States with study locations identified. Each chapter also includes a map of the specific area explored in its study. We start our exploration of the West by examining vowel production in California. California is, in fact, one of the more extensively studied states in terms of Western speech, with recent work by Eckert (2008), Hall-Lew (2009, 2011), Podesva (2011), and Kennedy and Grama (2012), as well as early work by DeCamp (1958–59), the California Style Collective (e.g., Hinton et al. 1987; Moonwomon 1987), Luthin (1987), and Hagiwara (1997). Such work laid the foundation for the chapters included here, but this collection moves beyond the coastal urban speech described in such works to include more understudied areas inland and also to investigate perceptual aspects of vowel variation.

Chapter 2, "The Low Vowels in California's Central Valley," by D'Onofrio, Eckert, Podesva, Pratt, and Van Hofwegen, examines the vowels from the state's interior. This study, in contrast to most previous research

TABLE 1.1
B–T Frame Guide

Wells Keyword	*U.S. English*	*B–T Frame*	*Wells Keyword*	*U.S. English*	*B–T Frame*
KIT	ɪ	BIT	GOOSE	u	BOOT
DRESS	ɛ	BET	PRICE	aɪ	BITE
TRAP	æ	BAT	CHOICE	ɔɪ	BOY
LOT	ɑ ~ a	BOT	MOUTH	aʊ	BOUT
CLOTH	ɔ ~ a	BOUGHT	NEAR	ɪɹ ~ iɹ	BEER
THOUGHT			SQUARE	ɛɹ	BARE
STRUT	ʌ	BUT	START	ɑɹ	BAR
FOOT	ʊ	BOOK	NORTH	ɔɹ	BORE
NURSE	ɜɹ	BURT	FORCE	oɹ	
FLEECE	i	BEET	CURE	ʊɹ	BURR
FACE	e	BAIT	LETTER	əɹ	
GOAT	o	BOAT	COMMA	ə	

FIGURE 1.1
The Western United States

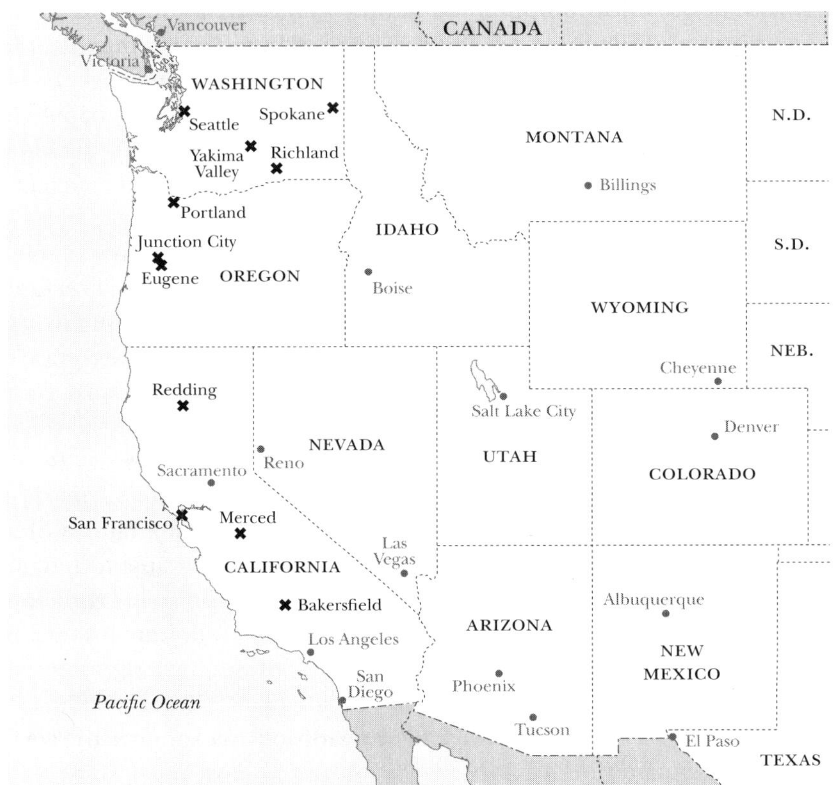

in California, investigates variation in the low vowels in three nonurban inland communities in the Central Valley: Bakersfield, Merced, and Redding (see figure 1.1). Focusing on /æ/, /ɑ/, and /ɔ/, the authors find that all three low vowel classes appear to be undergoing change, conditioned by community and sex in particular ways for each vowel class. While they find variation across all three communities that suggests they are in line with larger California norms, their work reveals that speakers in these sites have taken different routes to the contemporary vowel space. In other words, though similar to the vowel norms reported in other research on English in California, subtle differences indicated that "place" as locally defined is important in shaping the vowel system of these speakers

Chapter 3, "Between California and the Pacific Northwest: The Front Lax Vowels in San Francisco English," by Cardoso, Hall-Lew, Kementchedjhieva, and Purse, moves back to the coast, closely examining vowel variants in contemporary San Francisco speech, an urban community that, in early work, did not always show consistent Western speech features (e.g., exhibiting resistance to the low back vowel merger). Here, the area is revisited to explore the presence or absence of two Western U.S. English features in San Francisco: the retraction of the short front vowels and prenasal /æ/ raising found elsewhere in California and the prevelar raising of /ɛ/ and /æ/, features more often associated with Pacific Northwest English. In addition to providing an updated look at vowel variants first noted by Hinton et al. (1987) and building on earlier work by Hall-Lew (2010, 2011), Cardoso et al. also consider the role of ethnic group membership on participation in vowel variation, in particular comparing European Americans and Chinese Americans living in the same San Francisco neighborhood.

Moving beyond production norms, chapter 4, "'Do I Sound Like a Valley Girl to You?': Perceptual Dialectology and Language Attitudes in California," by Villarreal, examines what Californians themselves hear when listening to and rating speakers from various parts of the state. While often noted by outsiders as a salient speech variety (for example, *Saturday Night Live*'s parody "The Californians"), Californians' own perception of their speech, and in particular how it is affected by vowel positions, has not been widely studied. In this chapter, Villarreal examines residents' own perceptions of California speech to find how accurately Californians recognize speakers from different areas of the state and where they assess the most correct or pleasant speech to be located. A unique aspect of this research compared to earlier perceptual dialectology studies in California is its use of speech stimuli with varying concentrations of California vowel features, such as /æ/ retraction and /o/ fronting. This chapter provides a sense of how the vowel variants discussed in the earlier chapters on California vowels are viewed by Californians themselves.

Our next chapters move out of California and turn to the Pacific Northwest. Arguably the youngest of the continental North American dialect regions, the Pacific Northwest (including Washington, Oregon, and Idaho) has been subject to ongoing, variable linguistic input since the introduction of English to the region. While California's early migratory flows were predominantly from Eastern cities, such as New York, and Ohio coupled with substantial European and Mexican settlement, the Pacific Northwest had more early transnational migration by travelers originating from states in the American Midwest (including Illinois, Iowa, Indiana, Ohio), New England, and the American South. In addition, both Washington and Oregon, the states included in this volume, had substantial and diverse Native American populations that contributed to the diversity of speech in each area. In the chapters on Oregon and Washington speech, we see that modern Pacific Northwest speech still lays claim to some unique features but variably also shows evidence of the vowel norms found in California.

We start our exploration of the Pacific Northwest just south of the border with Canada. In chapter 5, "The Vowels of Washington State," Wassink examines Washington State English from the perspective of both previously noted Pacific Northwest features and more general Western features, such as back vowel fronting and the low back vowel merger. The study pays close attention to advancement of a feature first noted by Carroll Reed (1961, 561) in data collected for the Linguistic Atlas of the Pacific Northwest in 1953–63, the raising of /æ/ in voiced prevelar contexts, referred to as prevelar raising by Wassink et al. (2009). Here Wassink finds that the change has advanced beyond its distribution in Reed's day. One key distinctive aspect of the Pacific Northwest is its particular type of cultural diversity. Washington is unlike Eastern states such as Pennsylvania and New York, where strong ethnic enclaves formed not long after initial settlement. Interethnic contact has been a sustained part of Washington State history. Data from a multiethnic sample of 73 Washingtonians, distributed throughout the western, central, and eastern parts of the state, show widespread participation in Western features, as well as the newer changes specific to the Pacific Northwest.

From there, we move to Oregon, a state situated between Washington State and California. It is this placement, this proximity to multiple dialect influences, that informs "Variation in West Coast English: The Case of Oregon," by Becker, Aden, Best, and Jacobson. Examining the speech of 34 Oregonians, Becker et al. examine prevelar raising, a feature previously associated with Washington State, as well as features such as /o/ fronting and the low back vowel merger considered to be more panregional. Finally, the authors look for any evidence of the California vowel features discussed in the initial chapters, such as front short vowel retraction. Their work finds a linguistic melting pot of sorts in Oregon, with aspects of Washington State and California features, as well as general Western features, variably realized, though most are not fully instantiated. Using a perceptual map task, their research also suggests this variation in degree of participation in regional norms depends on speakers' ideologies about accent; that is, respondents whose map task suggests an ideology of nonaccent show different vowel realization than other speakers.

The final study, "Investigating the Development of the Contemporary Oregonian English Vowel System," by McLarty, Kendall, and Farrington, complements the research of Becker and colleagues by examining three generational cohorts of Oregon speakers to trace the development of the current Oregonian vowel configuration. With an eye toward tracking how vowel classes have changed over the course of the twentieth century, McLarty et al. use both contemporary speakers and archival speakers recorded in 1967 (years of birth, 1890–1914) for the *Dictionary of American Regional English* (*DARE* 1985–2013). They observe in both the contemporary sample and the archival data well-established Western features, such as the low back vowel merger, as well as newly noted features in neighboring states, such as short front vowel retraction and /o/ fronting, to establish which features are most relevant to Oregon speech and the time depth of those features.

In the chapters that follow, we hope to provide an impetus to other language scholars and dialectologists to look more closely at the complexity of larger vowel patterns as realized in local communities. Though much of this work is descriptive, the volume takes the important first steps toward understanding the vowel changes that have moved through the Western United States this past century and that continue to shape speech in the Western states.

REFERENCES

Bowie, David. 2008. "Acoustic Characteristics of Utah's CARD-CORD Merger." *American Speech* 83.1: 35–61. doi:10.1215/00031283-2008-002.

Conn, Jeff. 2006. "Dialects in the Mist (Portland, OR)." In *American Voices: How Dialects Differ from Coast to Coast*, edited by Walt Wolfram and Ben Ward, 149–55. Malden, Mass.: Blackwell.

DARE. Dictionary of American Regional English. 1985–2013. Edited by Frederic G. Cassidy and Joan Houston Hall. 6 vols. Cambridge, Mass.: Belknap Press of Harvard University Press.

DeCamp, David. 1958–59. "The Pronunciation of English in San Francisco." *Orbis* 7: 372–91; 8: 54–77.

Di Paolo, Marianna, and Alice Faber. 1990. "Phonation Differences and the Phonetic Content of the Tense-Lax Contrast in Utah English." *Language Variation and Change* 2.2: 155–204. doi:10.1017/S0954394500000326.

Eckert, Penelope. 2008. "Where Do Ethnolects Stop?" *International Journal of Bilingualism* 12.1–2: 25–42. doi:10.1177/13670069080120010301.

Faber, Alice, and Marianna Di Paolo. 1995. "The Discriminability of Nearly Merged Sounds." *Language Variation and Change* 7.1: 35–78. doi:10.1017/S0954394500000892.

Fought, Carmen. 1999. "A Majority Sound Change in a Minority Community: /u/-Fronting in Chicano English." *Journal of Sociolinguistics* 3.1: 5–23. doi:10.1111/1467-9481.t01-1-00060.

Fridland, Valerie, and Tyler Kendall. 2012. "Exploring the Relationship between Production and Perception in the Mid Front Vowels of U.S. English." *Lingua* 122.7: 779–93. doi:10.1016/j.lingua.2011.12.007.

Fridland, Valerie, and Toby Macrae. 2008. "Patterns of /uw/, /ʊ/, and /ow/ Fronting in Reno, Nevada." *American Speech* 83.4: 432–54. doi:10.1215/00031283-2008-030.

Hagiwara, Robert. 1997. "Dialect Variation and Formant Frequency: The American English Vowels Revisited." *Journal of the Acoustical Society of America* 102.1: 655–58. doi:10.1121/1.419712.

Hall-Lew, Lauren. 2005. "One Shift, Two Groups: When Fronting Alone Is Not Enough." In "Selected Papers from NWAVE 32," edited by Maciej Baranowski, Uri Horesh, Keelan Evans, and Giang Nguyen. *University of Philadelphia Working Papers in Linguistics* 10.2: 105–16. http://repository.upenn.edu/pwpl/vol10/iss2/9/.

———. 2009. "Ethnicity and Phonetic Variation in a San Francisco Neighborhood." Ph.D. diss., Stanford University. http://www.lel.ed.ac.uk/~lhlew/Hall-Lew_2009.pdf.

———. 2010. "Ethnicity and Sociolinguistic Variation in San Francisco." *Language and Linguistics Compass* 4.7: 458–72. doi:10.1111/j.1749-818X.2010.00207.x.

———. 2011. "The Completion of a Sound Change in California English." In *Proceedings of the 17th International Congress of Phonetic Sciences (ICPhS XVII), 17–21 August 2011, Hong Kong*, edited by Wai-Sum Lee and Eric Zee, 807–10. Hong Kong: City University of Hong Kong. https://www.internationalphoneticassociation.org/icphs-proceedings/ICPhS2011/OnlineProceedings/RegularSession/Hall-Lew/Hall-Lew.pdf.

Hinton, Leanne, Birch Moonwomon, Sue Bremner, Herb Luthin, Mary Van Clay, Jean Lerner, and Hazel Corcoran. 1987. "It's Not Just the Valley Girls: A Study of California English." In *Berkeley Linguistics Society: Proceedings of the Thirteenth Annual Meeting, February 14–16, 1987*, edited by Jon Aske, Natasha Beery, Laura Michaelis, and Hana Filip, 117–28. Berkeley, Calif.: Berkeley Linguistics Society. doi:10.3765/bls.v13i0.1811.

Kendall, Tyler, and Valerie Fridland. 2012. "Variation in Perception and Production of Mid Front Vowels in the U.S. Southern Vowel Shift." *Journal of Phonetics* 40.2: 289–306. doi:10.1016/j.wocn.2011.12.002.

Kennedy, Robert, and James Grama. 2012. "Chain Shifting and Centralization in California Vowels: An Acoustic Analysis." *American Speech* 87.1: 39–56. doi:10.1215/00031283-1599950.

Labov, William. 1994. *Principles of Linguistic Change.* Vol. 1, *Internal Factors.* Cambridge, Mass.: Blackwell.

Labov, William, Sharon Ash, and Charles Boberg. 2006. *The Atlas of North American English: Phonetics, Phonology, and Sound Change.* Berlin: Mouton de Gruyter.

Luthin, Herbert. 1987. "The Story of California (ow): The Coming-of-Age of English in California." In *Variation in Language: NWAV-XV at Stanford; Proceedings of the Fifteenth Annual Conference on New Ways of Analyzing Variation*, edited by Keith M. Denning, Sharon Inkelas, Faye C. McNair-Knox, and John R. Rickford, 312–24. Stanford, Calif.: Dept. of Linguistics, Stanford University.

Moonwomon, Birch. 1987. "Truly Awesome: (ɔ) in California English." In *Variation in Language: NWAV-XV at Stanford; Proceedings of the Fifteenth Annual Conference on New Ways of Analyzing Variation*, edited by Keith M. Denning, Sharon Inkelas, Faye C. McNair-Knox, and John R. Rickford, 325–36. Stanford, Calif.: Dept. of Linguistics, Stanford University.

Podesva, Robert J. 2011. "The California Vowel Shift and Gay Identity." *American Speech* 86.1: 32–51. doi:10.1215/00031283-1277501.

Reed, Carroll E. 1961. "The Pronunciation of English in the Pacific Northwest." *Language* 37.4: 559–64. doi:10.2307/411357.

Terrell, Tracy D. 1976. "Some Theoretical Considerations on the Merger of the Low Vowel Phonemes in American English." *Proceedings of the Second Annual Meeting of the Berkeley Linguistics Society*, edited by Henry Thompson, Kenneth Whistler, Vicki Edge, Jeri J. Jaeger, Ronya Javkin, Miriam Petruck, Christopher Smeall, and Robert D. Van Valin Jr., 350–59. Berkeley, Calif.: Berkeley Linguistics Society. doi:10.3765/bls.v2i0.2302.

Wassink, Alicia, Robert Squizzero, Mike Scanlon, Rachel Schirra, and Jeffrey Conn. 2009. "Effects of Gender and Style on Fronting and Raising of /æ/, /eː/ and /ɛ/ before /g/ in Seattle English." Paper presented at the 38th annual meeting of New Ways of Analyzing Variation (NWAV 38), Ottawa, Oct. 22–25.

Wells, J. C. 1982. *Accents of English 1: An Introduction.* Cambridge: Cambridge University Press.

Yaeger-Dror, Malcah, and Erik R. Thomas, eds. 2009. *African American English Speakers and Their Participation in Local Sound Changes: A Comparative Study.* Publication of the American Dialect Society 94. Durham, N.C.: Duke University Press.

2. THE LOW VOWELS IN CALIFORNIA'S CENTRAL VALLEY

ANNETTE D'ONOFRIO, PENELOPE ECKERT, ROBERT J. PODESVA, TERESA PRATT, *and* JANNEKE VAN HOFWEGEN

IN *THE ATLAS OF NORTH AMERICAN ENGLISH*, Labov, Ash, and Boberg (2006) outline a vast Western dialect area that includes just about everything west of the hundredth meridian. This is based primarily on the presence of the low back merger and the absence of salient features of other North American dialects. This volume represents an effort to complicate the dialect picture of the West, and this chapter seeks to complicate the dialect picture of California specifically.

Studies in the fifties, sixties, and seventies asked whether distinct dialects were developing in the West and focused on the Eastern origins of dialect features found in the West. Metcalf (1972, 28) concluded that indeed a regional dialect was emerging among young native-born Californians, but rather than yet another strongly distinctive dialect, this one was an emerging standard—"the general American of the future." He went on to say that California English "has modified itself to maintain a structure of its own while remaining as unobtrusive as possible." There is little question in 2016 that there is indeed a specifically California English, and a more obtrusive one than Metcalf was hearing. The variety spoken in the coastal cities has gained widespread attention thanks to the place of coastal California in the American imaginary. In what follows, we will shift attention to the rural Central Valley, the heartland of California.

Recent studies of coastal California have shown a robust vowel shift with three primary components:

1. The low back merger of BOT and BOUGHT (Hinton et al. 1987; Labov, Ash, and Boberg 2006; Hall-Lew 2009, 2013; Kennedy and Grama 2012).
2. The lowering and backing of the front lax vowels BIT, BET, and BAT in oral contexts (Hinton et al. 1987; Hagiwara 1997; Eckert 2008; Kennedy and Grama 2012).
3. The fronting of BOOT, PUT, BOAT, and BUT (Hinton et al. 1987; Hagiwara 1997; Fought 1999; Hall-Lew 2009; Eckert 2011; Kennedy and Grama 2012).

Publication of the American Dialect Society 101 DOI 10.1215/00031283-3772879

These changes constitute what has been referred to as the California Vowel Shift (CVS). Recent work (Geenberg 2014; Podesva et al. 2015), along with the present study in California's Central Valley, shows that this shift is not limited to the coast, and examination of the geographical breadth of California will eventually provide a more continuous view of developments throughout California. The first two of these components are shared with dialects in the Northwest and Canada, and other chapters in this volume take up the extent to which they are found outside of California. While we will continue to refer to developments in California as the California Vowel Shift, continuing work throughout the West will clarify whether there is actually one "Western Shift" or whether there is (more likely) a shared basis with different developments in some areas of the West.

The dialects of the West all have their structural origins in what Labov (1991) has called the "Third Dialect," based on a potentially stable configuration of the low vowels. Labov identified two pivot points, the front and back of the bottom of the vowel space, whose outcomes distinguish the three dialects. At the time of Labov's study, dialects of the West, parts of the East centering around Boston and Pittsburgh, and all of Canada shared singular phonemes at each of the pivot points. A single BAT phoneme (before nonnasals) in the front and merged BOT and BOUGHT in the back created a trapezoid, with fewer distinctions among the back vowels than the front. This configuration created stability by blocking major shifts among the mid and high vowels, but Labov noted that observations of BOOT fronting in California diminished the claim of general stability. More recent work on Canadian and Western dialects has established that this was in fact not a stable situation, for while the low back merger continues, BAT has moved out of its front corner into the territory of BOT, setting off a backing and lowering of the remaining lax front vowels BIT and BET. In what follows, we will focus on the pivot points—the low back merger and the lowering and backing of BAT—as the foundation of the CVS in particular and Western vowel systems more generally.

The low back merger was noted early on in coastal California (Metcalf 1972), and Labov, Ash, and Boberg (2006) shows the merger in Sacramento and the coastal cities of Southern California, but not in Fresno, Bakersfield, or San Francisco. More recent local studies find the merger well advanced among young speakers on the coast in both the south (Kennedy and Grama 2012) and in San Francisco (Hall-Lew 2013). Early observations of this merger (Metcalf 1972; Hinton et al. 1987) noted that BOUGHT was lowering and fronting, but Eckert (2010) found the merged vowel raising and backing among preadolescent speakers in San Jose.

The position of the merged vowel is closely tied to the position of BAT, and a backed outcome of BOT/BOUGHT is generally believed to have set a pull chain in motion (Clarke, Elms, and Youssef 1995; Boberg 2005; Bigham 2010; Roeder and Gardner 2013).[1] If Labov's Third Dialect was characterized by a broad-based trapezoid, the backing of BAT now narrows the base. Boberg (2011) has found that with the raising of BOT/BOUGHT, BAT in Canada has come to occupy the position as the lowest vowel in the system, converting the trapezoid to a triangle. Van Hofwegen (2015) has found this pattern among some speakers in California as well.

In the present study, we examine the relative and absolute location of the low vowels in relation to one another in California's Central Valley. We ask also whether these vowels pattern the same up and down the Central Valley.

METHODS

The data for this study consist of sociolinguistic interviews conducted in 2010–12 with residents of three communities in inland California: Bakersfield, Merced, and Redding. These field sites, shown in figure 2.1, mark the south, center, and north of the Central Valley, respectively. Interviews were conducted by student and faculty fieldworkers as part of the Stanford Linguistics Department's Voices of California dialectology project (http://web.stanford.edu/dept/linguistics/VoCal/). The initial aims of the project were to document dialect patterns in lesser studied parts of the state, particularly noncoastal and less urban areas. According to the U.S. Department of the Interior, the highly agricultural Central Valley produces a quarter of the nation's table food, supplying a majority of its fruits, vegetables, nuts, and dairy. Decisions about the regulation of these industries are made largely by legislators in Sacramento, elected primarily by those living in the more populous coastal cities, which has engendered feelings of disenfranchisement among many residents of the valley. It is unsurprising, then, that economic, social, and political orientations are more uniform among valley communities than they are between these communities and (sometimes geographically closer) coastal cities.

We examine the speech of 54 white residents, 18 from each community (evenly split by sex).[2] The ages of the 9 speakers representing each combination of field site and sex (e.g., women from Bakersfield) are evenly distributed across the adult lifecourse, from 18 to 80 years of age. Recordings were made at a sampling rate of 44.1 kHz and 16 bits, using solid state digital recorders (Marantz PMD660, Zoom H2, or Sony PCM-M10) and

FIGURE 2.1
Map of the Three Inland California Field Sites

directional lapel microphones (Audio Technica AT831b or Audio Technica ATPro70).

All interviews were orthographically transcribed in either Transcriber (Barras et al. 2001) or ELAN (Wittenburg et al. 2006), and forced alignments were generated using FAVE (Rosenfelder et al. 2011). Using the resultant textgrid in Praat (Boersma and Weenink 2012), potential tokens for all vowels of interest were extracted by script. The set of vowels included the target low vowels (BAT, BOT, and BOUGHT) and the remaining high corners of the vowel space for the purposes of normalization (BEET and POOL, which we use to refer to the BOOT vowel preceding /l/, a phonological context that impedes fronting). For each speaker, we manually adjusted the vowel onset and offset for up to 25 tokens per vowel class per speaker. Tokens were selected, in order, beginning 15 minutes into the interview. No more than two tokens per lemma were selected. We excluded function words, vowels lasting less than 75 ms, vowels preceded by other vowels, glides, and /r/, and vowels followed by other vowels, glides, and liquids. In cases where fewer than 25 tokens met these criteria, we first sampled tokens from the first 15 minutes of the interview, and then permitted a third token per lemma. A total of 5,399 tokens was considered. Measurements of the first five formants, fundamental frequency, and duration were then taken by script, and formant tracking errors were hand-corrected. Formant measurements were converted to a bark scale (Traunmüller 1997) and then normalized using the Fabricius, Watt, and Johnson (2009) method using the vowels package (Kendall and Thomas 2012) in R.[3]

We constructed a number of mixed-effects linear regression models using the lme4 package (Bates et al. 2014) in R, depending on the component of the CVS in question. For the backing of BAT, the response variable was BAT F2; lower values are assumed to correlate with greater backing. To quantify the BOT-BOUGHT merger, we calculated the Euclidean distance between each token of BOT and the same speaker's mean for BOUGHT; lower values are indicative of greater merger. We focused on the distance from individual BOT tokens to the speaker's mean BOUGHT (rather than the reverse) because the BOT vowel shows stronger social conditioning than BOUGHT, the reasons for which we discuss below. We did not measure the (speaker-level) degree of merger (e.g., with Pillai scores, as in Hall-Lew 2009) so that we could additionally take into account the linguistic factors (at the token-level) conditioning the distance between BOT and BOUGHT. For the raising of BOT, the response variable was BOT F1; lower values are indicative of greater raising. To gauge the extent to which BOUGHT is raised or lowered, we examined the F1 of BOUGHT; lower values indicate raising, while higher values indicate lowering. Finally, to ascertain the lowest vowel in the vowel space, for each speaker we calculated the difference between the mean BAT F1 and the mean BEET F1 and subtracted this from the difference between the mean BOT F1 and the mean BEET F1. Negative values indicate that the distance between BAT and BEET is greater than the distance between BOT and BEET, in other words that BAT is the lowest vowel in the vowel space; positive values indicate that BOT is the lowest vowel in a speaker's vowel space. We examine the F1 of the low vowels relative to BEET rather than simply normalized F1 because the former locates vowel height in a (phonological) system of contrasts, rather than in vowel space blind to contrast. For all models, we included age, sex, field site, and vowel duration[4] (log-transformed to meet the parametric statistics normality assumption) as fixed effects. Random effects (all intercepts) were included for speaker, lexical item, and preceding and following segments.

RESULTS

Results of the models indicate that social factors condition community-wide patterns for all three low vowel classes (BAT, BOT, and BOUGHT). Regression tables summarize these models for each measure. While we include the linguistic factors of duration and surrounding phonological environment as control predictors in these models, we focus here on the patterning of these variables according to the social factors of speaker age, sex, and site in the Central Valley.

BAT. We assess the movement of the BAT vowel in nonprenasal contexts by focusing on the front-back dimension of the vowel space, analyzing normalized F2. Note that the method of normalization we used converts Hertz values to a scale between 0 and 2. The regression predicting normalized F2 of BAT indicates main effects of speaker age, sex, and field site, with no significant interactions among the social factors (table 2.1). The main effect of speaker age shows retraction of BAT in apparent time, with BAT F2 decreasing significantly as speaker age decreases (indicating retraction in younger speakers as compared to older speakers). Furthermore, the model indicates that female speakers show significantly backer BAT vowels (lower F2) than male speakers. Finally, the main effect of field site indicates that speakers from Merced exhibited BAT vowels that are significantly less retracted than their Bakersfield and Redding counterparts. Following other work on the CVS, speakers in the Central Valley appear to be adopting BAT-retraction over time, with male speakers and speakers from Merced maintaining relatively more conservative, fronter BAT vowels.

BOT-BOUGHT DISTANCE. We measure distance between BOT and BOUGHT for a given speaker by analyzing the Euclidean distance between each of that speaker's BOT vowel productions and that speaker's mean BOUGHT vowel. BOUGHT was selected as the anchor, as BOT showed greater social conditioning than BOUGHT (see below). We then assess the degree to which

TABLE 2.1
Summary of Main Effects on BAT Normalized F2

	Estimate	*Std. Dev.*	*DF*	*T-Value*	*P-Value*
(Intercept)	1.04	0.0281	0.0243	36.991	<.0001
Log duration	0.0105	0.0043	1220	2.432	.0152
Sex = Male	0.0480	0.0118	49	4.067	.0002
Age	0.0016	0.0003	49.1	5.078	<.0001
Site = Merced	0.0334	0.0145	49	2.308	.0253
Site = Redding	−0.0032	0.0145	49.1	−0.218	.8282

social factors predict this distance, with smaller distance indicating vowel classes more likely to be merged and greater distance indicating more likely to be distinct. The regression analysis shows only a significant interaction between speaker sex and age in predicting BOT-BOUGHT distance (table 2.2). Details of this interaction are shown in figure 2.2.

Both males and females show a decrease in BOT-BOUGHT distance with a decrease in age, suggesting that the distance between these vowels is decreasing over time: younger speakers are more likely to be merged

TABLE 2.2
Summary of Main Effects on Euclidean Distance between BOT and Mean BOUGHT

	Estimate	*Std. Dev.*	*DF*	*T-Value*	*P-Value*
(Intercept)	0.0574	0.0279	38.1	2.061	.03996
Log duration	0.0027	0.0049	87.6	0.564	.57316
Sex = Male	−0.0366	0.0215	53.2	−1.705	.09395
Age	0.0005	0.0003	54.9	1.573	.12136
Sex(M) × Age	0.0013	0.0005	53.8	2.891	.00553

FIGURE 2.2
Euclidean Distance between BOT and Speaker Mean BOUGHT

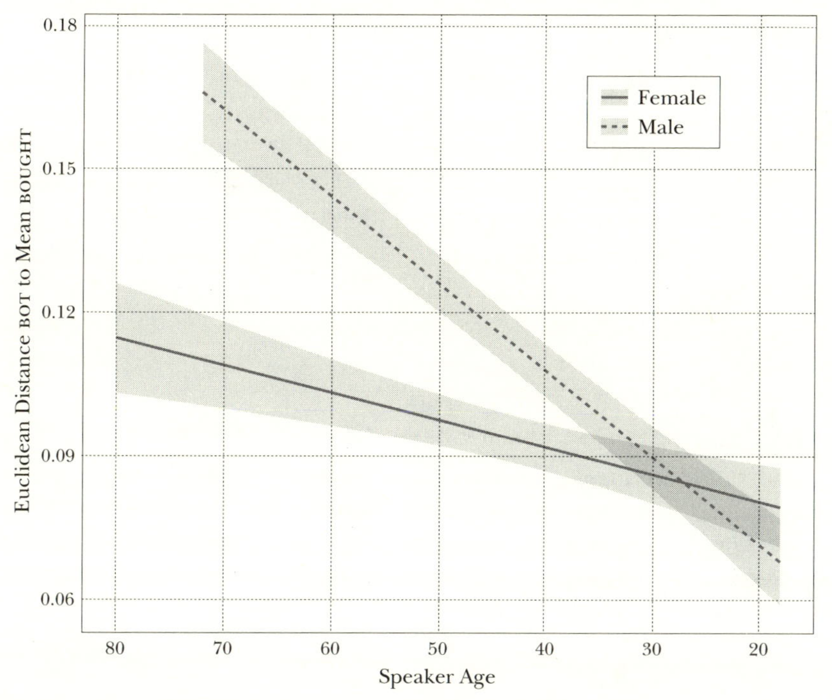

than older speakers. However, the interaction between sex and age shows that age is a more significant predictor of BOT-BOUGHT distance for males than for females. As figure 2.2 demonstrates, the distance between BOT and BOUGHT is more rapidly decreasing over time for males than for females. The figure shows that older males maintain a larger distance between the two vowels—or BOT-BOUGHT distinction—than older females. Yet in the youngest speakers, there is no discernible sex difference: both males and females maintain BOT and BOUGHT vowels that are relatively close to one another. For this measure, field site is not a significant predictor.

BOUGHT. This observable apparent-time movement of BOT and BOUGHT closer to one another yields the question of how, in the vowel space, this movement is achieved. More specifically, the distance between BOT and BOUGHT could decrease via the movement of BOT upward in the vowel space, the movement of BOUGHT downward in the vowel space, or both occurring simultaneously. Previous work in urban, coastal California has shown support for the BOT-BOUGHT merger being achieved primarily via the lowering of BOUGHT (Hall-Lew 2013). We thus investigate changes in BOUGHT height in our data over apparent time, as well as other social factors conditioning this variable's patterning.

Changes in BOUGHT height over time and across social groups are assessed by modeling predictors of normalized BOUGHT F1. The regression analysis shows age to be a significant predictor of BOUGHT F1, and site to be a marginally significant predictor, with no significant interactions (table 2.3).

While other studies have found BOUGHT lowering in California, our data show that as speaker age decreases, BOUGHT F1 decreases, indicating that BOUGHT is in fact raising across apparent time. This result suggests that, in these sites, the BOT-BOUGHT merger is not achieved via the lowering of BOUGHT. The marginal effect of site indicates that for Merced speakers, BOUGHT remains relatively lower (i.e., higher F1) than for speakers in Red-

TABLE 2.3
Summary of Main Effects on BOUGHT Normalized F1

	Estimate	*Std. Dev.*	*DF*	*T-Value*	*P-Value*
(Intercept)	1.27	0.0491	0.0645	25.901	<.0001
Log duration	0.0024	0.0092	993	–0.356	.7221
Sex = Male	0.0201	0.0131	50.2	1.533	.1314
Age	0.0007	0.0004	51.2	2.092	.0414
Site = Merced	0.0305	0.0160	49.5	1.911	.0619
Site = Redding	0.0190	0.0160	49.9	1.185	.2416

ding and Bakersfield. No significant sex effect was found for this variable, though males showed a tendency for higher BOUGHT vowels as compared to their female counterparts.

BOT. The regression analysis of BOT height, as quantified by normalized BOT F1, indicates that the apparent-time decrease in distance between BOT and BOUGHT in these sites appears to be achieved primarily by the raising of the BOT vowel. Speaker age, sex, and field site are significant predictors of BOT F1, with no significant interactions (table 2.4).

The age effect of the model for this variable shows that as age decreases, BOT F1 decreases, indicating BOT raising over apparent time. Males are significantly less likely to produce raised variants of BOT than females. The effect of site indicates that Merced speakers remain relatively more conservative than Redding and Bakersfield speakers, with Merced speakers being significantly less raised than speakers in the other two sites.

The social factors predicting BAT retraction, BOT-BOUGHT distance, BOUGHT height, and BOT height show consistent patterns, such that when sex is found as a significant predictor, males remain more conservative than females, and when site is found as a significant predictor, Merced speakers remain more conservative than Redding and Bakersfield speakers.

LOWEST VOWEL. Finally, we examine the lower bound of the vowel space in the F1 dimension, investigating the potential for an apparent-time shift from a trapezoidal vowel space, with BAT and BOT at similar heights, to a triangular space, with BAT as the lowest vowel, as proposed by Boberg (2011) in the Canadian Shift.

We model the lowest vowel in the vowel space by examining the relative height difference between a given speaker's highest front vowel (the BEET vowel) and their BOT vowel in F1, as compared to the difference between that speaker's BEET and their BAT vowel in F1. This was calculated by speaker as BOT F1 distance to BEET minus that speaker's BAT F1 distance

TABLE 2.4
Summary of Main Effects on BOT Normalized F1

	Estimate	*Std. Dev.*	*DF*	*T-Value*	*P-Value*
(Intercept)	1.15	0.0414	0.0539	27.817	<.0001
Log duration	0.0172	0.0073	0.0012	2.353	.0188
Sex = Male	0.0504	0.0129	49.6	3.908	.0003
Age	0.0017	0.0004	50.4	4.763	<.0001
Site = Merced	0.0413	0.0158	49.3	2.622	.0116
Site = Redding	0.0055	0.0158	49.4	0.347	.7298

to BEET. The regression shows age and site as significant predictors of this difference (table 2.5). These significant trends are more clearly demonstrated in figure 2.3, which plots raw normalized BOT and BAT F1 (height) together, by age and site.

The significant age effect in table 2.5 indicates that as speaker age decreases, BAT distance from BEET is relatively greater than BOT distance from BEET. In other words, BAT is repositioned as relatively lower than BOT in apparent time. This result is unsurprising, given our finding that BOT is raising over time. Figure 2.3 demonstrates that while BOT and BAT are produced at similar heights for the oldest speakers in each site, BOT raises dramatically in apparent time, leaving BAT the lowest vowel in the vowel space. The significant site effect in the regression indicates that, again, Merced is relatively more conservative than the other two sites in this reconfiguring of the low vowel anchor. As shown in figure 2.3, while BOT is clearly raising over time, leaving BAT the lower vowel for the youngest Merced speakers, the height gap between the two vowels, even in the youngest speakers, is much smaller than that of Bakersfield and Redding speakers.

SUMMARY OF RESULTS. Taken together, these results indicate that all low vowel classes implicated in the CVS are undergoing change, conditioned by site and sex in particular ways for each vowel class. To summarize, BAT is retracting over time in all three sites and is the lowest vowel in the vowel space of young speakers across the sites. BOT is raising in all three field sites, and its distance from BOUGHT is decreasing over time, suggesting a greater degree of overlap among BOT and BOUGHT in the vowel space. Finally, in Bakersfield and Redding, BOUGHT is raising along with BOT, though BOT has raised at a faster rate. These apparent-time changes are shown together in figure 2.4.

Figure 2.4 demonstrates the relative co-occurrence of these changes, illustrating main effects for F1 of BOT, F1 of BOUGHT, and F2 of BAT over time for each of the three field sites. Measurements are plotted such that

TABLE 2.5
Summary of Main Effects on Mean BOT F1 Distance to FLEECE Minus BAT F1 Distance to FLEECE

	Estimate	*Std. Dev.*	*T-Value*	*P-Value*
(Intercept)	0.0127	0.0217	5.84	<.0001
Sex = Male	–0.0264	0.0139	–1.90	.0633
Age	–0.0013	0.0004	–3.43	.0012
Site = Merced	–0.0450	0.0170	–2.64	.0110
Site = Redding	0.0049	0.0171	0.29	.7744

FIGURE 2.3
Normalized F1 of BOT and BAT

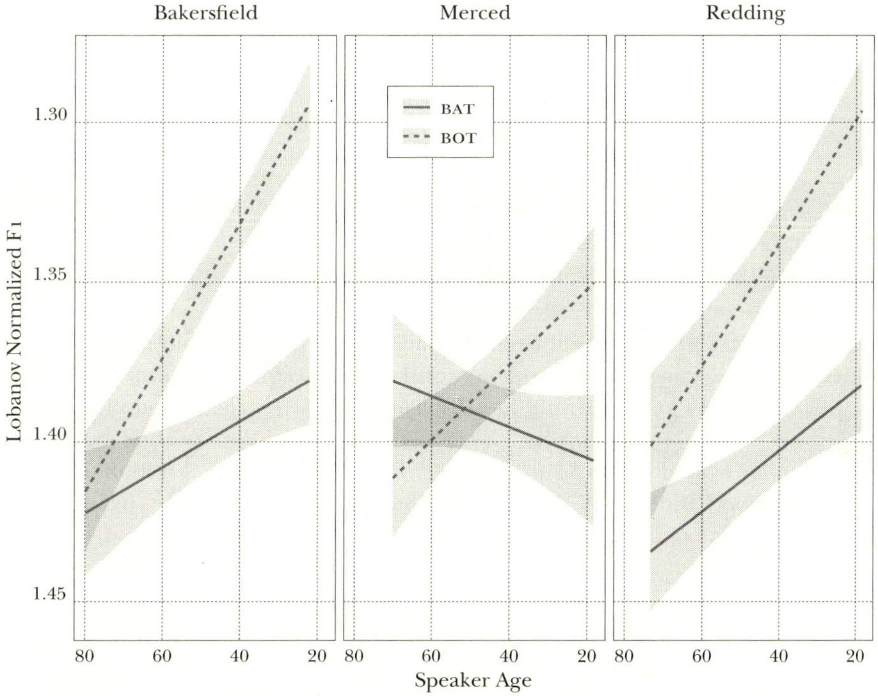

increasing trend lines for BOT and BOUGHT indicate raising (i.e., lower F1) over time, while increasing trend lines for BAT indicate retraction (i.e., lower F2). That is, as BAT retracts (F2 decreases for younger speakers), BOT raises (F1 decreases for younger speakers). This pattern appears across all three field sites.

The relative raising of BOT toward BOUGHT, however, differs across sites, suggesting that speakers in these sites have taken different routes to the contemporary California-shifted vowel space. In Redding, even the oldest speakers appear to have BOT and BOUGHT classes that are situated closely together, at least in the F1 dimension. In Bakersfield and Merced, however, the oldest speakers produce distinct BOT and BOUGHT classes (again in the F1 dimension), with BOT lower in the vowel space than BOUGHT. Over time, in conjunction with the retraction of BAT, BOT raises to BOUGHT. In these sites, the decrease in distance between BOT and BOUGHT does not predate BAT retraction, but rather co-occurs with BAT retraction. In both situations, this suggests that the youngest speakers' vowel spaces are characterized by a merged BOT and BOUGHT and a retracted BAT and that the latter is left as the lowest vowel in the system.

FIGURE 2.4
Normalized F1 of BOT and BOUGHT and Normalized F2 of BAT

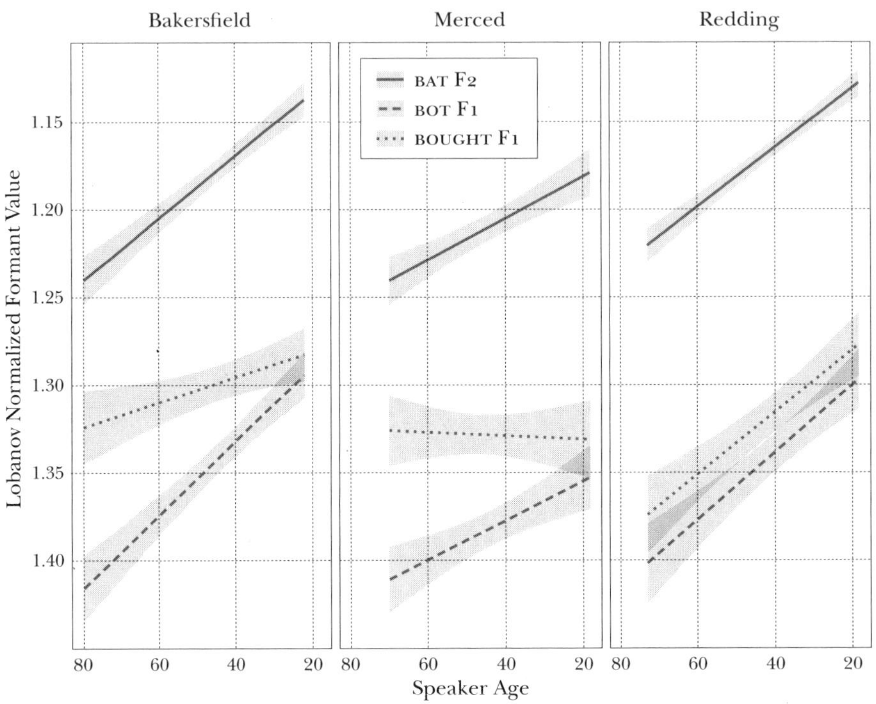

DISCUSSION

At this point, we can draw some conclusions about what the lower vowel space looks like, at least for inland Californians. We can talk about this space in terms of its general shape (i.e., how the whole region is patterning). And we can discuss site-specific patterns, specifically the different shift trajectories for the low vowels between Redding in the north and Merced and Bakersfield to the south.

Regarding the general patterns, we have shown that across the Central Valley there is evidence of BAT retraction and BOT raising (figure 2.4). At first glance, it is clear that all three field sites have experienced dramatic change in the low vowel space over the past 60 years of apparent time. In fact, as figure 2.3 shows, BAT is now the lowest vowel in the space across the region.

The finding of BAT retraction in inland California is perhaps not surprising, since BAT lowering/retraction has been attested in urban/coastal areas of the state (Hinton et al. 1987; Hagiwara 1997; Eckert 2008; Kennedy and Grama 2012). Both wave and hierarchical diffusion models for sound change would predict that less urban areas would initially lag behind, but eventually catch up to, changes observed in urban centers. The data are insufficient at this point to assess the extent of difference between inland and coastal California with respect to relative actuation times and degree of change for this feature. However, our data show that Central Valley 50-year-old speakers retract BAT; Hinton et al.'s 1986-era San Francisco Bay Area speakers (a comparable age cohort to present-day 50-year-olds) likewise exhibited BAT retraction. Apparently, this component of the CVS is a statewide phenomenon and has been around for some time.

As figure 2.4 shows, all three field sites in the Central Valley show significant change in BOT F1 over time, such that there is significant overlap with BOUGHT in younger speakers. This indicates BOT-BOUGHT merger, with these vowels now together occupying a higher position than elsewhere in the United States.[5] Conventional wisdom (see Thomas 2001; Gordon 2005) about low back merger in American dialects (at least for white speakers) is that the merged vowel is typically produced low and back in the vowel space—firmly in BOT territory. In Canadian dialects, however, the merged vowel is realized higher in the vowel space, resulting in a triangular (rather than trapezoidal) vowel system (Boberg 2011), with BAT as the lowest vowel. In inland California, we find a similar triangular vowel system, with clear indication of F1 change (raising) for BOT and little to no movement for BOUGHT. Figure 2.5 illustrates this triangular space for two female Redding speakers in our sample.

This finding contrasts with previous work on the low back merger in California in urban coastal centers, which has suggested that the merger occurs via encroachment of BOUGHT into BOT territory. Studies as early as DeCamp (1953) and then Moonwomon (1991) noted BOUGHT lowering/fronting but did not observe any change in BOT. Likewise, in more recent work, Hall-Lew (2013, 384) finds in San Francisco that "[w]hile [BOT] remains low and central, [BOUGHT] is fronter and lower among younger speakers, with a decrease in the acoustic distance between the vowels." Conversely, in the Central Valley, we have evidence of BOUGHT being relatively stable while BOT raises—exactly the opposite of what has been found on the coast. Thus, while we do find a marked decrease in distance between the two vowels, which strongly suggests the presence of the low back merger and confirms some involvement in the CVS (in which the merger is a hallmark feature), we find the location of these vowels to be different from what has been reported for the coast.

When we look more closely at the individual vocalic patterns for the three field sites, we begin to also see some site-specific patterns sugges-

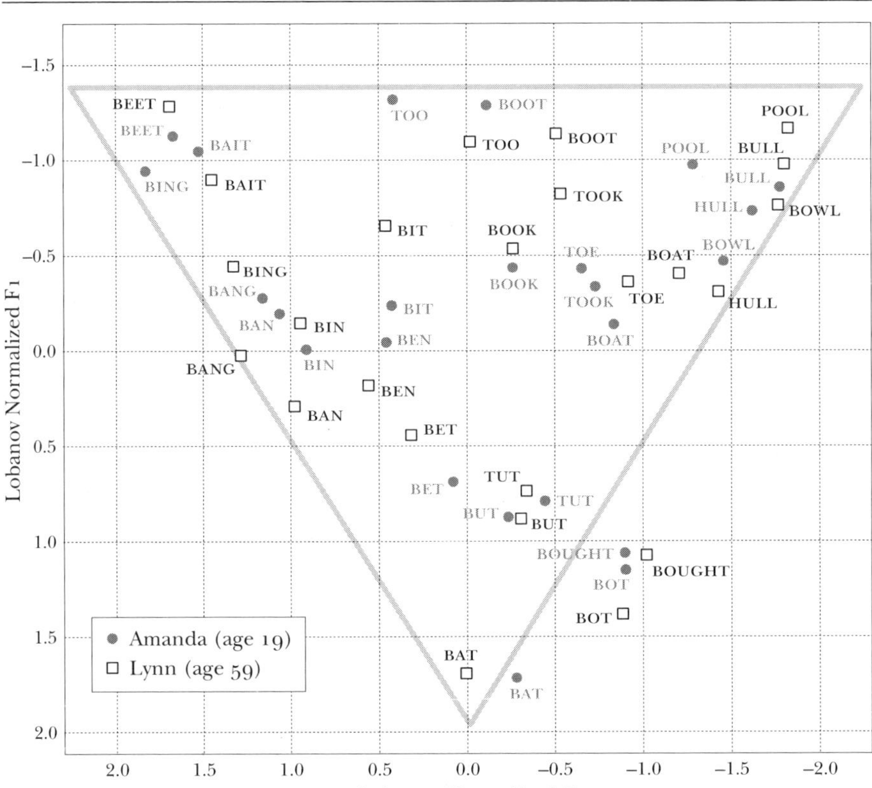

FIGURE 2.5
Triangular Vowel Spaces for Two Female Speakers from Redding

tive of further regional variation. Clearly, across the Central Valley, as BAT retracts, BOT raises. As figure 2.4 shows, trend lines (i.e., degree of change over time) for these vowels are robustly sloped for all field sites. But what about BOUGHT? Specifically, did BOT and BOUGHT merge prior to BAT retraction and prior to BOT raising? Delving more deeply into the patterns represented by these trend lines, we find two different possibilities for the shifting of these vowels in different parts of inland California.

The first pattern can be seen in Redding (figure 2.4). The BOUGHT vowel raises dramatically over time in Redding, but not in Merced and only marginally in Bakersfield. In fact, for the oldest Redding speakers, BOT and BOUGHT are in a very similar place in terms of F1, suggesting that even the oldest speakers do not distinguish these vowels in production. The parallel trend lines for BOT and BOUGHT over time in Redding suggest that BOT and BOUGHT moved closer together at some mid-F1 level before even the oldest speakers were born, leaving room for BAT retraction in turn. Following that, they both raise as BAT retracts. The process occurs in two stages, as illustrated in figure 2.6.

For Merced and Bakersfield, however, the shift appears to have proceeded differently. Here (figure 2.4) the oldest speakers have clearly distinct low back vowels; BOT is notably lower than BOUGHT. Then, over time, BOT raises to meet BOUGHT, resulting in apparent merger for younger speakers. Thus, in Merced and Bakersfield, we have BAT retraction and BOT raising occurring at roughly the same time. This results in a relatively high position for BOT and BOUGHT, which gives BAT plenty of room to retract and anchor the low vowel space. Figure 2.7 illustrates this process.

CONCLUSION

In sum, this study has not only revealed the current status of the low vowel system in inland California, but it has also uncovered regional variation, both in terms of how the Central Valley patterns differently from the coast and in terms of how the northern Central Valley (Redding) differs from the mid/southern Central Valley (Bakersfield and Merced).

First, we have shown that across the Central Valley, the low vowels have reconfigured over the last 60 years of apparent time, such that BAT is firmly the lowest vowel in the system and the distance between BOT and BOUGHT has decreased significantly, suggesting merger. We have also shown how the Central Valley has diverged from coastal, urban centers with respect to the placement of the low back vowels. While the merger in coastal California may be characterized by BOUGHT lowering and relative BOT stability (DeCamp 1953; Moonwomon 1991; Hall-Lew 2009), the Central Valley

FIGURE 2.6
Relative Timing and Position of BOT, BOUGHT, and BAT Movement in Redding

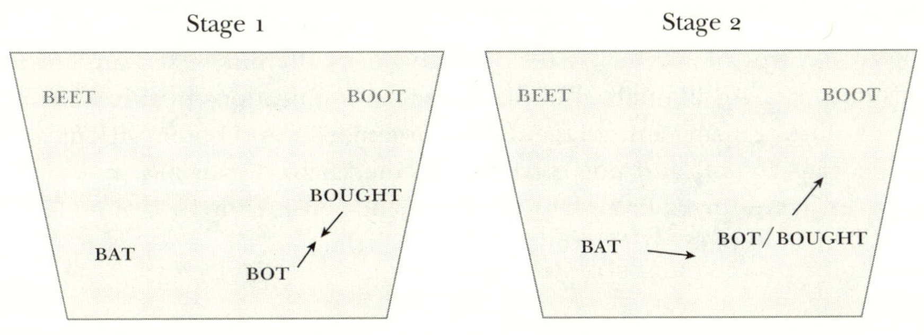

FIGURE 2.7
Relative Timing and Position of BOT, BOUGHT, and BAT Movement in Merced and Bakersfield

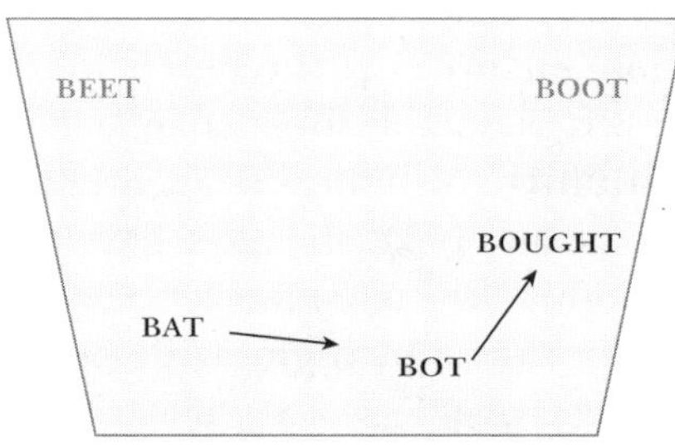

exhibits the exact opposite phenomenon: BOT raises and BOUGHT is fairly stable. Finally, we have noted how even within the Central Valley there is a north/south divide in terms of the relative timing/manner of these movements and the corresponding behavior of BAT. In the north, our data suggest that the low back vowels approach each other before the retraction of BAT, while in the south we find BAT to be retracting simultaneously with BOT raising toward BOUGHT.

In further work, we hope to delve more deeply into the social factors that play a role in this regional differentiation. For example, we find significant sex differences for all features in this study, such that females lead males in BAT retraction, BOT raising, and decreasing distance between BOT and BOUGHT. This is not altogether surprising, given the prominent role women play in innovating/propagating sound change (Labov 2001), but gender plays out differently across the state, particularly between urban and rural contexts. We cannot necessarily take for granted that our findings are comparable with those of Kennedy and Grama (2012) and Hall-Lew (2009) in coastal urban locales.

Additionally, the phonetic and phonological ramifications of our findings remain to be determined. The issue of whether the CVS occurs as a pull chain or a push chain (Kennedy and Grama 2012) could only be resolved via an analysis of the front lax vowels. Future investigations of shifting in the front lax vowel system should better illuminate the answer to this question. Additionally, the phonological implications of this study in terms of recognizing a fundamentally reorganized vowel system (triangular versus trapezoidal) and potentially respecified features for BAT and BOT/BOUGHT in California English (see Roeder and Gardner 2013) are yet to be explored, and we leave that for future work.

Last, though overall the patterns here parallel those which have been observed among speakers in urban coastal areas of the state, there are differences across field sites in the current data that beg further investigation. As we reported here, even within the Central Valley, one particular site, Merced, is significantly more conservative than the others. This resonates with other work on the Voices of California corpus to date. For example, Pratt (2015) has found Merced to be less advanced than Bakersfield for BOOT fronting. As the field site with the closest proximity to the San Francisco Bay Area, and given the positive orientations to the city expressed by Merced residents in interviews, Merced's relative conservatism is surprising and warrants more investigation.

Our work in the Central Valley is yielding a picture of developments along the north-south axis of California, and collaboration with our colleagues in Oregon and Washington will integrate these findings into a broader north-south perspective. Of particular interest are developments in Redding, which is a powerful link to the Northwest. The fact that the low back vowels merged in Redding considerably earlier than in Merced or Bakersfield suggests that the merger may have its center farther north (see McLarty, Kendall, and Farrington 2016 [this volume] for some evidence to this effect). Furthermore, we have noted occurrences of a raised BEG vowel in Redding (see Wassink 2016 [this volume]). Redding may well be orienting linguistically to the north, because while it is at the northern rim of the Central Valley, it is not culturally or ecologically part of the valley. The mountain forest environment extending from Redding to the north constitutes an ecological zone that extends well into southern Oregon. This has yielded a distinct culture and considerable alienation from the parts of either state outside of that zone. This alienation is palpable throughout the area and led to a secession movement in the first half of the twentieth century centered in Redding. This movement, to combine northern California and southern Oregon into the state of Jefferson, endures to this day. Early settlement patterns, furthermore, bound northern California to southern Oregon. The Applegate Trail brought people to southern Oregon via northern California and continued to serve as a conduit bringing Oregonians into northern California for the gold rush. The ultimate goal of this work is to integrate findings in California with those in other areas of the West. Needless to say, there can be no dialectology of California that is independent of the dialectology of the West more generally, and there can be no account of vowel systems that is independent of regional social history and life.

NOTES

Many thanks to the Richard A. Karp Foundation and Stanford University for funding data collection. This study would not have been possible without the tireless efforts of the 34 Voices of California fieldworkers. Thanks are also due to the audience at the 2015 Meeting of the American Dialect Society as well as to this volume's editors for helpful feedback. Finally, we acknowledge the time and insight shared with us by the Voices of California field participants.

1. This is in keeping with Labov's generalization (e.g., Labov 1991, 29) that mergers set off pull chains and block push chains. Kennedy and Grama (2012), however, have argued for a push chain set in motion by BAT backing.
2. We use the term "sex" as a proxy for sex class, by which we mean a nonbiological binary classification.
3. Although Fabricius, Watt, and Johnson (2009) find that the Lobanov (1971) normalization method performs marginally better than their own, the latter requires the inclusion of the entire range of vowel classes in a speaker's vowel space. We elected to prioritize the number of speakers in our sample over the number of vowels sampled for each speaker, and therefore follow Fabricius, Watt, and Johnson's (2009) method.
4. Vowel duration was treated as a fixed effect under the assumption that articulatory targets are more fully reached at longer durations.
5. We remain agnostic about whether this BOT-BOUGHT merger is by approximation, transfer, or expansion.

REFERENCES

Barras, Claude, Edouard Geoffrois, Zhibiao Wu, and Mark Liberman. 2001. "Transcriber: Development and Use of a Tool for Assisting Speech Corpora Production." *Speech Communication* 33.1–2: 5–22. doi:10.1016/S0167-6393(00)00067-4.

Bates, Douglas, Martin Maechler, Ben Bolker, and Steven Walker. 2014. lme4: Linear Mixed-Effects Models Using "Eigen" and S4. R package. Version 1.1-7. http://CRAN.R-project.org/package=lme4.

Bigham, Douglas S. 2010. "Correlation of the Low-back Merger and TRAP-retraction." In "Selected Papers from NWAV 37," edited by Kyle Gorman and Laurel MacKenzie. *University of Pennsylvania Working Papers in Linguistics* 15.2: 21–31. http://repository.upenn.edu/pwpl/vol15/iss2/4/.

Boberg, Charles. 2005. "The Canadian Shift in Montreal." *Language Variation and Change* 17.2: 133–54. doi:10.1017/S0954394505050064.

———. 2011. "Reshaping the Vowel System: An Index of Phonetic Innovation in Canadian English." In "Selected papers from NWAV 39," edited by Meredith Tamminga. *University of Pennsylvania Working Papers in Linguistics* 17.2: 21–29. http://repository.upenn.edu/pwpl/vol17/iss2/4/.

Boersma, Paul, and David Weenink. 2012. Praat: Doing Phonetics by Computer. Version 5.3.07. http://www.praat.org.

Clarke, Sandra, Ford Elms, and Amani Youssef. 1995. "The Third Dialect of English: Some Canadian Evidence." *Language Variation and Change* 7.2: 209–28. doi: 10.1017/S0954394500000995.

DeCamp, David. 1953. "The Pronunciation of English in San Francisco." Ph.D. diss., University of California, Berkeley.

Eckert, Penelope. 2008. "Where Do Ethnolects Stop?" *International Journal of Bilingualism* 12.1–2: 25–42. doi:10.1177/13670069080120010301.

———. 2010. "Affect, Sound Symbolism, and Variation." In "Selected Papers from NWAV 37," edited by Kyle Gorman and Laurel MacKenzie. *University of Pennsylvania Working Papers in Linguistics* 15.2: 70–80. http://repository.upenn.edu/pwpl/vol15/iss2/9/.

———. 2011. "Language and Power in the Preadolescent Heterosexual Market." *American Speech* 86.1: 85–97. doi:10.1215/00031283-1277528.

Fabricius, Anne H., Dominic Watt, and Daniel Ezra Johnson. 2009. "A Comparison of Three Speaker-Intrinsic Vowel Formant Frequency Normalization Algorithms for Sociophonetics." *Language Variation and Change* 21.3: 413–35. doi:10.1017/S0954394509990160.

Fought, Carmen. 1999. "A Majority Sound Change in a Minority Community: /u/-Fronting in Chicano English." *Journal of Sociolinguistics* 3.1: 5–23. doi:10.1111/1467-9481.t01-1-00060.

Geenberg, Katherine. 2014. "What It Means to Be Norcal Country: Variation and Marginalization in Rural California." Ph.D. diss., Stanford University.

Gordon, Matthew J. 2005. "The Midwest and West: Phonology." In "The Americas and the Caribbean," edited by Edgar W. Schneider, in *A Handbook of Varieties of English*, vol. 1, *Phonology*, edited by Edgar W. Schneider, Kate Burridge, Bernd Kortmann, Rajend Mesthrie, and Clive Upton, 338–50. Berlin: Mouton de Gruyter.

Hagiwara, Robert. 1997. "Dialect Variation and Formant Frequency: The American English Vowels Revisited." *Journal of the Acoustical Society of America* 102.1: 655–58. doi:10.1121/1.419712.

Hall-Lew, Lauren. 2009. "Ethnicity and Phonetic Variation in San Francisco English." Ph.D. diss., Stanford University.

———. 2013. "'Flip-Flop' and Mergers-in-Progress." *English Language and Linguistics* 17.2: 359–90. doi:10.1017/S1360674313000063.

Hinton, Leanne, Birch Moonwomon, Sue Bremner, Herb Luthin, Mary Van Clay, Jean Lerner, and Hazel Corcoran. 1987. "It's Not Just the Valley Girls: A Study of California English." In *Berkeley Linguistics Society: Proceedings of the Thirteenth Annual Meeting, February 14–16, 1987*, edited by Jon Aske, Natasha Beery, Laura Michaelis, and Hana Filip, 117–28. Berkeley, Calif.: Berkeley Linguistics Society. doi:10.3765/bls.v13i0.1811.

Kendall, Tyler, and Erik R. Thomas. 2012. Vowels: Vowel Manipulation, Normalization, and Plotting. R package. Version 1.2. http://CRAN.R-project.org/package=vowels.

Kennedy, Robert, and James Grama. 2012. "Chain Shifting and Centralization in California Vowels: An Acoustic Analysis." *American Speech* 87.1: 39–56. doi:10.1215/00031283-1599950.

Labov, William. 1991. "The Three Dialects of English." In *New Ways of Analyzing Sound Change*, edited by Penelope Eckert, 1–44. San Diego, Calif.: Academic Press.

———. 2001. *Principles of Linguistic Change*. Vol. 2, *Social Factors*. Oxford: Blackwell.

Labov, William, Sharon Ash, and Charles Boberg. 2006. *The Atlas of North American English: Phonetics, Phonology, and Sound Change*. Berlin: Mouton de Gruyter.

Lobanov, Boris M. 1971. "Classification of Russian Vowels Spoken by Different Speakers." *Journal of the Acoustical Society of America* 49.2B: 606–8. doi:10.1121/1.1912396.

McLarty, Jason, Tyler Kendall, and Charlie Farrington. 2016. "Investigating the Development of the Contemporary Oregonian English Vowel System." In *Speech in the Western States*, vol. 1, *The Coastal States*, edited by Valerie Fridland, Tyler Kendall, Betsy Evans, and Alicia Beckford Wassink, 135–57. Publication of the American Dialect Society 101. Durham, N.C.: Duke University Press. doi:10.1215/00031283-3772934.

Metcalf, Allan A. 1972. "Directions of Change in Southern California English." *Journal of English Linguistics* 6: 28–33. doi:10.1177/007542427200600104.

Moonwomon, Birch. 1991. "Sound Change in San Francisco English." Ph.D. diss., University of California, Berkeley. http://escholarship.org/uc/item/6qz10226.

Podesva, Robert J., Annette D'Onofrio, Janneke Van Hofwegen, and Seung Kyung Kim. 2015. "Country Ideology and the California Vowel Shift." *Language Variation and Change* 27.2: 157–86. doi:10.1017/S095439451500006X.

Pratt, Teresa. 2015. "BOOT-Fronting in Inland California: The Role of Trajectory Measurements in Characterizing Vowel Quality." Paper presented at the annual meeting of the Linguistic Society of America, Portland, Ore., Jan. 8–11.

Roeder, Rebecca V., and Matt Hunt Gardner. 2013. "The Phonology of the Canadian Shift Revisited: Thunder Bay and Cape Breton." In "Selected papers from NWAV 41," edited by Aaron Freeman. *University of Pennsylvania Working Papers in Linguistics* 19.2: 161–70. http://repository.upenn.edu/pwpl/vol19/iss2/18/.

Rosenfelder, Ingrid, Joe Fruehwald, Keelan Evanini, and Jiahong Yuan. 2011. FAVE (Forced Alignment and Vowel Extraction) Program Suite. http://fave.ling.upenn.edu.

Thomas, Erik R. 2001. *An Acoustic Analysis of Vowel Variation in New World English*. Publication of the American Dialect Society 85. Durham, N.C.: Duke University Press.

Traunmüller, Hartmut. 1997. "Auditory Scales of Frequency Representation." Department of Linguistics, Stockholm University. http://www.ling.su.se/staff/hartmut/bark.htm.

Van Hofwegen, Janneke. 2015. "The New Normal: Multi-modal Distributions Signifying Loci of Vocalic Stylization." Paper presented at the annual meeting of the Linguistic Society of America, Portland, Ore., Jan. 8–11.

Wassink, Alicia Beckford. 2016. "The Vowels of Washington State." In *Speech in the Western States*, vol. 1, *The Coastal States*, edited by Valerie Fridland, Tyler Kendall, Betsy Evans, and Alicia Beckford Wassink, 77–106. Publication of the American Dialect Society 101. Durham, N.C.: Duke University Press. doi:10.1215/00031283-3772912.

Wittenburg, Peter, Hennie Brugman, Alberts Russel, Alex Klassmann, and Han Sloetjes. 2006. "ELAN: A Professional Framework for Multimodal Research." In *LREC 2006: 5th International Conference on Language Resources and Evaluation*, 1556–59. http://www.lrec-conf.org/proceedings/lrec2006/pdf/153_pdf.pdf.

ANNETTE D'ONOFRIO is an assistant professor in the Department of Linguistics at Northwestern University. She holds a Ph.D. from Stanford University. Her research explores the ways that linguistic styles are tied to social categories and personae both in perception and in production. Her primary research focus uses experimental paradigms to investigate how sociophonetic variation and sociolinguistic style are represented cognitively. She also studies the macro-social, local, and ideological factors that condition phonetic variation and change in regional dialects. She has conducted fieldwork and analyses across inland California through Stanford's Voices of California project and is currently beginning fieldwork in the Chicagoland area. E-mail: donofrio@northwestern.edu.

PENELOPE ECKERT is the Albert Ray Lang Professor of Linguistics and Anthropology at Stanford University. Her research focuses on the social meaning of variation, seeking out the relation between the indexical use of variation at the local level and the patterning of variation at the macro-sociological level. She examines the meaning of variation through its use in stylistic practice, approaching variation as a robust semiotic system that draws on a wide range of linguistic material. She is also an active participant in Stanford's Voices of California project, examining English dialectology across California. She is author of *Jocks and Burnouts: Social Identity in the High School* (Teachers College Press, 1989), *Linguistic Variation as Social Practice* (Blackwell, 2000), and *Language and Gender* (Cambridge University Press, 2003 [2nd ed., with Sally McConnell-Ginet, 2013]). E-mail: eckert@stanford.edu.

ROBERT J. PODESVA is an assistant professor in the Department of Linguistics at Stanford University. He holds degrees from Stanford University (Ph.D., M.A.) and Cornell University (B.A.) and has been an assistant professor at Georgetown University. His research examines the social significance of variation in the domains of segmental phonetics, prosody, and voice quality. He has a particular interest in how phonetic resources participate in the construction of identity, most notably gender, sexuality, race, and their intersections. His latest projects focus on the social meaning of nonmodal voice qualities in interactional contexts and sociolinguistic variation in inland California and Washington, D.C. He has coedited *Research Methods in Linguistics* (with Devyani Sharma; Cambridge University Press, 2013), *Language and Sexuality: Contesting Meaning in Theory and Practice* (with Kathryn Cambpell-Kibler, Sarah Roberts, and Andrew Wong; CSLI Publications, 2001), and a special issue of *American Speech* on sociophonetics and sexuality (with Penelope Eckert; *AS* 86.1 [Spring 2001]). E-mail: podesva@stanford.edu.

TERESA PRATT is a Ph.D. candidate in the Department of Linguistics at Stanford University. Through her work with the Voices of California project at Stanford, she has conducted sociolinguistic fieldwork throughout the Central Valley and studied phonetic variation in California English in these communities. In addition, she has studied actors' performances of California English with an interest in the interplay of phonetic variables and the embodied stereotypes associated with California. Her research interests include sociophonetics, sociolinguistic style, and embodiment. E-mail: tcpratt@stanford.edu.

JANNEKE VAN HOFWEGEN is a Ph.D. candidate in linguistics at Stanford University. A sociolinguist primarily, she focuses her research on ethnic and world varieties of English. At Stanford, she is a contributing member of the Voices of California research team, where she documents and analyzes sociophonetic variation in the as-yet understudied California inland (nonurban) dialect region, with particular attention paid to minority ethnic and LGBT communities. In addition to her work at Stanford, she is an associate on the North Carolina Language and Life Project (NCLLP), where she studies morphosyntactic variation in African American English from a one-of-a-kind longitudinal sample of African American children, as well as sociophonetic variation in both African American and Chicano Englishes. E-mail: jmvanhof@stanford.edu.

3. BETWEEN CALIFORNIA AND THE PACIFIC NORTHWEST: THE FRONT LAX VOWELS IN SAN FRANCISCO ENGLISH

AMANDA CARDOSO, LAUREN HALL-LEW,
YOVA KEMENTCHEDJHIEVA, *and* RUARIDH PURSE

English in the western united states has been described as largely homogenous, primarily based on the BOT/BOUGHT merger and its contrast with the Northern Cities and the South (Labov 1991). However, as the current volume demonstrates, differentiation within Western U.S. English can be found, based on certain distinct features. One example is San Francisco English, where a delayed acquisition of the low back merger has led to San Francisco English being identified as distinct from other Western varieties (Labov, Ash, and Boberg 2006). The current investigation focuses on the presence or absence of two other Western U.S. English features in San Francisco: the front lax vowels in the California Vowel Shift (CVS) (Kennedy and Grama 2012) and prevelar raising of BET and BAT characteristic of the Pacific Northwest English (Wassink 2016 [this volume]). Previous work has shown that San Franciscans participate in other features characteristic of the CVS, such as the fronting of BOOT and BOAT (Hall-Lew 2009, 2011), as well as the low back vowel merger (Moonwomon 1991; Hall-Lew 2013). However, these back vowel features do little to speak to the distinctiveness of California English vis-à-vis the rest of the Western United States, because all three changes have also been found in other Western states (e.g., Hall-Lew 2005; Labov, Ash, and Boberg 2006). While the front vowel shift is potentially more distinctive to California, evidence of its occurrence in San Francisco is still preliminary (Hall-Lew et al. 2015). Furthermore, while prevelar raising has been shown to occur as far south as Oregon (Becker et al. 2016 [this volume]), there has been no investigation as to whether this feature might be found in San Francisco; perhaps it could be a feature distinguishing Northern and Southern California Englishes. In short, the lack of evidence for the features associated with San Francisco English and on its relationship to other varieties in the Western United States demon-

Publication of the American Dialect Society 101 DOI 10.1215/00031283-3772890

strates the need for further study of this variety, which the present chapter undertakes.

THE CALIFORNIA VOWEL SHIFT. The CVS involves a lowering and retraction of BIT and BET, a fronting of BOOT and BOAT, a merger of BOT and BOUGHT, a fronting of BUT, and a "nasal split" whereby BAN (BAT before nasals) raises and fronts and BAT before nonnasals lowers and retracts (Eckert 2004). Much of the research surrounding the CVS focuses on only a subset of these features. The only investigation (before the current volume) that considers nearly all of them was Hinton et al. (1987). Their study was based on 22 participants from different areas of California, a majority of whom were middle-class, non-Hispanic European Americans ("Anglos") from the San Francisco Bay Area. The present chapter represents a follow-up to their findings for the front lax vowels. We focus on 22 speakers from a single neighborhood in San Francisco, with equal numbers of Chinese Americans

FIGURE 3.1
San Francisco, California, in Its Regional Context

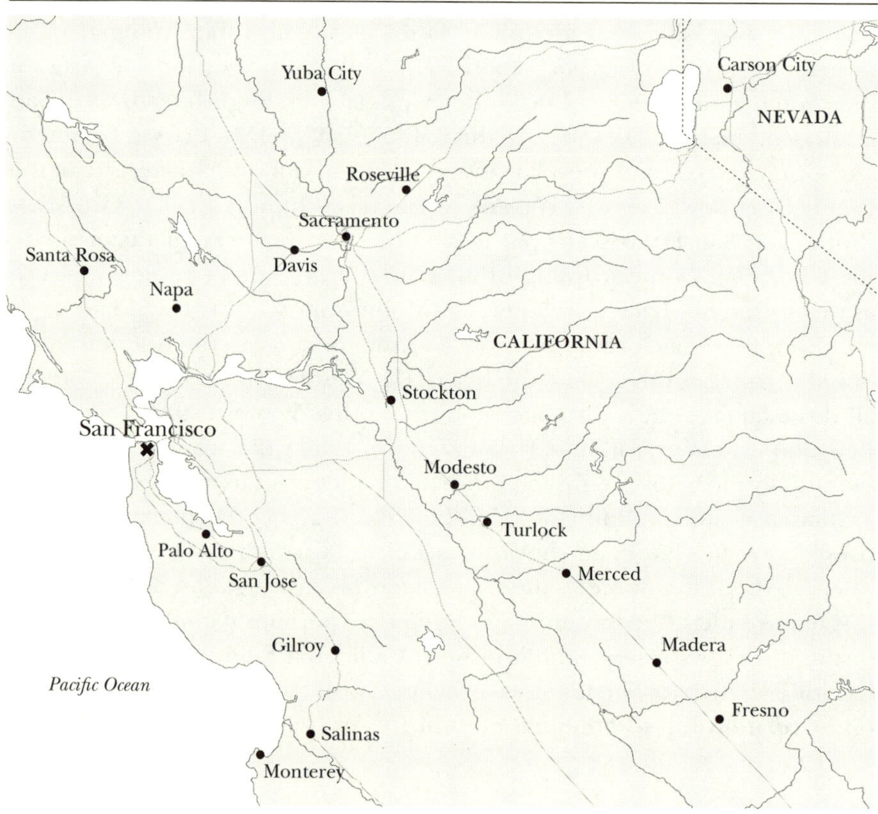

and European Americans. Gender and ethnicity have both been shown to be significant predictors of the CVS across the state of California and within San Francisco specifically.

Previous work outside of San Francisco has found evidence of the CVS in both Northern and Southern Californian communities. The back vowel system, especially the fronting of BOOT, has so far garnered the most attention. The fronting of both BOOT and BOAT was documented in California by Hinton et al. (1987). Fought (1999) documented fine social conditioning of BOOT fronting based on a sample of 32 Mexican American young adults in Los Angeles, with the most fronted variants being produced by non-gang-affiliated women. BOOT and BOAT fronting is also reported in a study of one Vietnamese American gay man from Orange County (Podesva 2011). In the speech of 130 Californians from Redding, younger and country-oriented residents have fronter variants of BOAT (Podesva et al. 2015). In all cases, the fronting of these vowels is inhibited by a following /l/ and promoted by a preceding coronal consonant (e.g., Hall-Lew 2011; Podesva et al. 2015). Podesva et al. (2015) suggest that the fronting of BOAT following coronals preceded BOAT fronting in other environments.

The same speaker in Podesva's (2011) study also showed evidence of the BAT "nasal split," a feature documented phonetically for the speech of 20 ethnically diverse preadolescents in Northern California (Eckert 2008). In Eckert's study, girls with the most local social capital had the greatest amount of prenasal BAT raising and preoral BAT retraction, but only in the social context where those features indexed desirable social qualities. Podesva et al. (2015) find that younger country-oriented Redding residents have the most raised prenasal BAT; there is no similar effect found for preoral BAT retraction, which is backer for younger speakers overall.

The lowering of the BIT and BET vowels has received relatively less attention before the present volume. An investigation of 13 speakers from a range of Californian locations provides some evidence for the lowering of BIT, BET, and BAT (Kennedy and Grama 2012). They found that women were leading men in these changes in progress, but their sample was mostly European American, and they did not test for any effects of ethnic difference.

Features of the CVS have been attested in San Francisco English. The fronting of BOOT and BOAT is the clearest result (Hall-Lew 2009, 2011), with apparent time correlations for BOOT after noncoronal segments and for BOAT in all conditions; BOOT after coronals is the furthest front but is not correlated with speaker year of birth and thus may have gone to completion (Hall-Lew 2011). Women lead men in the fronting of BOAT, but not in the fronting of BOOT. The apparent-time correlation for BOOT after noncoronals is particularly robust among Chinese American women and not so among European American women; ethnic differences among men are less marked.

Despite findings that suggest that San Francisco does not exhibit the BOT/BOUGHT merger (Labov, Ash, and Boberg 2006), other studies have found evidence of vowel coalescence in midpoint F1/F2 space, correlating with speaker year of birth (Moonwomon 1991; Hall-Lew 2009). This shift appears to be realized by a fronting and lowering of BOUGHT in apparent time, with no apparent-time change in the quality of the BOT vowel (Hall-Lew 2013); acoustically, this may differentiate the change from that occurring in California's Central Valley, where the merger results from raising of BOT (D'Onofrio et al. 2016 [this volume]) or elsewhere in California, where the merger has been described as resulting from a retraction of BOT (Eckert 2004). In San Francisco, there is no difference between men and women with respect to low back vowel production, but the change in apparent time is much stronger and the extent of acoustic coalescence greater among the Chinese Americans than among the European Americans (Hall-Lew 2013). This ethnic difference may go part of the way to explaining why the results in Hall-Lew (2013) differ from the results obtained by Labov, Ash, and Boberg (2006), who included only (non-Hispanic) European Americans in the San Francisco speaker sample.

Little is known about the status of San Francisco's front vowels. A preliminary investigation of the front lax vowels in San Francisco using word lists and reading passages demonstrates that certain front lax vowels may be participating in the CVS (Hall-Lew et al. 2015). Here we provide a more in-depth examination of the front lax vowels in San Francisco using interview data from the same participants. Furthermore, other possible conditioning environments are investigated to determine the relationship of San Francisco English to other varieties in the Western United States. Specifically, we take a first look at the pre-/g/ environment, which is a conditioning environment for BET and BAT raising in Pacific Northwest varieties (Wassink 2016 [this volume]; Cardoso 2016).

PREVELAR RAISING. Prevelar raising (or "tensing") refers to a phenomenon found in many varieties in the United States and Canada (Labov, Ash, and Boberg 2006) whereby the front lax vowels BAT and BET are raised before voiced velar consonants (BAG and BEG, respectively). This process is reported to affect BAG in a wide range of locations across North America, including Wisconsin (Bauer and Parker 2008; Benson, Fox, and Balkman 2011), Washington State (Reed 1952; Labov, Ash, and Boberg 2006), Oregon (Conn 2000; Becker et al. 2016 [this volume]), Michigan (Roeder 2009), and across Canada (Labov, Ash, and Boberg 2006; Boberg 2008). However, the co-occurrence of BAG and BEG raising is much more geographically constrained. It has been reported in the Atlantic States (Kurath and McDavid 1961), Oregon (Becker et al. 2016 [this volume]), Washington State (Wassink et al. 2009; Freeman 2014; Wassink 2016 [this volume]), and British Columbia in Canada (Gregg 1957; Cardoso 2016). These dialects have a raised variant of BAG and BEG in words such as *bag* and *egg*; the resultant productions are closer to [ɛ] for BAG and [e] for BEG.

To our knowledge, the only report of a variety that exhibits BEG raising without BAG raising is in Nevada (Fridland, Kendall, and Fickle 2015). BEG raising alone was initially thought to occur in British Columbia, as earlier descriptions of this variety only make mention of BEG raising without reporting BAG raising (Gregg 1957), but further investigation provides evidence for the presence of both (Cardoso 2016).

Recent investigations of raising in Washington State find that BEG, and potentially BAG, may be merging with BAIT (Wassink et al. 2009; Freeman 2014; Wassink 2015; Wassink 2016 [this volume]). This is not reported for the other nearby locations with prevelar raising—British Columbia in Canada (Cardoso 2016) and Oregon (Becker et al. 2016 [this volume]). Wassink et al. (2009) find that gender is a factor in the extent to which these prevelar front vowels merge; males tend to have a three-way merger between BEG, BAG, and BAIT (Wassink et al. 2009; Freeman 2014), whereas females tend to merge BEG and BAIT. Freeman (2014) and Wassink (2015) report that raising of BAG and BEG is evident in speakers of all ages but that older speakers produce a raised midpoint while younger speakers produce a relatively more diphthongal vowel. Oregon also shows evidence of gender and age differences in raising of BEG and BAG (Becker et al. 2016 [this volume]), whereby older speakers are found to produce the most raising for both vowels, as well as the most fronting of BAG. They also find that women are leading in fronting of BEG.

This evidence of prevelar raising in the Englishes north of California has emerged relatively recently. Given that there has been no investigation of prevelar raising in Northern California and that there is little information about the front lax vowels in San Francisco, a thorough examination of those vowels should include analysis of the pre-/g/ environment. By investigating whether San Francisco participates in prevelar raising, it is possible to gain a better understanding of the outer limits of prevelar raising and the relationship between San Francisco and the varieties to the north of the city. The pattern in Washington State and British Columbia specifically predicts that BEG and BAG vowels should front and raise for all speakers and diphthongize for younger speakers, whereas the pattern in Oregon suggests that only the fronting of BEG is a change in progress. If there is a prevelar pattern in San Francisco, we might expect it to pattern more like Oregon than Washington State.

In contrast to prevelar raising, the CVS specifically predicts that BET and BAT before nonnasal segments, like /g/, should retract and lower. Other evidence also predicts that BIT should similarly retract and lower, except when preceding velar nasals (Eckert 2004). The present analysis of the front lax vowels in San Francisco, therefore, also allows for further comparison of the similarities and differences between San Francisco English and other Californian Englishes. Will it pattern with the rest of California, as in BOOT and BOAT, or will it appear somewhat distinct, as in the BOT/BOUGHT distinction?

METHODOLOGY

The speaker sample is equally stratified across age, binary gender, and ethnic heritage. A balanced sample is useful in distinguishing between purely linguistic features and those features that are influenced by sociolinguistic conditioning. Vowels are taken from interview speech to augment the results of the read speech data analyzed in Hall-Lew et al. (2015). A detailed statistical analysis on the results using linear mixed-effects models is performed on single first- and second-formant measurements for each vowel class.

PARTICIPANTS. The speaker sample consists of 22 native San Franciscans born between 1932 and 1991 and interviewed by the second author in 2008–9 (table 3.1). All speakers in the current sample were interviewed individually in their homes or places of work, and interviews ranged in length from 37 to 138 minutes. Analysis of these speakers' read speech

TABLE 3.1
Speaker Sample and Demographics

	N	*Years of Birth*
Chinese	11	
female	6	1932–91
male	5	1962–91
White	11	
female	6	1942–91
male	5	1941–90

(word lists and reading passages) has been conducted in a preliminary investigation of the front vowel system (Hall-Lew et al. 2015); here we focus on unstructured interview speech.

Previous work on San Francisco English indicates that the back vowel features of the CVS are progressing in apparent time at a faster rate among women than among men, and at a faster rate among Asian or Chinese Americans than among European Americans (Hall-Lew 2009, 2011, 2013). While previous samples have included some Asian Americans of mixed, non-Chinese, or specifically non-Cantonese heritage, the current sample of Chinese San Franciscans includes only native English speakers of Cantonese heritage to better control for variation in ethnic identity (see also Wong and Hall-Lew 2014). The term "white" is used here to refer to all speakers who identify as "white," "Anglo," or "Caucasian." All speakers are English dominant, and some are variably bilingual (in both ethnic groups). Level of bilingualism has not been a predictor of English vowel variation in previous related studies (Hall-Lew 2009) and so was not considered as a factor here. Because of the nature of the interview sample, there is one fewer man than woman in each speaker subsample; this is particularly unfortunate for the group of Chinese men, who have no representation in their oldest cohort. Previous work (e.g., Hall-Lew 2013) has filled this gap with a nonnative English speaker who we decided to exclude from the current study.

MEASUREMENT, NORMALIZATION, AND MODELING. In contrast to all previous work on sound change in San Francisco English, which relied on a much smaller hand-aligned data set (except for Hall-Lew et al. 2015), the current data set has been automatically phone-aligned and all vowel measurements have been automatically extracted using FAVE (Rosenfelder et al. 2014). To produce results comparable with the read speech results (Hall-Lew et al. 2015), the current analysis uses the single-point FAVE defaults for F1 and F2. These measurements are all taken at the one-third point in the vowel duration for those lexical sets under analysis here: BIT, BET, and BAT.

The initial data set included all possible vowel classes but was trimmed for consistency: all tokens immediately preceded by (n = 12,717) or followed by (n = 9,340) a noise were deleted; all tokens without primary lexical stress (n = 10,529) were deleted; the word *yeah* (n = 23) was deleted; and measurement errors (n = 1,118) were deleted. The final data set contains 79,343 vowel tokens, 23,716 of which correspond to the three front lax vowels.

The front lax vowels are divided into a number of categories based on following phonological environment to directly compare predictions made by previous work on the CVS and on prevelar raising. Table 3.2 presents the

TABLE 3.2
Vowel Subcategories, Descriptions, and Number of Tokens of Each

Vowel	*Category*	*Description*	*No. of Tokens*
BIT	BIT2	all BIT except before nasals and /g/	5,157
	BIN	BIT before /m/ and /n/	1,080
	BING	BIT before /ŋ/	607
	BIG	BIT before /g/	172
BET	BET2	all BET except before nasals and /g/	6,052
	BEN	BET before /m/ and /n/	2,121
	BEG	BET before /g/	15
BAT	BAT2	all BAT except before nasals and /g/	6,031
	BAN	BAT before /m/ and /n/	2,286
	BANG	BAT before /ŋ/	180
	BAG	BAT before /g/	15

revised lexical sets for the current study and the number of tokens in each. Previous research on the CVS (Hinton et al. 1987; Hall-Lew et al. 2015) and on prevelar raising (Baker, Mielke, and Archangeli 2008; Cardoso 2016) indicated that preceding environment may affect vowel productions. The preceding environment is included in the statistical analysis of the target vowels but is not taken into account in the categories in table 3.2.

Evidence from previous research on prevelar raising suggests that BET and BAT are raised to the same extent or more before /ŋ/ compared to before /g/ due to a further lowering of the F1 induced by velum lowering (Baker, Mielke, and Archangeli 2008; Cardoso 2016). The current investigation only has one token of BET before the velar nasal. Therefore, it is not possible to comment on the status of BET before velar nasals at this time, and no subcategory for this vowel with a following /ŋ/ is included in the analysis.

Prevelar raising has mostly been investigated in word list and reading passage speech or experimental perception tasks, such as semantic differentials (Wassink et al. 2009; Cardoso 2016; Wassink 2015; Becker et al. 2016 [this volume]), but has generally not been investigated in interview speech. The token numbers in table 3.2 indicate why this is so; there are vastly fewer naturally occurring instances of BEG and BAG than there are for any of the other lexical sets. Across all 22 speakers, we find only 15 tokens of BEG and BAG, compared to 253 tokens of BET before /k/ and 801 tokens of BAT before /k/. In fact, 13 of the speakers in the current sample have no instances of BAG, 11 have no instances of BEG, and 2 have no instances of BIG. Because prevelar environments were not included in the reading passage and word list during the 2008–9 fieldwork, we have to rely on these interview speech occurrences for the analysis. Therefore, only a preliminary investigation into prevelar raising in San Francisco English will be possible. On the other hand, the sample does provide ample tokens to present a detailed account of San Francisco's relationship to the more general front lax vowel features of the CVS.

FAVE measurements for the initial data set were normalized in R using the Lobanov method in the Vowels.R package (Kendall and Thomas 2009–14). A statistical analysis of the data was performed using linear mixed-effects models, built using the step() function in the lmerTest package (Kuznetsova, Brockhoff, and Christensen 2014). The dependent variables for all models were normalized F1 and F2 measurements, with each vowel (indicated as BIT, BET, and BAT in the following findings), vowel subcategory (indicated as lexical sets provided in table 3.2), and formant modeled separately. The linguistic constraints included in each initial model are PRECEDING and FOLLOWING phonological environment, each coded as a single factor encompassing both manner and place features, where relevant. The models for each overall vowel (BIT, BET, BAT) have following oral velars as a single factor encompassing voice, as well as place and manner. The social constraints, included both as fixed main effects and as interaction effects, were YOB (speaker year of birth), SEX (male, female), and ETHNICITY (Chinese, white). Random effects included SPEAKER and WORD. In the models involving the BET vowel, the following phonological environment nasal_velar was removed, as there was only one token of BET before /ŋ/ and the models could not converge with this token included. Furthermore, BEG and BAG were not modeled independently to BET and BAT due to the small number of tokens.

RESULTS

See appendix for a subset of the mixed effects models significance tables. The linguistic and social factors that are significant predictors of the models differ for each of the vowels and vowel subcategories (see table 3.2), in ways similar to those seen in Hall-Lew et al. (2015) for the reading passage and word list data. Overall, preceding and following environments are significantly correlated with normalized F1 and F2 measurements for all three front lax vowels; all indicate known phonetic coarticulatory effects.

Results from linear mixed-effects models indicate that the pre-/g/ environment is a conditioning factor for BET F2 and BAT F1 (figure 3.2). BEG is fronter than BET2 tokens; BAG is higher than BAT2. However, BAG is not raised to the same extent as BANG or BAN. Figure 3.2 includes BAIT for com-

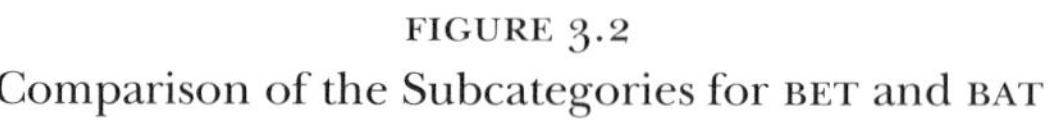
FIGURE 3.2
Comparison of the Subcategories for BET and BAT

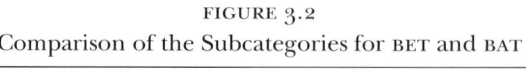

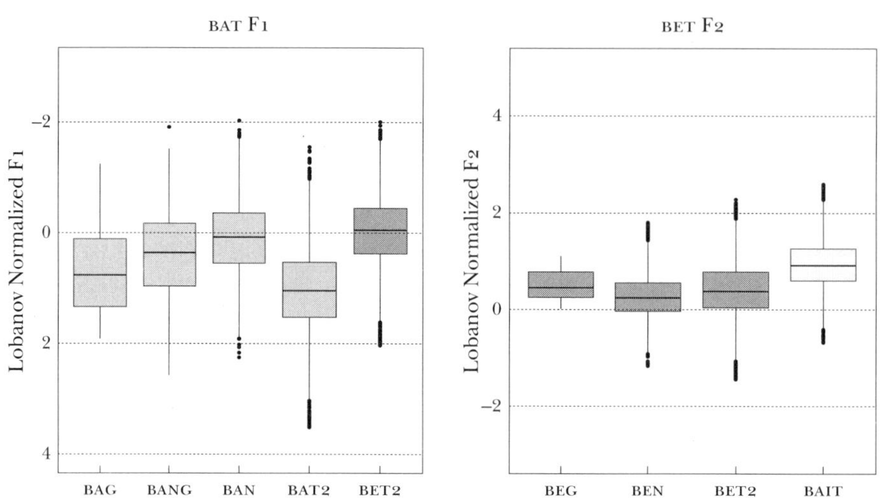

parison of the BET results, and BET2 for comparison with BAT. Note that these effects do not directly correspond to descriptions for other varieties with prevelar raising. Statistical analysis of the pre-/g/ environment in these vowels, BEG or BAG, are not available, but graphical representations suggest that BEG is not fronted to the extent of BAIT, and BAG is not raised to the extent of BET.

BIG, which is generally not included in discussions of prevelar raising, does not show signs of raising or fronting relative to BIT. The results for BIT show that BIT2, BIN, and BIG are all lower and retracted and that BING productions are raised. These findings correspond well to descriptions of the CVS (Eckert 2008; Kennedy and Grama 2012). Gender is a predictor of the respective models for BING F1, with women favoring the more advanced variant. Year of birth is not a predictor for any of the BIT models, suggesting that lowering and retraction of BIT2, BIN, and BIG and raising of BING is not a change in progress. Rather, there is a phonologically conditioned split in BIT (with gender effects for some variable productions), where the criteria for the split are different from those for BAT (i.e., the trigger for raising is a following velar nasal, not just any nasal).

BET is higher and fronter when preceded by an oral velar onset, in line with Hinton et al. (1987) and Hall-Lew et al. (2015). Similar to Hall-Lew et al. (2015), BET is also higher and fronter when preceded by an apical nasal onset but does not raise (or front) before nasals. In fact, BEN and BET2 produce almost identical results in the statistical analysis; there is no BET nasal split. As a result of the MERRY-MARY-MARRY merger (see Labov, Ash, and Boberg 2006), which San Francisco appears to participate in, BET2 tokens are higher before liquids than other environments. Note that 85% (*n* = 2,920) of the BET2 tokens before liquids are BET followed by /r/, such as *there,* rather than BET followed by /l/.

BAT2 productions are lowest and most retracted both when preceded by liquids as well as when followed by liquids, which in the case of BAT2 are mostly /l/ (preceded by /l/, *n* = 107, 70%; followed by /l/, *n* = 123, 90%). There is also substantial lowering of BAT before /k/, which suggests that the raising of BAG is not purely due to phonetic coarticulation. Overall, BAT is found to be lowering and retracting in accordance with the CVS, except before oral voiced velars (BAG). We also find evidence of the nasal split, where BAN is higher and fronter than all of the other BAT subcategories. This raising and fronting is most inhibited when the nasal in BAN is an /m/ or when the onset consonant is a liquid.

The three social constraints included in the current analysis (year of birth, binary gender, and ethnicity) are discussed below in turn.

CHANGE IN APPARENT TIME: SPEAKER YEAR OF BIRTH. Speaker year of birth is found to significantly correlate with F1 measurements of BET2, BAT2, and F2 measurements of BEN. In the preliminary study on the front vowels using read speech, BAT F2 and BAN F1 are also correlated with year of birth

FIGURE 3.3
Significant Fixed Effects of Year of Birth

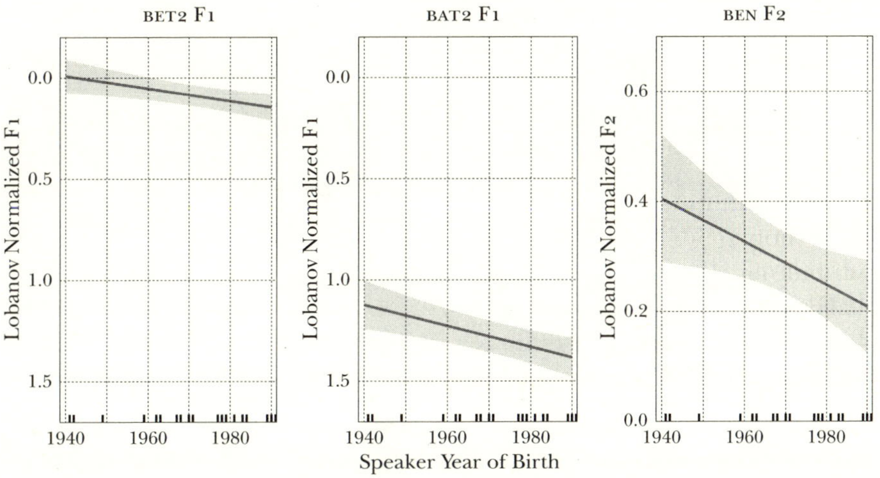

(Hall-Lew et al. 2015), which is not borne out in the current study. Figure 3.3 plots year of birth from 1932 to 1991 on the *x*-axis and normalized formant values on the *y*-axes, reversed for BET2, BAT2 (so a lower *y*-value indicates a lower vowel), and standard for BEN F2 (where a lower *y*-value indicates a retracted vowel). All of the correlations shown achieve statistical significance in model comparisons.

The current results in combination with the read speech results provide substantial evidence that BET lowering and the BAT nasal split are both advancing in apparent time in San Francisco English, in line with other Californian varieties.

CHANGE IN APPARENT TIME: SPEAKER GENDER. Speaker gender is significantly correlated with BING F1, and F2 measurements of BAT2 (figure 3.4), and an interaction between year of birth and gender is a significant predictor in the model of BANG F1 (figure 3.5). In all cases, the more advanced or nonstandard productions are attributable to the female speakers, which evidences the well-documented phenomenon of female-led changes in progress that has been found for other aspects of the CVS (in San Francisco and elsewhere) and in sound change studies more generally. Furthermore, these results support the finding for read speech (Hall-Lew et al. 2015) that BAT retraction is a change in progress being led by females. Figure 3.4 shows the results of the linear-mixed effects model for the predictor GENDER in BING F1, and F2 of BAT2. Speaker gender is plotted on the *x*-axis and the dependent variable along the *y*-axis. As before, the *y*-axis for the

FIGURE 3.4
Significant Fixed Effects of Speaker Gender

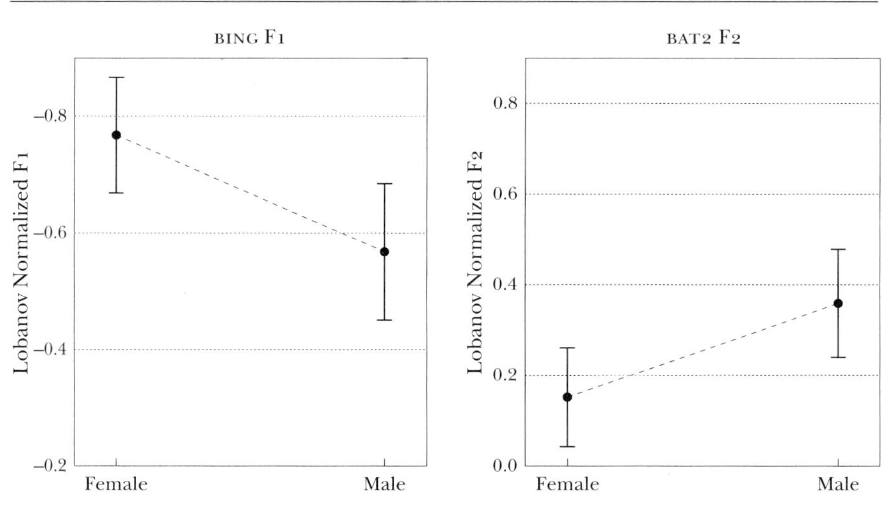

FIGURE 3.5
Significant Interaction between Year of Birth and Speaker Gender

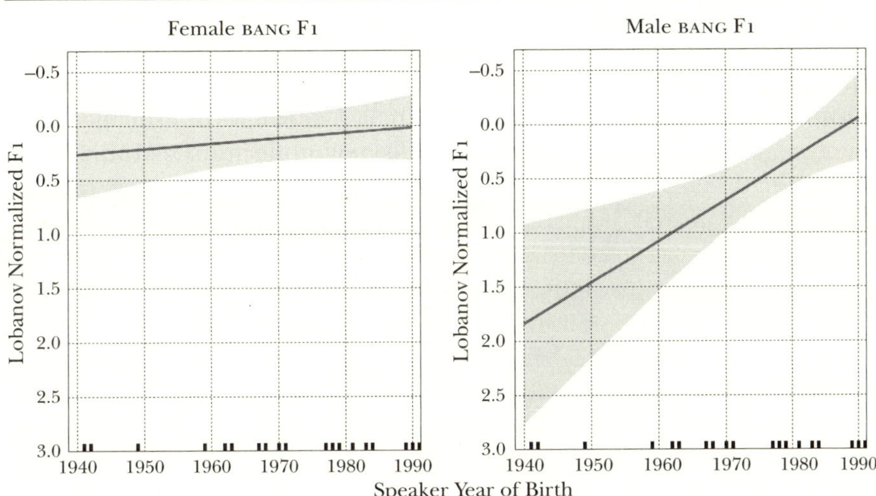

BING F1 plot has been reversed so that values that are lower represent lower vowel productions and the lower values on the *y*-axis for BAT2 F2 represent retracted variants.

BANG F1 is the only vowel subcategory to show a significant interaction of gender and year of birth. As can be seen in figure 3.5, male speakers are lagging behind with a robust apparent time correlation toward the high stable female norm.

CHANGE IN APPARENT TIME: SPEAKER ETHNICITY. Previous research on San Francisco English provides evidence of change in progress being led by Chinese Americans: the apparent-time correlation is more robust, and the most advanced variants are also acoustically more advanced than in the European American cohort (Hall-Lew 2009, 2011, 2013). In this study, BAT2 and BAN F1 values are significantly correlated with ethnicity (figure 3.6; note that *y*-axis values are not matched between vowels). Chinese American speakers show lower productions of BAN and higher productions of BAT2 than European American (white) speakers; in other words, less of a nasal split. Thus, while the apparent-time correlations have appeared stronger among Chinese Americans for some of the back vowel changes (Hall-Lew 2009, 2013), in BAT we see the opposite pattern (see also Eckert 2008). Hall-Lew et al. (2015) found that variation was not significantly correlated with ethnicity in read speech; however, we see here that in interview speech an ethnic difference obtains.

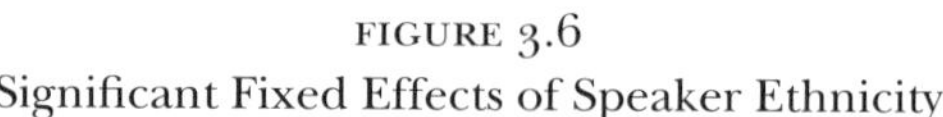
FIGURE 3.6
Significant Fixed Effects of Speaker Ethnicity

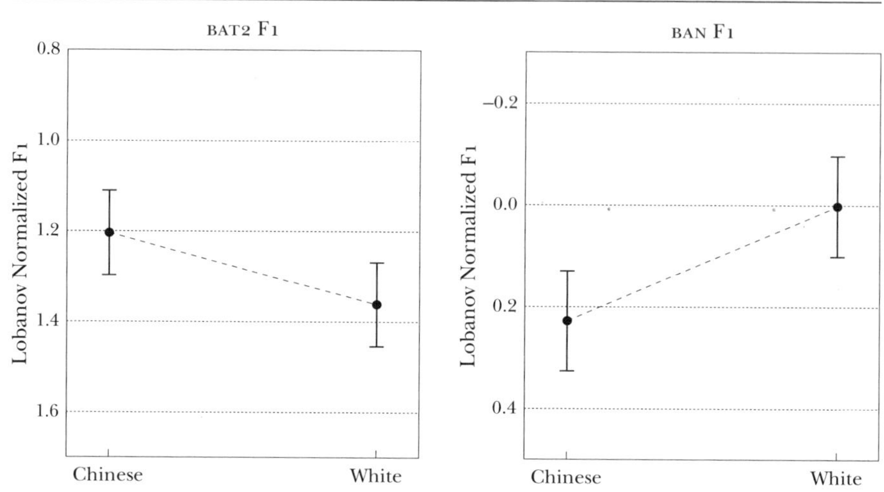

TABLE 3.3
Summary of Significant Social Effects

Social Factor	*Linguistic Variable*	*Direction of Effect*
Year of birth	BET2 F1	young lowering
	BAT2 F1	young lowering
	BEN F2	young retracting
Gender	BING F1	females raised
	BAT2 F2	females retracted
Ethnicity	BAN F1	white raising
Year of Birth × Ethnicity	BAT2 F1	young and white lowering
Year of Birth × Gender	BANG F1	females stable and high, young males raising

SUMMARY. A summary of the social factors that are correlated with the vowel subcategories is presented in table 3.3. See appendix for a subset of the mixed effects models significance tables.

DISCUSSION

SAN FRANCISCO AND PREVELAR RAISING. The preliminary investigation of pre-/g/ environments suggests that aspects of prevelar raising occur in San Francisco English, though not exactly in the same ways as in Oregon, Washington State, and British Columbia. Here, all three front lax vowels were investigated in the pre-/g/ environment. Studies of prevelar raising have generally not included BIT in the analysis, and in the present study the prevelar subclass BIG is found not to participate in raising. However, similar to other studies, both BAT and BET are conditioned by the following /g/. While BEG is fronted compared to BET2 and BEN, BAG's raised position relative to BAT2 is not so dramatic as the raising of BANG and BAN. Fronting is the main distinguishing characteristic of BEG, similar to the findings for Oregon (Becker et al. 2016 [this volume]), while raising mainly differentiates BAG from BAT2 (excluding BAN and BANG).

These findings may indicate that San Francisco English is participating in aspects of prevelar raising found in the Pacific Northwest. If this is the case, then the outer limits of prevelar raising might be within Northern California, which is much further south than has generally been assumed. Alternatively, the results may indicate that San Francisco is participating in the CVS but that the shift of BET and BAT is inhibited in pre-/g/ environments. In this hypothesis, BET and BAT are lowering and retracting in accordance with the CVS, but BAG and BEG are inhibited, potentially as a result of coarticulatory pressures.

Coarticulatory pressure has been used as an explanation for prevelar raising in some varieties (see, for example, Baker, Mielke, and Archangeli 2008), such that raising results from the lowering of F1 and raising of F2 characteristic of vowels followed by /g/. There is also evidence that the velar pinch effect, which affects both pre-/k/ and pre-/g/ contexts, differs in duration for pre-/k/ contexts versus pre-/g/ contexts. The pre-/g/ context has a longer velar pinch resulting in a diphthongal variant (see Cardoso 2016; Freeman 2014; Wassink 2015). In contrast, the velar pinch in pre-/k/ vowels is much shorter (Cardoso 2016). It is possible that this mismatch in velar pinch duration might account for why prevelar raising, or CVS inhibition, appears to affect only those vowels before /g/ and not those before /k/.

A larger sample of tokens across all speakers would be required to test these two hypotheses, as well as any sociolinguistic factors that may be affecting prevelar raising. Therefore, this preliminary investigation can only confirm that for a subset of speakers, BEG tokens are further front compared to BET in other environments, and BAG tokens are raised compared to BAT before other nonnasal consonants.

SAN FRANCISCO AND THE CALIFORNIA VOWEL SHIFT. Regardless of the status of the pre-/g/ environments, the overall results suggest that San Francisco English is participating in those front vowel changes that have been most robustly documented as part of the CVS: the lowering and retraction of

BET and the BAT nasal split (Eckert 2004, 2008; Podesva 2011; Kennedy and Grama 2012). This pairs well with previously reported results of San Francisco's participation in back vowel fronting (Hall-Lew 2009, 2011), as well as the evidence that the same speakers are gradually merging BOT and BOUGHT in apparent time (Hall-Lew 2009, 2013). Taken together, we present here further evidence to argue against a characterization of contemporary San Francisco English as a dialect isolate (cf., Labov, Ash, and Boberg 2006).

The specific results for BET show that the vowel (including BEN and BEG) is retracting in apparent time; additionally, BEN is itself retracting, and BET2 (excluding both BEN and BEG) is lowering. The specific results for BAT show that the lexical subset that excludes prevelars and prenasals, BAT2, is lowering in apparent time. Since we do not see the prenasal context (BAN) raising in apparent time, the data only present evidence for half of a BAT nasal split process. We would also expect to see significant correlations with year of birth on the F2 dimension, which did not obtain here. This is particularly perplexing because the analysis of read speech (Hall-Lew et al. 2015) does show an apparent-time correlation for BAT F2 (and, actually, not for BAT F1). It could be that these incongruent results reflect a simple problem of too little data, and future work will endeavor to test for this possibility.

Two dimensions that do not correlate with speaker year of birth do correlate with speaker gender: BING is higher among females than males, and BAT2 is retracted more among females than males.

Overall, these results and those of Hall-Lew et al. (2015) provide evidence that San Francisco English is participating in changes in apparent time similar to other Californian Englishes, distinguishing it from the Pacific Northwest (Wassink 2015). At the same time, the relatively more raised productions of BEG and BAG potentially place San Francisco also within the northwest U.S. varieties, although more data are needed to test for apparent-time correlations for these rarely occurring lexical items.

One aspect of the CVS that has not been previously reported is found here for the lexical subset BANG (BAT before velar nasals), where BANG is found to be raising in apparent time and differentiated by speaker gender. For the female speakers, this appears to be a completed change, as the vowel is uniformly high and height does not covary with speaker year of birth. For the male speakers, we see a robust apparent-time correlation, with older males showing lower productions of BANG and younger males moving toward the stable female production pattern.

Lastly, while ethnicity was not found to correlate with any of the read speech results, here it is found to be a significant predictor for the lowering of BAT2 and raising of BAN. This results in a difference between the nasal split for Chinese American and European American speakers, where the change is more advanced for the latter than the former. This is the first time a CVS change in San Francisco English has been found to be less robust in the Chinese American subsample, in contrast to changes where the apparent-time change was stronger for the Chinese Americans, as with the low back merger (Hall-Lew 2013) or where there was no ethnic difference as with BOOT fronting (Hall-Lew 2011). However, it does pair well with findings, such as those of Eckert (2008), where in certain Northern Californian contexts, the BAT nasal split was argued to index social meanings associated with white or otherwise non-Chicano social persona. The present finding, therefore, presents an update to previous claims about ethnicity and sound change in San Francisco: while the majority status of Chinese Americans in the local community might predict the leading of local sound changes by members of that ethnic group, this might not be the case for any instances of sound changes that index ethnic persona that are at odds with Chinese American identity. A full investigation of these issues is beyond the scope of the present study and is left for future work.

CONCLUSIONS

This chapter presents an analysis of the front lax vowels of San Francisco English based on unscripted, spontaneous interview speech from 22 men and women of various ages and ethnic backgrounds. The results suggest that San Francisco English is participating in the California Vowel Shift with respect to the lowering and retraction of the BET vowel and the BAT nasal split. These changes are socially conditioned, such that women are leading in the retraction changes, and European Americans are leading Chinese Americans in both BAT retraction and the raising of BAN. The results also show preliminary evidence for a kind of prevelar raising for both vowels, although this might be better described as an inhibition of retraction and lowering rather than a raising movement per se. We also find the first evidence for a robust, gender-stratified change in the raising of BANG, specifically. Overall, San Francisco English seems to exhibit precisely the Northern Californian vowel system one would expect.

APPENDIX

Mixed Effects Models: Subset of Significant Effects

Model	*Level*	*Estimate*	*Standard Error*	*t-Value*	*Stat. Sig.*
Following Environment					
BAT F1	(Intercept)	1.01008	0.15824	6.383	***
	nasal_apical	–0.65432	0.13823	–4.734	***
	nasal_labial	–0.61948	0.15126	–4.095	***
	nasal_velar	–0.37582	0.16816	–2.235	*
	liquid	0.05776	0.16153	0.358	
	oral_apical	0.48567	0.13979	3.474	***
	oral_labial	0.63088	0.14408	4.379	***
	palatal	0.31340	0.15788	1.985	*
	oral_vd_velar	–0.11471	0.23593	–0.486	
	oral_vl_velar	0.64851	0.14476	4.480	***
BET F2	(Intercept)	–0.26366	0.21659	–1.217	
	nasal_apical	0.47170	0.21276	2.217	*
	nasal_labial	0.35435	0.22329	1.587	
	liquid	0.48368	0.21239	2.277	*
	oral_apical	0.41145	0.21196	1.941	
	oral_labial	0.34814	0.21324	1.633	
	palatal	0.38520	0.22118	1.742	
	oral_vd_velar	0.62452	0.26029	2.399	*
	oral_vl_velar	0.49593	0.21597	2.296	*
Social Factors					
BET2 F1	(Intercept)	–6.100	2.111	–2.890	**
	yob	0.003107	0.001071	2.902	**
BEN F2	(Intercept)	7.876	3.303	2.385	*
	yob	–0.003928	0.001675	–2.345	*
BING F1	(Intercept)	–0.76774	0.05054	–15.190	***
	gen_male	0.19997	0.07809	2.561	*
BAT2 F2	(Intercept)	–0.045178	0.085624	–0.528	
	gen_male	0.207316	0.077883	2.662	*
BAN F1	(Intercept)	0.40185	0.10288	3.906	***
	ethnic_white	–0.22584	0.07100	–3.181	**
BAT2 F1	(Intercept)	–13.058573	3.877716	–3.131	**
	yob	0.006986	0.001962	3.373	**
	ethnic_white	0.164214	0.054565	3.271	**
BANG F1	(Intercept)	10.234874	11.260901	0.909	
	yob*gen_male	–0.033075	0.013601	–2.432	*

$^{*}p < .05$; $^{**}p < .01$; $^{***}p < .001$

NOTE

The automatic alignment and extraction of vowel data is only possible due to long hours of initial orthographic transcription. Our thanks go to research funds from the 2009–10 Andrew W. Mellon postdoctoral fellowship which funded transcription by RAs Claire Drohan, Annabel Schwenk, and Amanda Wall, as well as to the 2010–11 PPLS Pilot Scheme which funded transcription by RAs Keelin Murray and the first author. A special note of thanks goes to RAs Julie Saigusa and Kieran Wilson, who, along with the authors of this paper, volunteered their time to project transcription during 2014–15. We also thank Josef Fruehwald and the editors and other contributors to this collection for the conversations that made this paper possible. Lastly, the biggest debt goes to those speakers whose voices are represented here. All shortcomings are our own.

REFERENCES

Baker, Adam, Jeff Mielke, and Diana Archangeli. 2008. "More Velar than /g/: Consonant Coarticulation as a Cause of Diphthongization." In *Proceedings of the 26th West Coast Conference on Formal Linguistics*, edited by Charles B. Chang and Hannah J. Haynie, 60–68. Somerville, Mass.: Cascadilla Proceedings Project.

Bauer, Matt, and Frank Parker. 2008. "/æ/-Raising in Wisconsin English." *American Speech* 83.4: 403–31. doi:10.1215/00031283-2008-029.

Becker, Kara, Anna Aden, Katelyn Best, and Haley Jacobson. 2016. "Variation in West Coast English: The Case of Oregon." In Fridland et al. 2016, 107–34. doi:10.1215/00031283-3772923.

Benson, Erica J., Michael J. Fox, and Jared Balkman. 2011. "*The Bag That Scott Bought*: The Low Vowels in Northwest Wisconsin." *American Speech* 86.3: 271–311. doi:10.1215/00031283-1503910.

Boberg, Charles. 2008. "Regional Phonetic Differentiation in Standard Canadian English." *Journal of English Linguistics* 36.2: 129–54. doi:10.1177/0075424208316648.

Cardoso, Amanda. 2016. "Pre-velar Raising in Western Canadian Dialects." Unpublished manuscript.

Conn, Jeffrey. 2000. "Portland Dialect Study: The Story of /æ/ in Portland." Master's thesis, Portland State University.

D'Onofrio, Annette, Penelope Eckert, Robert J. Podesva, Teresa Pratt, and Janneke Van Hofwegen. 2016. In Fridland et al. 2016, 11–32. doi:10.1215/00031283-3772879.

Eckert, Penelope. 2004. "Vowel Shifts in Northern California and the Detroit Suburbs." http://www.stanford.edu/~eckert/vowels.html.

———. 2008. "Where Do Ethnolects Stop?" *International Journal of Bilingualism* 12.1–2: 25–42. doi:10.1177/13670069080120010301.

Fought, Carmen. 1999. "A Majority Sound Change in a Minority Community: /u/-Fronting in Chicano English." *Journal of Sociolinguistics* 3.1: 5–23. doi:10.1111/1467-9481.t01-1-00060.

Freeman, Valerie. 2014. "Bag, Beg, Bagel: Prevelar Raising and Merger in Pacific Northwest English." University of Washington Working Papers in Linguistics, 32. http://depts.washington.edu/uwwpl/vol32/freeman_2014.pdf.

Fridland, Valerie, Tyler Kendall, Betsy Evans, and Alicia Beckford Wassink, eds. 2016. *Speech in the Western States.* Vol. 1, *The Coastal States.* Publication of the American Dialect Society 101. Durham, N.C.: Duke University Press.

Fridland, Valerie, Tyler Kendall, and Craig Fickle. 2015. "It's Nev-ae-da, Not Nev-ah-da!" Paper presented at the annual meeting of the American Dialect Society, Portland, Ore., Jan. 8–11.

Gregg, Robert J. 1957. "Notes on the Pronunciation of Canadian English as Spoken in Vancouver, BC." *Journal of the Canadian Linguistic Association* 3.1: 20–26.

Hall-Lew, Lauren. 2005. "One Shift, Two Groups: When Fronting Alone Is Not Enough." In "Selected Papers from NWAVE 32," edited by Maciej Baranowski, Uri Horesh, Keelan Evans, and Giang Nguyen. *University of Philadelphia Working Papers in Linguistics* 10.2: 105–16. http://repository.upenn.edu/pwpl/vol10/iss2/9/.

———. 2009. "Ethnicity and Phonetic Variation in a San Francisco Neighborhood." Ph.D. diss., Stanford University. http://www.lel.ed.ac.uk/~lhlew/Hall-Lew_2009.pdf.

———. 2011. "The Completion of a Sound Change in California English." In *Proceedings of the 17th International Congress of Phonetic Sciences (ICPhS XVII), 17–21 August 2011, Hong Kong,* edited by Wai-Sum Lee and Eric Zee, 807–10. Hong Kong: City University of Hong Kong. https://www.internationalphoneticassociation.org/icphs-proceedings/ICPhS2011/OnlineProceedings/RegularSession/Hall-Lew/Hall-Lew.pdf.

———. 2013. "'Flip-Flop' and Mergers-in-Progress." *English Language and Linguistics* 17.2: 359–90. doi:10.1017/S1360674313000063.

Hall-Lew, Lauren, Amanda Cardoso, Yova Kemenchedjieva, Kieran Wilson, Ruaridh Purse, and Julie Saigusa. 2015. "San Francisco English and the California Vowel Shift." In *The Scottish Consortium for ICPhS 2015: Proceedings of the 18th International Congress of Phonetic Sciences.* Glasgow, U.K.: University of Glasgow. http://www.icphs2015.info/pdfs/Papers/ICPHS0591.pdf.

Hinton, Leanne, Birch Moonwomon, Sue Bremner, Herb Luthin, Mary Van Clay, Jean Lerner, and Hazel Corcoran. 1987. "It's Not Just the Valley Girls: A Study of California English." In *Berkeley Linguistics Society: Proceedings of the Thirteenth Annual Meeting, February 14–16, 1987,* edited by Jon Aske, Natasha Beery, Laura Michaelis, and Hana Filip, 117–28. Berkeley, Calif.: Berkeley Linguistics Society. doi:10.3765/bls.v13i0.1811.

Kendall, Tyler, and Erik R. Thomas. 2009–14. Vowels: Vowel Manipulation, Normalization, and Plotting in R. R Package. Version 1.2-1. Available on http://lingtools.uoregon.edu/norm/.

Kennedy, Robert, and James Grama. 2012. "Chain Shifting and Centralization in California Vowels: An Acoustic Analysis." *American Speech* 87.1: 39–56. doi:10.1215/00031283-1599950.

Kurath, Hans, and Raven I. McDavid. 1961. *The Pronunciation of English in the Atlantic States: Based upon the Collections of the Linguistic Atlas of the Eastern United States.* Ann Arbor: University of Michigan Press.

Kuznetsova, Alexandra, Per B. Brockhoff, and Rune H. B. Christensen. 2014. Package lmerTest. CRAN. http://cran.rproject.org/web/packages/lmerTest/.

Labov, William. 1991. "The Three Dialects of English." In *New Ways of Analyzing Sound Change*, edited by Penelope Eckert, 1–44. San Diego, Calif.: Academic Press.

Labov, William, Sharon Ash, and Charles Boberg. 2006. *The Atlas of North American English: Phonetics, Phonology, and Sound Change.* Berlin: Mouton de Gruyter.

Moonwomon, Birch. 1991. "Sound Change in San Francisco English." Ph.D. diss., University of California, Berkeley. http://escholarship.org/uc/item/6qz10226.

Podesva, Robert J. 2011. "The California Vowel Shift and Gay Identity." *American Speech* 86.1: 32–51. doi:10.1215/00031283-1277501.

Podesva, Robert J., Annette D'Onofrio, Janneke Van Hofwegen, and Seung Kyung Kim. 2015. "Country Ideology and the California Vowel Shift." *Language Variation and Change* 27.2: 157–86. doi:10.1017/S095439451500006X.

Reed, Carroll E. 1952. "The Pronunciation of English in the State of Washington." *American Speech* 27.3: 186–89. doi:10.2307/453476.

Roeder, Rebecca. 2009. "The Effects of Phonetic Environment on English /æ/ among Speakers of Mexican Heritage in Michigan." In *Toronto Working Papers in Linguistics* 31," edited by Richard Compton and Monica Irimia. http://twpl.library.utoronto.ca/index.php/twpl/article/view/6090.

Rosenfelder, Ingrid, Joseph Fruehwald, Keelan Evanini, Scott Seyfarth, Kyle Gorman, Hilary Prichard, and Jiahong Yuan. 2014. FAVE 1.1.3. Zenodo. doi:10.5281/zenodo.9846.

Wassink, Alicia Beckford. 2015. "Sociolinguistic Patterns in Seattle English." *Language Variation and Change* 27.1: 31–58. doi:10.1017/S0954394514000234.

———. 2016. "The Vowels of Washington State." In Fridland et al. 2016, 77–106. doi:10.1215/00031283-3772912.

Wassink, Alicia, Robert Squizzero, Mike Scanlon, Rachel Schirra, and Jeffrey Conn. 2009. "Effects of Gender and Style and on Fronting and Raising of /æ/, /e:/ and /ɛ/ before /g/ in Seattle English." Paper presented at the 38th annual meeting of New Ways of Analyzing Variation (NWAV 38), Ottawa, Oct. 22–25.

Wong, Amy Wing-mei, and Lauren Hall-Lew. 2014. "Regional Variability and Ethnic Identity: Chinese Americans in New York City and San Francisco." In "New Perspectives on Linguistic Variation and Ethnic Identity in North America," edited by Lauren Hall-Lew and Malcah Yaeger-Dror. Special issue, *Language and Communication* 35.1: 27–42. doi:10.1016/j.langcom.2013.11.003.

AMANDA CARDOSO is currently a teaching fellow at the University of Leeds and has held posts at the University of York and Newcastle University. Her research considers the interaction of phonetics/phonology, dialectology, and sociolinguistics and the development of phonological patterns referencing historical and contemporary evidence. Her Ph.D. disseration, written in 2015 at the University of Edinburgh, focused on the emergence and development of phonologically conditioned variation of /aɪ/ and /aʊ/ in the variety of English spoken in Liverpool, United Kingdom. Various qualitative and quantitative techniques are employed, such as dynamic vowel measurements, linear-mixed effects models, and the analysis of historical census data. Cardoso has further research projects on phonological conditioning of lenition in Liverpool English and on Western Canadian varieties, specifically focusing on prevelar raising of /æ/ and /ɛ/ and Canadian Raising. E-mail: a.b.cardoso@sms.ed.ac.uk.

LAUREN HALL-LEW is lecturer in linguistics and English language in the School of Philosophy, Psychology, and Language Sciences at the University of Edinburgh. Her Ph.D. dissertation, written in 2009 at Stanford University, focused on back vowel variation in English spoken in the Sunset District of San Francisco, California. This continuing project examines the role of social identity and language change, particularly examining the potential for social meaning to influence the trajectory of a change, as well as the dialectological relationship between San Francisco and its adjacent geographic regions. Hall-Lew's other research projects consider the role of political party identity in predicting synchronic variation, the commodity value of language in tourism, and issues in sociophonetic methodologies. E-mail: lauren.hall-lew@ed.ac.uk.

YOVA KEMENTCHEDJHIEVA is an M.S. student in natural language processing at the University of Edinburgh. E-mail: s1233656@ed.ac.uk.

RUARIDH PURSE is a Ph.D. student in linguistics at the University of Pennsylvania working in phonetics, phonology, and sociolinguistics. In particular, his research is concerned with the articulatory realities of variable phenomena and the notion of systematic articulatory variation. This work explores how grammar and physiological limitations influence observed patterns of variation and if their respective effects can be isolated. Further, the discussion of whether representations in speech should be articulatory or acoustic—of central concern to phonetics and phonology—would be enhanced by an understanding of the way speakers might exhibit articulatory variation with little or no acoustic consequence. E-mail: rupurse@sas.upenn.edu.

4. "DO I SOUND LIKE A VALLEY GIRL TO YOU?" PERCEPTUAL DIALECTOLOGY AND LANGUAGE ATTITUDES IN CALIFORNIA

DAN VILLARREAL

As THE CHAPTERS in this volume demonstrate, vowel features play an important role in sociolinguists' understanding of California as a unique dialect region of Western U.S. English. However, this research leaves open the question of whether California vowels matter as much to speakers of California English as they do to sociolinguists; that is, how do vowels play a role in Californians' linguistic self-perceptions? The present study aims to address this question through the lens of folk linguistics by using a dialect recognition task (Williams, Garrett, and Coupland 1999).

FOLK LINGUISTICS AND PERCEPTUAL DIALECTOLOGY

The object of study in folk linguistics is nonlinguists' responses to language, whether in the form of overt commentary or unconscious reactions. Of particular importance to this study is the subfield of perceptual dialectology, which seeks to understand speakers' mental maps of linguistic variation over geographical spaces (Preston 1996). One method for eliciting these mental maps is simply to ask for them directly by giving respondents a map of a region (e.g., the United States, Ohio) and asking them to indicate where people speak differently. The results of these map-drawing tasks reveal not only where respondents find regional speech to be salient, but also attitudes toward these regions. One North Carolinian respondent, for example, labeled a portion of the Northeastern United States "Boston & New York & New Jersey: fast & rude" (Preston 1996, 308). These attitudes are rarely presented in ways that are coherent with the phrasing of linguistic description, but they nevertheless indicate the shape of folk-linguistic belief. Such is true of a Chicagoan's label for California: "High Class partying Slobs & Stuck up sound" (Preston 1996, 307). While a "stuck up sound," of course, has no inherent linguistic reality, to this particular Chicagoan it

Publication of the American Dialect Society 101 DOI 10.1215/00031283-3772901

is sufficiently self-evident to function as a linguistic descriptor that his audience is assumed to readily recognize.

Other perceptual dialectology methodologies utilize auditory stimuli to investigate the relationship between variation and perception of speaker region. Plichta and Preston (2005) found that listeners from Michigan and Indiana were able to distinguish BITE tokens on a fine-grained continuum between monophthongal [a] and diphthongal [aɪ], attributing more monophthongal tokens to more Southern speakers. Such sensitivity to fine phonetic detail may be surprising in light of the relatively crude, under-detailed labels found on hand-drawn maps (e.g., "Potatoe Land" for Idaho [Preston 1996, 308]); as Plichta and Preston suggest, however, distinctive features may be perceptually available to listeners even in the absence of overt folk-linguistic commentary.

Finally, perceptual dialectology studies have demonstrated the usefulness of comparing how dialects are perceived by both IN-GROUP members (speakers of that dialect) and OUT-GROUP members (speakers not of that dialect). Allbritten (2011, 186), for example, found that perceptions of Southernness and rurality strengthened with an increase in Southern features, indicating that rurality is connected to the notion "sounding Southern." Not all features created this effect uniformly, however; while (ing) did not affect Southerners' perceptions, non-Southerners perceived [ɪn] samples significantly more Southern than [ɪŋ] samples. Whereas [ɪn] plays into non-Southerners' percepts of Southern speech, Southerners do not necessarily view themselves as [ɪn] users. In other words, with respect to (ing), Southerners (in-group perceivers) have a different notion of "sounding Southern" than do non-Southerners (out-group perceivers). This is a finding quite relevant in California since, as I will discuss shortly, in-group and out-group perceptions of California English differ in substantial ways.

FOLK LINGUISTICS OF CALIFORNIA. Similar to the South, California is another region for which the folk-linguistic beliefs of out-group perceivers (i.e., non-Californians) are rather different than those of in-group perceivers. In short, non-Californians align California speech with persistent cultural tropes that index Southern California, whereas Californians identify greater distinctions within the state and de-emphasize these tropes. Seventeen percent of the Michigan respondents surveyed by Preston (1996, 305) identified a California speech region on hand-drawn maps. Labels for the state included "not so much a diff[erent] lang[uage] but completly diff words: totally rad etc." (310), "Fer-Sher [for sure] Valley People" (308), and (for a small area roughly west of Fresno) "valley girl" (307). The latter two labels apparently respond to the "Valley Girl" stereotype popularized by Frank

Zappa's popular 1982 song of the same name ("Valley" referring to the suburban San Fernando Valley north of Los Angeles).

A limited amount of perceptual dialectology research has investigated Californians' perceptions. Fought (2002) found that Californian students do not share Michiganders' notion of Upper Midwestern speech as "standard"—indeed, Fought's data call into question whether Californians share even the same underlying schema of "standardness" as Michiganders. Whereas New England states were more likely to be labeled "proper English," Western states (especially California) were more likely to be labeled "good/better/best English." Fought attributes this apparent contradiction to Californians' acknowledgment of marked speech within the state but overall linguistic security: "Californians seem to see their own speech in a fairly positive light, as natural and relaxed, but with its positive value tempered by the idea that it is also not 'accurate' speech in some sense, and that it reflects the negative aspects of the surfers and the Valley girls" (132).

Bucholtz et al. (2007) restrict their analytic scope to California, collecting Californian students' hand-drawn maps of the state itself. Many maps included a north/south division, which typically surfaced as an opposition between the state's two most populous regions: the San Francisco Bay Area and the Los Angeles area. This distinction often rested on the intensifier/quantifier *hella*, reported to be far more prevalent in the Bay Area and often derided by nonusers, but linguistic features otherwise received rather little overt comment. Chinese and "Diverse" also featured prominently in the Bay Area, and few dialects of English received particular mention (other than "Ebonics" in Los Angeles and "Spanglish" inland and in San Diego). Folk-linguistic labels also included "surfers" and "Valley girls" in Southern California, but most frequently mentioned was "hicks"—a stereotype of California speech that is not well known outside the state—in the least populous parts of the state: Northern California and inland. These regions were also subject to substantial erasure (Irvine and Gal 2000): "*Almost no one lives here*; *Does Anyone Live Out Here?*; *No man's land*; *Nothing—oppression, ennui, desert*; and *DEATH VALLEY (NO ONE SPEAKS)*" (Bucholtz et al. 2007, 338). In general, Californians' perceptions of California speech appear to hinge more on social differences than simply sociolinguistic or geographic differences.

DIALECT RECOGNITION. In Williams, Garrett, and Coupland's (1999) original study of dialect recognition, adolescent listeners in six regions of Wales were asked to rate speakers from each region on affective scales (e.g., likability, "Welshness") and guess speakers' regional origin.

The overall rate at which listeners accurately recognized speakers' regions was roughly 25%, but some speakers were accurately recognized at a far higher or lower rate. (Here and below, I use ACCURATE RECOGNITION to refer to correctly identifying a speaker's region of origin.) The authors' analysis of likability ratings helps to explain this variation in accurate-recognition rates, as the speakers who were rated most likable were also more likely to be identified as belonging to a listener's in-group (whether or not this was actually true). Cardiff listeners, for example, found Northwest speaker 2 more likable than Northwest speaker 1 and misidentified Northwest speaker 2 (but not Northwest speaker 1) as a Cardiffian. From this pattern, the authors find evidence for a social-psychological CLAIMING effect, with individuals grouping themselves with those they find desirable (356).

In pairing regional identification with affective scales, this type of task demonstrates that dialect recognition is a sociolinguistic process rather than a purely phonetic process; that is, when listeners make a judgment on where a speaker is from, they are not simply matching the speaker to preexisting acoustic templates of regional speech, but they are also drawing on their attitudes toward certain regions, including their own region. The present study uses a similar task to investigate attitudes toward vowel variation in California English, as well as which attributes are claimed by Californians as marking their regional in-group.

VOWEL VARIATION IN CALIFORNIA ENGLISH

The two phonetic innovations that are most associated with California English are the low back vowel merger, a general feature of Western dialects (Labov, Ash, and Boberg 2006), and the so-called California Vowel Shift (CVS) (Eckert 2008; Holland 2014). In short, the vowel features associated with what has often been referred to as the CVS involve mid and high back vowels fronting, mid and high front short vowels lowering and retracting, and a nasal split for BAT such that it raises and fronts prenasally (BAN) but retracts elsewhere. Kennedy and Grama's (2012) more recent study found that BOOT has fronted extensively, overlapping in F2 with BAT and BET. Another possible feature of California English is prelateral mergers between tense/lax pairs, such as *pool-pull*, *hole-hull*, and *pull-hole* (Guenter 2000; Holland 2014); Labov, Ash, and Boberg (2006, 285–86) mentions these mergers as a possible Western feature, which accords with studies finding these mergers in the Mountain West (e.g., in Utah [Baker and Bowie 2010]).

Whereas most studies of California English have investigated speakers from either the Bay Area or Southern California (assuming that either group adequately stands in for the state as a whole), recent studies have begun to address potential intrastate variation in California vocalic features. Hall-Lew (2009) investigated phonetic variation in a single neighborhood of San Francisco. Holland (2014) compared speakers from the Bay Area, Southern California, and the inland Central Valley but found little evidence for intrastate vocalic differences. D'Onofrio et al. (2016 [this volume]) find evidence that the merged BOT/BOUGHT vowel occupies the higher and more retracted space of /ɔ/ in the Central Valley as opposed to /ɑ/ in coastal California.

An important caveat about the CVS is that its currently accepted formalization generalizes over phonetic environments and words (save for the BAT/BAN nasal split). It is possible that finer details of linguistic conditioning (such as the multiple linguistic constraints on sociolinguistic variables [e.g., Guy 1980]) may reveal regional differences in a way that broader vowel categories do not. Holland (2014, 17) finds that BEN is fronted relative to BET for Southern California and Central Valley natives, but not Bay Area speakers. Recent work on San Francisco English suggests that front lax vowels are raising in the pre-/ŋ/ environment (Cardoso et al. 2016 [this volume]). Labov, Ash, and Boberg (2006, 68, map 9.5) also show striking intrastate variation in the PIN-PEN merger; whereas almost all Caucasian speakers in coastal cities exhibit no merger, four of five Fresno and Bakersfield speakers (all Caucasian) are fully merged. In sum, little evidence currently exists to suggest major intrastate differences in California English; however, it is possible that future work may uncover intrastate differences.[1]

THE PRESENT STUDY

This study aims to reconcile the findings uncovered in previous sociolinguistic work on California English (especially the variants associated with the CVS) with folk-linguistic perceptions by investigating the role that vowels play in Californians' perceptions of California English. Using Williams, Garrett, and Coupland's (1999) dialect recognition task as a model, the present study asked respondents to "place" speakers in one of five regions (four Californian regions and one catchall "outside California" region) and rate speakers on semantic differential scales for affective traits. Unlike Williams, Garrett, and Coupland's task, however, the stimuli in this study were identical in content, meaning listeners responded primarily to vocalic variation among speakers. The data were analyzed to find how accurately Californians recognize speakers from across the state, who they perceive to be its "best" speakers, and which traits they associate most strongly with speakers they perceive to be a Californian or a member of their own regional group.

METHODS

Before conducting the recognition task, it was first necessary to define the regions of California that would be used. Stimuli were acquired from two sources: the Nationwide Speech Project corpus (NSP) (Clopper and Pisoni 2006) and a small corpus of newly recorded speakers. Fifty-three listeners participated in the recognition task, and the responses of 41 listeners were analyzed.

REGIONS. The four Californian regions defined in this study are Far Northern California (FN), the Bay Area (BA), the Lower Central Valley (CV), and Southern California (SC) (see figure 4.1).[2] Although the existing evidence for intrastate differences in California English is minimal, these regions were selected on the basis of economic, geographic, and ethnolinguistic differences—in other words, sociocultural factors that Wolfram and Schilling-Estes (2006, 29–35) identify as being responsible for dialect differentiation. The two most populous regions, Southern California and the Bay Area, are heavily urbanized, whereas the Lower Central Valley is mostly farmland (with the exception of its two largest cities, Fresno and Bakersfield) and Far Northern California is mostly undeveloped forest. Speakers in different regions also experience different language-contact situations, as nearly half of all residents of the Bay Area, Lower Central Valley, and Southern California reside in households where English is not spoken.[3] These regions also enjoy rather different folk-linguistic status among both Californians and non-Californians. Californians typically construct difference along a north-south dichotomy (Fought 2002; Bucholtz et al. 2008), often erasing the less-urbanized Far Northern California and Lower Central Valley (Bucholtz et al. 2008), whereas to outsiders Southern California linguistic stereotypes tend to stand in for the state as a whole (e.g., Preston 1996).

SPEAKERS AND STIMULI. The stimuli were short sound clips drawn from 12 Caucasian speakers: two speakers (one female and one male) from each California region and four speakers (two females and two males) from outside the state. The male Bay Area speaker, both Southern California speakers, and all four non-Californian speakers were recorded as part of the NSP

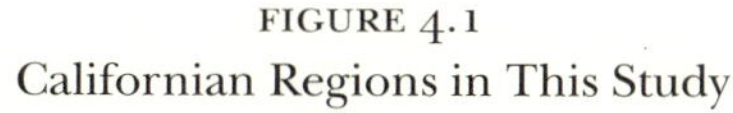

FIGURE 4.1
Californian Regions in This Study

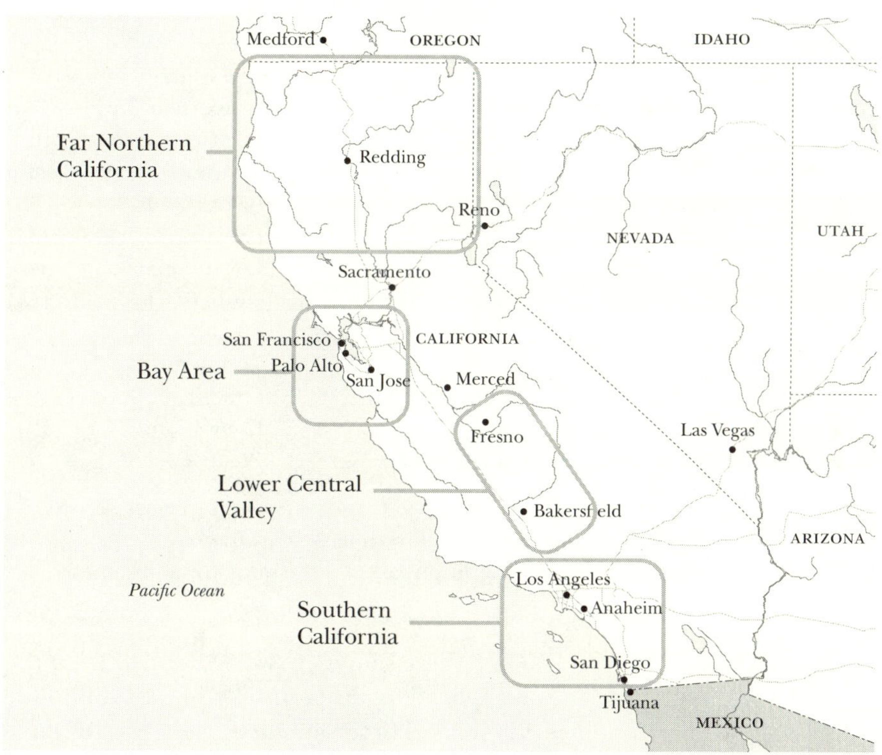

corpus. To complete the stimulus sample, 10 additional Californian speakers, students at Northern California University (NCU) (a pseudonym) were recruited via social networks. Speakers were required to self-identify as Caucasian, speak English natively, have lived in the same region their entire lives (prior to attending NCU), be between 18–29 years of age, and report normal speech and hearing. Five NCU speakers were chosen for the recognition task based on their regional origin and use of Californian/Western vocalic features. Four speakers from the NSP's Mid-Atlantic region were chosen for the "outside California" region based on a lack of Californian/Western vocalic features. Table 4.1 displays information on the speakers.

The NCU speakers were recorded following similar procedures to the NSP, under my supervision. Unlike the NSP, NCU speakers only participated in one task: recording the 102 sentences from the NSP's high-probability sentence list in randomized order. Four of these sentences, 9, 43, 83, and 36, were chosen for the stimuli based on 10 CVS/Western features.

TABLE 1
Speakers Included in Recognition Task

Region/Corpus	*Code*	*Gender*	*Age*[a]	*Hometown*	*Order*[b]
California					
Northern California Univ.	FN1	F	21	Red Bluff	1
Northern California Univ.	FN2	M	28	Grass Valley	7
Northern California Univ.	BA1	F	21	San Geronimo	6
Nationwide Speech Project	BA2	M	19	San Mateo	3
Northern California Univ.	CV1	F	22	Bakersfield	9
Northern California Univ.	CV2	M	21	Fresno	8
Nationwide Speech Project	SC1	F	20	Los Angeles	4
Nationwide Speech Project	SC2	M	18	Santa Clarita	11
Mid-Atlantic					
Nationwide Speech Project	Out1	F	18	Middletown, N.J.	5
Nationwide Speech Project	Out2	F	18	Oradell, N.J.	12
Nationwide Speech Project	Out3	M	18	Long Island, N.Y.	10
Nationwide Speech Project	Out4	M	18	Plainview, N.Y.	2

a. Age is listed at the time of recording. Nationwide Speech Project recordings were completed in 2003; Northern California University in 2013.
b. Order of presentation in the recognition task was the same for all listeners.

For each speaker (NSP and NCU), these sentences were sampled from the speaker's original sound file and spliced together into a stimulus sound file with 1-second intersentence intervals. These sentences are given in table 4.2 in order of presentation in the recognition task. As there was variation across speakers in baseline speech intensity and background noise, Praat (Boersma and Weenink 2013) was used to equalize files' intensity level to 60 dB and equalize background noise. All stimuli were around 10 seconds in duration.

TABLE 4.2
Sentences Chosen for Stimuli and CVS/Western Features Represented in Each

Sentence	*NSP #*[a]	*Features*
Follow this road around the bend.	9	BOAT, BET, BEN
The bloodhound followed the trail.	43	BUT, BAIL
The swimmer's leg got a bad cramp.	83	BIT, BET, BEG, BAT, BAN
Ruth had a necklace of glass beads.	36	BOOT, BAT (×2), BET

NOTE: Underlines indicate location of features; some features overlap (e.g., the vowel in *bend* could undergo either BET lowering or the PIN-PEN merger).
a. "NSP #" refers to the sentence number in the Nationwide Speech Project.

In controlling for the content of the sound clips, this study differed from Williams, Garrett, and Coupland (1999), which used excerpts from speakers' spontaneous narratives for stimuli.[4] Listeners' responses were thus tied only to phonological/prosodic differences among speakers, and the primary differences between speakers were vowel features.

To quantify these vowel differences, each stimulus was coded for the presence or absence of the CVS/Western features in table 4.2 using a three-point scale: 0 for nonshifted, 0.5 for partially shifted, and 1 for shifted. For BET, for example, [ɛ] would be coded 0, [ɛ̞] would be coded 0.5, and [æ̝] or [æ] would be coded 1. All of the non-Californian speakers also raised the vowels in *bad* and *glass* to varying degrees, a feature characteristic of a Mid-Atlantic short-*a* system (Labov, Ash, and Boberg 2006), so this feature was also coded for. These codes were then converted to indices to determine the degree to which stimuli contained CVS features (divided into front and back vowels), non-CVS Western features, and Mid-Atlantic *bad/glass* raising. Indices were calculated by dividing the sum of codes by the number of tokens and multiplying by 100; for example, CV1's stimulus was coded 1 for BOOT, 0 for BOAT, and 0.5 for BUT, so her CVS back index was 50. The CVS index was then calculated by averaging the CVS front index and CVS back index. Speakers' indices are displayed in table 4.3.

Speakers BA1 and SC1, for example, were the heaviest user of California-shifted vowels, with CVS indices of 66, whereas BA2 was the least California-shifted Californian, with a CVS index of 13. The CVS and *bad/glass* indices clearly differentiate the Californian and non-Californian speakers: all of the non-Californian speakers had lower CVS indices than the least

TABLE 4.3
Indices by Speaker

Speaker	*CVS Front*	*CVS Back*	*CVS*	*Other West*	*bad/glass*
FN1	25	67	46	33	0
FN2	25	33	29	0	0
BA1	81	50	66	0	0
BA2	25	0	13	17	0
CV1	25	50	38	100	0
CV2	31	83	57	0	0
SC1	31	100	66	0	0
SC2	19	33	26	17	0
Out1	13	0	6	0	100
Out2	19	0	9	17	75
Out3	0	17	8	17	50
Out4	6	17	11	0	75

California-shifted Californian, while all of the non-Californians and no Californians had at least some *bad/glass* raising. CV1 had a high rate of non-CVS Western features and was the only speaker to exhibit the PIN-PEN merger; in this respect, CV1 patterns as Labov, Ash, and Boberg (2006) predicts, as she is a second-generation Bakersfieldian. Aside from CV1's PIN-PEN merger, it is difficult to determine whether the Californian speakers are exemplars of their respective regions within the state due to the relative lack of previous findings on intrastate vocalic differences. However, this research attempts to ascertain whether Californians attach social meaning to vocalic features in the same way that Bucholtz et al. (2008) found that they attach social meaning to lexical differences.

RECOGNITION TASK. Fifty-three NCU undergraduates participated in the recognition task. The task consisted of 12 trials (following a practice trial) in which listeners guessed where each speaker was from and rated speakers from 1–6 on 14 semantic differential scales (see table 4.4). Most scales were selected to correspond to the "correctness" and "pleasantness" groupings found in perceptual dialectology studies (Preston 1996). Each trial lasted 60 seconds, with the sound clips played twice. Stimuli were presented in the same order to all listeners (displayed in table 4.1). Listeners then filled out a brief questionnaire, which included a space to list where they had lived and which of those places they considered their hometown.

ANALYSIS. Listeners' questionnaire responses were coded for hometown and mobility. Hometown categories were Far Northern California, the Bay Area, Lower Central Valley, Southern California, other California locations, non-Californian U.S. locations, and international locations. Mobility categories were nonmobile (listeners had never lived outside their home region of California), mobile across multiple regions of California, mobile across multiple states, and mobile across multiple countries.

TABLE 4.4
Semantic Differential Scales and Categories Used in Perceptual Task

Category	*Scales*
Correctness	smart–dumb; educated–uneducated; confident–not confident; good English–bad English; fast–slow; unaccented–accented
Pleasantness	attractive–unattractive; friendly–unfriendly; polite–rude; likable–not likable
Self-similarity	speaks like me–doesn't speak like me; familiar–unfamiliar
Place	Californian–not Californian; rural–urban

The data analysis fell into three broad categories: regional identification, affective scale ratings, and the interaction of identification and attitudes. Accurate-recognition rates were calculated for individual speakers, speaker regions, listener regions, and listener mobility. Identification rates were also investigated independently of accuracy, with special attention paid to PERCEIVED REGION (the region into which a plurality of listeners placed a speaker), IN-GROUP IDENTIFICATION RATES (the proportion of listeners from a given region who identify a speaker as being from their home region), and OUTSIDE IDENTIFICATION RATES (the proportion of California listeners who identify a speaker as being from outside the state).

Average ratings for affective traits were calculated by region in two ways: speakers' actual region and speakers' perceived region. To assess the presence of CLAIMING in California (as Williams, Garrett, and Coupland 1999 found in Wales), average ratings were also calculated for listeners from the two regions most heavily represented in the listener sample (the Bay Area and Southern California), and correlation tests were performed to compare average ratings with in-group identification rates. Finally, correlation tests were performed to compare Californian listeners' average ratings with outside identification rates.

RESULTS

A one-way ANOVA analysis of recognition revealed a significant effect of listener mobility on accurate recognition ($F(3, 49) = 3.83$, $p = .015$). Post-hoc Scheffé tests showed that listeners who had lived outside the United States were significantly less accurate than those who had moved among Californian regions and those who had lived in other U.S. states ($p < .05$). As a result, these 12 listeners were removed from the sample for the analyses described in this section; after removing these listeners, there was no significant effect of listener hometown ($F(4, 35) = 1.01$).

In the remaining 41-listener sample, Far Northern California ($n = 1$), the Lower Central Valley ($n = 2$), and outside California ($n = 4$) were underrepresented compared to the Bay Area ($n = 11$), Southern California ($n = 13$), and Greater Sacramento ($n = 10$). As a result, it was feasible to analyze in-group identification only for the Bay Area and Southern California.

REGIONAL IDENTIFICATION. The overall rate at which speakers' regions were accurately recognized was 31.2%, consistent with Clopper and Pisoni's (2004) 30% and Williams, Garrett, and Coupland's 25%. As table 4.5 shows, few listeners accurately recognized Californian speakers' region; for

TABLE 4.5
Percentage of Listeners Who Placed Speakers into Their Actual Region and Perceived Region

Speaker	*Actual Region*		*Perceived Region*	
FN1	Far North	19.5%	So. Cal.	39.0%
FN2	Far North	19.5%	Bay Area	26.8%
BA1	Bay Area	9.8%	Far North	34.1%
BA2	Bay Area	22.0%	Far North	31.7%
CV1	Cent. Valley	27.5%	Cent. Valley	27.5%
CV2	Cent. Valley	15.8%	Far North	42.1%
SC1	So. Cal.	48.8%	So. Cal.	48.8%
SC2	So. Cal.	24.4%	Bay Area	34.1%
Out1	Outside	61.0%	Outside	61.0%
Out2	Outside	25.0%	Cent. Valley	30.0%
Out3	Outside	70.0%	Outside	70.0%
Out4	Outside	31.7%	Outside	31.7%

NOTE: Shading indicates that perceived region matched actual region.

example, only 15.8% of listeners identified CV2, the male Lower Central Valley speaker, as from the Lower Central Valley. For six of eight Californian speakers, their perceived region (the region into which a plurality of listeners placed a speaker) did not match their actual region. For example, a plurality of listeners placed FN1, the female Far Northern California speaker, in Southern California (39.0%), whereas only 19.5% of listeners placed her accurately in Far Northern California. In contrast, listeners accurately recognized three of four non-Californian speakers; more than two-thirds of listeners identified Out3 as from outside California. Accurate-recognition rates ranged from 9.8% (BA1) to 70.0% (Out3).

To test whether listeners associated certain regions with the CVS or other features, Pearson correlations were calculated between the indices in table 4.3 and the rate at which speakers were placed into each region. There was a significant positive correlation between speakers' CVS index and the percentage of listeners who identified them as being from Southern California ($r = .69$, one-tailed $t_{10} = 3.05$, $p < .01$), although there was no significant correlation for the CVS front and CVS back indices; in other words, speakers who exhibited more CVS features were identified as being from Southern California at a higher rate.

Table 4.6 gives rates of in-group identification by Bay Area and Southern California listeners, as well as outside identification by all Californian listeners. Notably, over three-fourths of listeners from Southern California identified SC1 as a Southern Californian (76.9%), whereas no listeners from the Bay Area identified BA1 as from the Bay Area. Listeners from both the Bay Area (45.5%) and Southern California (53.8%) identified FN1 as an in-group speaker. It is not clear how these in-group identification patterns relate to vocalic variation within the sample; while Bay Area in-group identification correlated negatively with CVS indices and Southern California in-group identification correlated positively with CVS indices, these correlations did not reach significance.

Not surprisingly, Californian listeners identified the non-Californian speakers as from outside California at a higher rate than they identified Californian speakers as from outside the state; for example, 72.2% of Californian listeners identified Out3 as from outside California, compared to just 2.7% for FN1 and SC1. The Californian speaker with the highest outside identification rate was CV2 (25.7%), which surpassed that of Out2 (19.4%). Outside identification rates correlated significantly with *bad/glass* raising indices ($r = .72$, one-tailed $t_{10} = 3.30$, $p < .005$); in other words, listeners were generally more likely to identify speakers with *bad/glass* raising as being from outside California.

LANGUAGE ATTITUDES. Tables 4.7 and 4.8 give average affective scale ratings for each region; table 4.7 shows average ratings based on speakers' ACTUAL REGION (where speakers were actually from) and table 4.8 shows average ratings based on speakers' PERCEIVED REGION (listed in table 4.5). (Recall that scales ranged from 1–6.) Turning first to table 4.7, it is clear that Southern Californian speakers enjoyed favorable attitudes across the

TABLE 4.6
Ingroup Identification Rates for Bay Area and Southern California Listeners and Outside Identification Rates for All Californian Listeners

Speaker	*Ingroup Identification*		*Outside*
	Bay Area	*So. Cal.*	*Identification*
FN1	45.5%	53.8%	2.7%
FN2	9.1%	7.7%	16.2%
BA1	0.0%	30.8%	8.1%
BA2	36.4%	23.1%	8.1%
CV1	27.3%	30.8%	8.1%
CV2	0.0%	8.3%	25.7%
SC1	18.2%	76.9%	2.7%
SC2	45.5%	30.8%	0.0%
Out1	9.1%	15.4%	59.5%
Out2	27.3%	23.1%	19.4%
Out3	9.1%	0.0%	72.2%
Out4	9.1%	15.4%	32.4%

NOTE: Shading indicates in-group speakers.

TABLE 4.7
Average Affective Scale Ratings for Each Actual Region on a 6-Point Scale

	Actual Region				
Scales	*Far North*	*Bay Area*	*Cent. Valley*	*So. Cal.*	*Outside*
Correctness					
smart	3.94	3.66	3.72	4.31	3.58
educated	4.35	3.96	3.96	4.54	3.65
confident	3.85	3.46	3.61	4.23	3.46
good English	4.59	4.15	4.08	4.65	3.89
fast	3.48	3.52	3.38	3.83	2.76
unaccented	3.96	3.97	3.81	4.35	3.13
Pleasantness					
attractive	3.90	3.44	3.12	4.16	3.12
friendly	4.33	3.64	3.60	4.57	3.62
polite	4.43	3.77	3.68	4.52	3.87
likable	4.21	3.59	3.42	4.34	3.62
Self-similarity					
speaks like me	3.47	3.14	2.82	3.73	2.34
familiar	4.04	3.91	3.69	4.49	3.20
Place					
Californian	4.44	4.53	3.83	4.99	2.95
rural	2.89	3.09	3.56	2.43	3.87

NOTE: Average ratings for each scale are shaded from light to dark from highest to lowest, respectively.

board, ranking highest on correctness items, pleasantness items, self-similarity items, and "California-ness." Because non-Californians ranked lowest on almost all scales, it is useful to examine the second-lowest average ratings for each scale. Here, it appears that the Lower Central Valley is viewed as the least prestigious Californian region (especially on pleasantness) and that the Bay Area also lacks prestige. The scale RURAL–URBAN (neither side of which was assumed a priori to correspond to correctness, pleasantness, or "California-ness") shows the opposite pattern of the other scales, with Southern California ranking lowest and non-Californians ranking highest on rurality; it thus appears that urbanness carries an element of linguistic prestige to these listeners.

CVS indices did not correlate significantly with any scale ratings, but significant negative correlations were found between *bad/glass* raising indices and UNACCENTED, SPEAKS LIKE ME, FAMILIAR, and CALIFORNIAN ratings ($r_{\text{familiar}} = -.68$, $p < .01$; $r_{\text{speaks like me}} = -.72$, $r_{\text{unaccented}} = -.76$, $r_{\text{Californian}} = -.76$, $p < .005$).

TABLE 4.8
Average Affective Scale Ratings for Each Perceived Region on a 6-Point Scale

	Perceived Region				
Scales	*Far North*	*Bay Area*	*Cent. Valley*	*So. Cal.*	*Outside*
Correctness					
smart	3.65	4.35	3.90	3.89	3.45
educated	3.91	4.56	4.06	4.34	3.51
confident	3.50	4.23	3.77	3.85	3.31
good English	4.09	4.62	4.16	4.63	3.80
fast	3.43	3.76	3.57	3.54	2.47
unaccented	3.89	4.23	3.75	4.09	2.97
Pleasantness					
attractive	3.24	3.92	3.47	4.13	2.98
friendly	3.58	4.39	3.89	4.50	3.48
polite	3.73	4.52	3.99	4.43	3.74
likable	3.51	4.34	3.71	4.20	3.51
Self-similarity					
speaks like me	3.00	3.57	2.89	3.63	2.17
familiar	3.83	4.16	3.70	4.36	3.04
Place					
Californian	4.18	4.50	3.94	4.93	2.71
rural	3.36	2.66	3.47	2.65	3.93

NOTE: Average ratings for each scale are shaded from light to dark from highest to lowest, respectively.

INTERACTION OF IDENTIFICATION AND LANGUAGE ATTITUDES. Perhaps surprisingly, the average ratings by perceived region in table 4.8 show several differences from the average ratings by actual region. In particular, the Bay Area gains top ratings on 7 of 14 scales, including all correctness scales except GOOD ENGLISH. Southern California retains top ratings for self-similarity scales and "California-ness," and Far Northern California becomes the least prestigious Californian region. The low regard in which listeners hold non-Californian speakers is even more pronounced in these ratings.

An important result from Williams, Garrett, and Coupland (1999) was that listeners were more likely to identify likable speakers as a member of their own regional group (claiming). In the present data set, Pearson correlations between in-group identification rates and affective scale ratings (table 4.9) suggest claiming effects for Bay Area and Southern California listeners. Listeners from both regions rated speakers who they perceived to be from their regional in-group higher on CALIFORNIAN and SPEAKS LIKE ME. In addition, Bay Area listeners claimed the speakers who they rated

TABLE 4.9
Correlations between Ingroup/Outside Identification Rates (table 4.6) and Affective Scale Ratings

	In-Group		
Scales	*Bay Area*	*So. Cal.*	*Outside*
smart	.36	.05	–.43
educated	.39	.30	–.55
confident	.34	.21	–.46
good English	.52	.61	–.67*
fast	.34	.43	–.72**
unaccented	.50	.49	–.94***
attractive	.68*	.61	–.67*
friendly	.49	.51	–.42
polite	.49	.24	–.33
likable	.55	.23	–.38
speaks like me	.70*	.69*	–.87***
familiar	.58	.70*	–.83***
Californian	.72**	.78**	–.96***
rural	–.41	–.60	.72**

NOTE: In-group columns pertain to Bay Area or Southern California listeners only. Outside column includes all Californian listeners. Asterisks indicate significance (one-tailed t-test with df = 10): $^*p < .01$, $^{**}p < .005$, $^{***}p < .001$.

as more attractive, and Southern California listeners claimed the speakers who they rated as more familiar. Correctness was apparently not a factor in in-group identification for either group (with a virtually zero SMART correlation for Southern California).

Californian listeners' outside identification rates correlated significantly with eight attitudes scales. These correlations mostly suggested either a lack of correctness (BAD ENGLISH, SLOW, ACCENTED) or a sense of difference/distinction from the listener (DOESN'T SPEAK LIKE ME, UNFAMILIAR, NOT CALIFORNIAN). Unlike in-group identification, attitudes about (in)correctness, especially those relating to language, were implicated in outside identification.

DISCUSSION

It is clear from the correlations in table 4.9 that there are stronger attitudes associated with NOT being a Californian than being one, as correctness traits such as speaking "without an accent" are denied to non-Californian speakers even if such traits are not necessarily attached to Californian speakers. This result makes sense given the linguistic security exhibited in perceptual dialectology map-drawing studies by Californians (Fought 2002), as well as Western speakers more generally (Fridland and Bartlett 2006). Consistent with Fought's (2002) hand-drawn maps, these Californian listeners clearly had a notion of linguistic correctness as something non-Californians lack but did not ascribe correctness to Californians. The negative correlation between *bad/glass* raising and UNACCENTED indicates that listeners responded negatively to this non-Californian (and non-Western) feature, although *bad/glass* raising did not significantly affect listeners' responses to any other correctness trait.

The in-group correlations reveal that self-perceptions differ slightly between California's two most populous regions. Bay Area listeners claim the speakers who they also judge to be most attractive, Californian, and speaking like them; conversely, Southern California listeners claim the speakers who they also judge to be most familiar, Californian, and speaking like them. Interestingly, this creates a dispute between the regions, as each region believes their own speakers to be central (and other speakers peripheral) to a notion of sounding Californian. Southern Californians are apparently more comfortable staking a claim to the CVS itself, however, as the two speakers with the highest CVS indices (BA1 and SC1) had much higher in-group identification for Southern California listeners than Bay Area listeners.

These data are similarly mixed on which region is considered most linguistically prestigious; although Southern Californians are rated highest for correctness, pleasantness, and CALIFORNIAN scales, listeners ascribe higher correctness to speakers they believe to be from the Bay Area than those they believe to be from Southern California. This boost in correctness is in line with Bucholtz et al.'s (2008) finding that Northern California (including the Bay Area) is believed to feature the "best" English in California thanks to its educational institutions. More broadly, this result reinforces the general finding that folk beliefs about certain places can create a disconnect between what listeners assume they are hearing and what they actually hear (e.g., Niedzielski 1999). Bucholtz et al. also found a belief that Southern California has the "worst" English, which conflicts with the positive attitudes toward Southern California speakers found in the current study; it is possible that the factors cited as driving stigmatization ("slang" and ethnolinguistic diversity) were less relevant in the current study, as both word choice and ethnicity were invariant between speakers. Indeed, the degree to which a speaker used CVS features apparently had no effect on the affective scale ratings they received.

The less populous regions of California received less favorable ratings than the Bay Area or Southern California, a result that is perhaps not surprising in a schema where urbanness is a factor in prestige. As mentioned above, Lower Central Valley speakers were apparently confused with non-Californians, which may have something to do with the common erasure of this region (e.g., "Almost no one lives here" [Bucholtz et al. 2007, 338]). Despite the fact that most of the state is covered by farmland, forest, or desert, rural speakers are peripheral to a sense of "sounding Californian."

Finally, the recognition results show that Californians encounter substantial difficulty in identifying the regional origin of Californian speakers, as only two of eight Californian speakers were accurately recognized by a plurality of listeners. Californians may be better able to guess at the regional origin of speakers in naturalistic interactions, of course, as these may feature strong identifiers, such as Southern Californians' use of *the* preceding freeway names (Geyer 2001) or Northern Californians' use of *hella* (Fought 2002). While there was variation in Californian and Western vocalic features between the speakers in this sample, it is unclear how much of this variation can be attributed to regional origin versus the host of other social factors that can drive variation. As a result, a follow-up study utilized vowel resynthesis to create matched-guise stimuli differing only in their degree of California shifting (Villarreal 2016). This follow-up study thus isolates Californians' attitudes toward the CVS itself (including their perceptions of the regional origins of more or less shifted speakers) from the multitude of other inputs that contribute to sociolinguistic perception. Nevertheless, the present study provides a useful early picture of the role that vowels play in Californians' self-perceptions.

NOTES

I would like to acknowledge the support of my adviser, Bob Bayley, the graduate students at UC Davis, Cynthia Clopper, and Sara Thomas.

1. Indeed, three speakers in the present study (FN1, NC1, and SC2) display BEG raising in *leg*, an established feature of the Pacific Northwest (Becker et al. 2016 [this volume]; Wassink et al. 2009; Wassink 2016 [this volume]) that had not been systematically investigated in California at the time of this study. More recently, Cardoso et al. (2016 [this volume]) found that BEG did not significantly differ from BET in San Francisco.
2. Note that these regions exclude some parts of the state, mostly sparsely populated areas (the Sierra Nevada mountains, Mojave Desert), as well as Greater Sacramento, a region that could arguably be called part of the Central Valley, an extension of the Bay Area, or its own region.

3. Data retrieved from American Community Survey (U.S. Census Bureau) 2007–11 five-year estimates, table B16001, available at http://factfinder2.census.gov/.
4. The method used here has the possible drawback of failing to capture the full range of cross-regional differences, since the controlled nature of the recording encourages speakers to style-shift toward standard variants. This drawback was addressed in a follow-up study that drew stimuli from a retell task in order to induce more casual speech while controlling content (Villarreal 2016).

REFERENCES

Allbritten, Rachael. 2011. "Sounding Southern: Phonetic Features and Dialect Perceptions." Ph.D. diss., Georgetown University.

Baker, Wendy, and David Bowie. 2010. "Religious Affiliation as a Correlate of Linguistic Behavior." In "Selected Papers from NWAV 37," edited by Kyle Gorman and Laurel MacKenzie. *University of Pennsylvania Working Papers in Linguistics* 15.2: 1–10.

Becker, Kara, Anna Aden, Katelyn Best, and Haley Jacobson. 2016. "Variation in West Coast English: The Case of Oregon." In Fridland et al. 2016, 107–34. doi: 10.1215/00031283-3772923.

Boersma, Paul, and David Weenink. 2013. Praat: Doing Phonetics by Computer. Version 5.3.53. http://www.praat.org.

Bucholtz, Mary, Nancy Bermudez, Victor Fung, Lisa Edwards, and Rosalva Vargas. 2007. "Hella Nor Cal or Totally So Cal? The Perceptual Dialectology of California." *Journal of English Linguistics* 35.4: 325–52. doi:10.1177/0075424207307780.

Bucholtz, Mary, Nancy Bermudez, Victor Fung, Rosalva Vargas, and Lisa Edwards. 2008. "The Normative North and the Stigmatized South: Ideology and Methodology in the Perceptual Dialectology of California." *Journal of English Linguistics* 36.1: 62–87. doi:10.1177/0075424207311721.

Cardoso, Amanda, Lauren Hall-Lew, Yova Kementchedjhieva, and Ruaridh Purse. 2016. "Between California and the Pacific Northwest: The Front Lax Vowels in San Francisco English." In Fridland et al. 2016, 33–54. doi:10.1215/00031283-3772890.

Clopper, Cynthia G., and David B. Pisoni. 2004. "Some Acoustic Cues for the Perceptual Categorization of American English Regional Dialects." *Journal of Phonetics* 32.1: 111–40. doi:10.1016/S0095-4470(03)00009-3.

———. 2006. "The Nationwide Speech Project: A New Corpus of American English Dialects." *Speech Communication* 48.6: 633–44. doi:10.1016/j.specom.2005.09.010.

D'Onofrio, Annette, Penelope Eckert, Robert J. Podesva, Teresa Pratt, and Janneke Van Hofwegen. 2016. In Fridland et al. 2016, 11–32. doi:10.1215/00031283-3772879.

Eckert, Penelope. 2008. "Where Do Ethnolects Stop?" *International Journal of Bilingualism* 12.1–2: 25–42. doi:10.1177/13670069080120010301.

Fought, Carmen. 2002. "California Students' Perceptions of, You Know, Regions and Dialects?" In *Handbook of Perceptual Dialectology*, vol. 2, edited by Daniel Long and Dennis R. Preston, 113–34. Amsterdam: Benjamins. doi:10.1075/z.hpd2.13fou.

Fridland, Valerie, and Kathryn Bartlett. 2006. "Correctness, Pleasantness, and Degree of Difference Ratings across Regions." *American Speech* 81.4: 358–86. doi:10.1215/00031283-2006-025.

Fridland, Valerie, Tyler Kendall, Betsy Evans, and Alicia Beckford Wassink, eds. 2016. *Speech in the Western States.* Vol. 1, *The Coastal States.* Publication of the American Dialect Society 101. Durham, N.C.: Duke University Press.

Geyer, Grant. 2001. "'The' Freeway in Southern California." *American Speech* 76.2: 221–24. doi:10.1215/00031283-76-2-221.

Guenter, Josh. 2000. "What Is English /l/ Really?" In *Proceedings of the Twenty-Sixth Annual Meeting of the Berkeley Linguistics Society: General Session and Parasession on Aspect,* edited by Lisa J. Conathan, Jeff Good, Darya Kavitskaya, Alyssa B. Wulf, and Alan C. L. Yu, 113–20. Berkeley, Calif.: Berkeley Linguistics Society. doi:10.3765/bls.v26i1.1163.

Guy, Gregory R. 1980. "Variation in the Group and in the Individual." In *Locating Language in Time and Space,* edited by William Labov, 1–36. New York: Academic Press.

Hall-Lew, Lauren. 2009. "Ethnicity and Phonetic Variation in a San Francisco Neighborhood." Ph.D. diss., Stanford University.

Holland, Cory Lin. 2014. "Shifting or Shifted? The State of California Vowels." Ph.D. diss., University of California, Davis.

Irvine, Judith T., and Susan Gal. 2000. "Language Ideology and Linguistic Differentiation." In *Regimes of Language: Ideologies, Polities, and Identities,* edited by Paul V. Kroskrity, 35–84. Santa Fe, N.M.: School of American Research Press.

Kennedy, Robert, and James Grama. 2012. "Chain Shifting and Centralization in California Vowels: An Acoustic Analysis." *American Speech* 87.1: 39–56. doi:10.1215/00031283-1599950.

Labov, William, Sharon Ash, and Charles Boberg. 2006. *The Atlas of North American English: Phonetics, Phonology, and Sound Change.* Berlin: Mouton de Gruyter.

Niedzielski, Nancy. 1999. "The Effect of Social Information on the Perception of Sociolinguistic Variables." *Journal of Language and Social Psychology* 18.1: 62–85. doi:10.1177/0261927x99018001005.

Plichta, Bartek, and Dennis R. Preston. 2005. "The /ay/s Have It: The Perception of /ay/ as a North-South Stereotype in United States English." *Acta Linguistica Hafniensia* 37: 107–30. doi:10.1080/03740463.2005.10416086.

Preston, Dennis R. 1996. "Where the Worst English Is Spoken." In *Focus on the USA,* edited by Edgar W. Schneider, 297–360. Amsterdam: Benjamins.

Villarreal, Dan. 2016. "The Construction of Social Meaning: A Matched-Guise Investigation of the California Vowel Shift." Ph.D. diss., University of California, Davis.

Wassink, Alicia Beckford. 2016. "The Vowels of Washington State." In Fridland et al. 2016, 77–106. doi:10.1215/00031283-3772912.

Wassink, Alicia, Robert Squizzero, Mike Scanlon, Rachel Schirra, and Jeffrey Conn. 2009. "Effects of Gender and Style on Fronting and Raising of /æ/, /e:/ and /ɛ/ before /g/ in Seattle English." Paper presented at thc 38th annual meeting of New Ways of Analyzing Variation (NWAV 38), Ottawa, Oct. 22–25.

Williams, Angie, Peter Garrett, and Nikolas Coupland. 1999. "Dialect Recognition." In *Handbook of Perceptual Dialectology*, vol. 1, edited by Dennis R. Preston, 345–58. Amsterdam: Benjamins. doi:10.1075/z.hpd1.29wil.

Wolfram, Walt, and Natalie Schilling-Estes. 2006. *American English: Dialects and Variation*. 2nd ed. Malden, Mass.: Blackwell.

DAN VILLARREAL is a postdoctoral fellow in the Department of English at the University of Nevada, Reno. His research area is sociolinguistics, with particular emphasis on the social meanings of language variation. He was awarded a Presidential Honorary Membership by the American Dialect Society in 2014. E-mail: djvill@unr.edu.

5. THE VOWELS OF WASHINGTON STATE

ALICIA BECKFORD WASSINK

THIS CHAPTER PROVIDES a contemporary description of the vowels of Washington State, focusing on three important changes: fronting of /u:/ BOOT, merging of /ɔ~ɑ/ BOUGHT ~ BOT, and prevelar raising of /æg/ BAG and /ɛg/ BEG. One goal of the volume has been to explore the regional diversity of the West. In keeping with this, data are examined from locations in western, central, and eastern Washington to afford as broad a view of the state's contemporary dialect landscape as possible. This is accomplished first by considering data for a sample of metropolitan Seattle speakers in the western region of the state, then moving eastward. Washington is divided using what is often regarded as its major perceptual, geographic, and cultural boundary, the Cascade Mountain range. To its west are cosmopolitan areas of higher socioeconomic standing and liberal politics; to its east lie rural communities known for agriculture and conservative politics. Settlements in both parts of the state date back to the 1850s. Because one of the defining characteristics of Washington is its multiethnic composition, the study includes nonwhite ethnicities that have had a long and deep history in the state.

The dialectology literature has recorded very few descriptions of Washington State speech. The most extensive early research was completed by Carroll Reed in the 1950s, with smaller-scale studies by Mills (1950), Thomas (1958), and Foster and Hoffman (1966). The findings of these early reports guide the research questions addressed below and inform the choice of linguistic variables. After briefly summarizing current perspectives on the sociolinguistic landscape of the West, those early reports are summarized in order to provide context for the forms investigated. The vowel system descriptions will then proceed geographically, from study sites in western to those in eastern Washington. The chapter ends with an examination of Washington English in its regional context. The vowel changes presently underway in Washington State are compared to those observed for neighboring Oregon and California to the south and British Columbia, Canada, to the north. We will see that Washington speech exhibits important similarities with and differences from its neighbors along the Pacific Coast.

Publication of the American Dialect Society 101 DOI 10.1215/00031283-3772912

EARLY DIALECT LITERATURE ON ENGLISH IN THE PACIFIC NORTHWEST. Based on the findings of the TELSUR and other studies, Labov (1991) divides North America into three major dialect regions, defined by their participation, or lack thereof, in the Northern Cities Vowel Shift and the Southern Vowel Shift. The third dialect region, called "the West," in which Washington is included, is defined by its lack of participation in either of these vowel shifts. Its primary distinguishing features are the merger of /ɑ/ BOT and /ɔ/ BOUGHT and the fronting of /u:/ BOOT. As has been mentioned elsewhere in this volume, this means that the dialects of this broad Western region are believed to share a configuration in which a merged low vowel sits in the back corner of the vowel space and a single phone for nonnasal contexts of the BAT vowel sits in the low front corner (Labov 1991). But a review of the earliest scholarly descriptions of Washington State speech suggests that the low front corner has been more variable among Western varieties than this view suggests.

Arguably the youngest of the North American dialect regions, the Pacific Northwest has been subject to ongoing, variable linguistic input since the introduction of English to the region. Settlement by Caucasian Americans dates back only to the 1850s, with transnational migration by travelers originating in the American Midwest (including Illinois, Iowa, Indiana, Ohio), New England, and the American South (Sale 1976; Taylor 1994). Thus, the Upper and Lower North and the eastern New England dialects would seem to be the most logical donor regions for a Pacific Northwest variety of English.

Carver (1987, 205) wrote, "Western speech is both extremely young and still undergoing the modifications and leveling processes of a region in social flux. But this in itself contrasts its speech with that of the rest of the country." His focus was on lexical forms, on the basis of which he determined that the West showed Northern features complemented by ones from the South and Midland regions. However, Labov, Ash, and Boberg (2006, 284) assert on the basis of a phonological study that "there is nothing in the ANAE data to support the identification of [Carver's northwest] region as phonologically distinct from the rest of the West." Their assessment was that the region showed irregularity and lacked structure, though they stress there remained a need for more information to clarify the picture.

The most extensive early research into the phonological features of Pacific Northwest speech was conducted by Carroll Reed, director of the Linguistic Atlas of the Pacific Northwest (Reed 1965). Mills (1950) and Foster and Hoffman (1966) report smaller-scale studies, with the principal finding of *r*-insertion in words such as *squash* and *wash* for Washington speakers. These researchers, together with Thomas (1958), find that Washington speakers merged (er~ɛr) *Mary, dairy, merry.* Thomas (1958) provides transcriptions for 130 speakers reading the Rain Story, but reports no regionally diagnostic forms of note, with the possible exceptions of [hw] in *which* and [ɔ] in *horrid.* Reed (1965, 186) likens Washington speech to that of southern Illinois and Iowa. Critically, for the present discussion, he provides us with the only evidence on record of phonetic variation that might support the inference that sound change in these classes may have been at an early stage in the 1950s. Namely, Reed (1952) notes raising to mid-front [e] in /æ/ vowels occurring in a prevelar nasal context, *hang.* Later, Reed (1961, 561–62) reports raising of /ɛ, æ/ in another voiced prevelar stop context, /g/. The vowel produced in *egg* and *keg* was predominantly pronounced [ɛ, ɛᴵ] but infrequently as [e, eᴵ], and *bag* was "nearly evenly divided" between [æᴵ] and [æ], respectively. It is difficult to know exactly what the phonetic values of these forms were, as Reed only used the International Phonetic Alphabet in his later writings and did not comment on his transcription conventions. What we do know for certain is that Reed referred to these raised forms as "infrequent." But, we can be fairly certain the nucleus of BAG (in which the vowel preceded a voiced velar stop) was not observed to be higher than [æ].

THE RAISING OF (æ). The raising of (æ) is not unknown in American dialectology. Changes involving the tensing and raising of (æ) in the Northern Cities, for example, have solidified its status as a showcase variable (Labov, Ash, and Boberg 2006). Prevelar raising in particular is known to occur in some speakers in the American Midwest (see, e.g., Zeller 1997; Labov, Ash, and Boberg 2006; Benson, Fox, and Balkman 2011). The phonological *Atlas of North American English* (Labov, Ash, and Boberg 2006, 182) maps the nationwide distribution of (æg)-raising as found by this extensive survey. It provides a map showing several Northern locations where /æ/ in /g/ contexts were found to be higher than in /d/ contexts. One such speaker was found in Washington State. The survey also found raising of /æg/ to [eᴵg], but this is concentrated in Minnesota and Wisconsin. In Washington State, Labov, Ash, and Boberg also found one speaker with /æ/ before alveolar nasal /n/ higher than /æ/ before /d, g/, and another with /æ/ before nasal /n/ higher than /æ/ before /d/ which was in turn higher than /æ/ before /g/. It is understandable why these researchers would conclude that Washington English showed considerable dialect mixing rather than any emergent regional patterning. In Wassink and Riebold (2013), Wassink (2015), and Riebold (2015), we consider possible sources for these changes. The dialect literature shows no clear evidence of this pattern in the regions whose speakers settled the Pacific Northwest, making it difficult to argue that this pattern was inherited. Instead, we argue that the strongest motivation appears to be phonetic—rooted in the coarticulatory phenomenon referred to as the "velar pinch." Low vowels, such as /ɑ/ and /æ/, are raised before velar nasal [ŋ] and voiced stop [g]. Acoustically, F1 is lowered. In addition, F2 rises to approximate F3 (the visual "pinch" in a spectrogram for which the phenomenon is named) in the transition from vowel to consonant, which is associated with the auditory-perceptual impression of fronting. This is a language-general tendency, attested for other varieties of English, as well as Dutch, Spanish, and Tlingit (Fant 1960). Its status as a language-general tendency may help to explain the common, but lexically limited, raising in words like *leg* and *egg* that is observed in other American dialects.

In light of this, why focus on raising of /æg/ BAG in the Pacific Northwest? First, it appears that in Washington State, raised /æ/ occurs in all voiced prevelar environments, whereas it is lexically restricted elsewhere in the United States or occurs with implicational ordering, appearing first in alveolar environments and subsequently in velar ones. Second, discovery of regularity between speakers and subregions within the state and in neighboring states like Oregon (see Becker et al. 2016 [this volume]) would indicate that rather than heterogeneity with "no structure," a regional pattern is evolving. A larger speaker sample should help to further clarify whether interspeaker patterns among Washingtonians are as variable as was found by Labov, Ash, and Boberg (2006).

THE RAISING OF (ɛ). Although the phonetic realization of /ɛ/ BET is known to be highly variable across contemporary American dialects (Krezschmar 2004), /ɛ/ BET is typically found to be backing or lowering in American dialects (e.g., in the NCS [Gordon 2004]). Only anecdotal evidence exists of raising of /ɛ/ to [eˡ] in *egg*, *leg* to [eˡg, leˡg] occurring sporadically in other parts of the United States, but this raising appears to be lexically isolated. It is only in the Southern Shift reports that we find documentation of more productive /ɛ/-raising (Labov, Ash, and Boberg 2006, 248). Here, /ɛ/ raised and developed an in-glide to yield the stereotypically Southern [eɪə] *bet* as [beɪət]. Aside from these reports, mentions of /ɛ/-raising are rare. Reed's (1961) survey of Pacific Northwest English mentions raising of /ɛg/ to [ɛˡg] as was mentioned above, although he found these variants to be infrequent. As we show below, Seattle speakers show more widespread raising of /ɛg/ BEG. However, unlike raising of /æg/ BAG, /ɛg/-raising may continue to be a phonolexical pattern, that is, restricted to specific lexical items.

Having established our knowledge of the current distribution of the feature, we might ask about its origins. There are two problems in determining when and why raising of /ɛg/ BEG might have started. First, there is a long-standing lack of descriptive work investigating vowel changes in the Pacific Northwest (apart from Reed's work), which makes it difficult to trace the roots of regional innovations. In fact, Reed (1961) provides the only mention of /ɛg/-raising until Wassink et al. (2009). Second, as was true for /æg/ BAG, sociohistorical sources (via settler effects) for the (ɛ)-raising observed in the Seattle area appear to be unlikely. We have been unable to find any early dialect literature specifically mentioning raising of /ɛg/ BEG in the likeliest donor areas—Upper and Lower North—during the period of transnational migration.

Given the state of our knowledge at present, these two raising phenomena appear to be best-characterized as independent developments in the Pacific Northwest. With this background in mind, we will look below at the extent of prevelar raising in five ethnic groups of Washington speakers. We also explore, more broadly, these groups' participation in other features characteristic of the West.

SAMPLING CONSIDERATIONS. Having identified key phonological phenomena on which to concentrate, the question became WHOM to study? This volume seeks to address two key questions: What is the Western vowel system? and How diverse are Western speakers (both from other Westerners and non-Westerners)? Given the Pacific Northwest's unique cultural diversity, we cannot satisfactorily answer the second question for Washington State by focusing on a single area or on Caucasian American speakers only.

Common practice in dialectological research since the linguistic atlas projects of the 1920s was to select for study lifelong, nonmobile, older, rural, typically male community members who were assumed to best reflect local regional dialect markers (Wolfram and Schilling-Estes 2006, 20). This approach came under sharp criticism in the 1960s, but it can perhaps be defended given that these early projects focused on historical settlement and upon American departures from British English. However, the focus on speakers of Anglo descent has persisted, perhaps because it provides a way to narrow the scope of regional studies to English-speaking groups least likely to be influenced by foreign language forms and local social dialects representing nonmainstream social and ethnic groupings. However, Washington is unlike Eastern states such as Pennsylvania and New York, where strong ethnic enclaves formed not long after initial settlement and with them important mid-Atlantic ethnic sociolects (Reiff 1981). Interethnic contact has been a sustained part of Washington State history. Seasonal trading along the Pacific Coast brought early contact between Native American tribes, with the spread of Chinook Jargon, a trade variety based upon Chinook (and other Native American languages), French, and English, along the entire Pacific Northwest coastline, including Seattle and Portland (Mills 1950; Holton 2004). This variety was in use when the first Caucasians arrived and is believed to have influenced the English spoken in the region, as well as other Native American languages (Holton 2004). Sale (1976) described Seattle as rare among American urbanities: interethnic contact began fewer than 10 years after its initial founding in 1850. Thus, selecting one ethnic group risks poor generalizability of research results and is poorly motivated as a general sampling procedure in this setting. There is a very real possibility that nonwhite groups present from the founding of Washington territory influenced its variety of English and are suitable representatives of Washington speech. A decision was made to examine the extent of participation of several key ethnicities in Western vowel changes (including Pacific Northwest features). All are English-dominant native speakers. The approach is to assume that all speakers may have a range of linguistic resources available to them, including both mainstream forms (including the Pacific Northwest changes) and other forms used in more local communities of practice. In this chapter, we simply look for evidence of these in their systems and will take care to highlight ways they may interact with other features in speakers' linguistic repertoires.

An additional advantage to including speakers born outside of the Seattle area is fuller treatment of the regional diversity in the state. Evans (2011) presents a perceptual dialectological account of the places in the state where people believe English is spoken differently. Several clear patterns emerged. The Cascade Mountains were mentioned as a critical boundary, dividing the state into east and west. The "Cascade curtain" represents a geographic and political divide between "Westside liberals" and "Eastside republicans" (see, e.g., Nickels 2002). The eastern region has a history of agriculture, cattle farming, and rodeos and is associated with rural, "cowboy" culture. Evans (2011) found respondents frequently used the labels "Spanish," "country," or "hick" to describe this region. The major urban areas of Washington were also regarded as different linguistically, which Evans's respondents suggested may be because they are "blended from different cultures" and are the sites of universities, giving them a comparably higher concentration of "more educated" people. Western Washington was viewed as more internally differentiated, especially around metropolitan Seattle. Thus, the east-west division adopted here reflects lay perceptions of intrastate differentiation.

SEATTLE AREA (WESTERN WASHINGTON)

SPEAKERS. The general locations of the field sites for the English in the Pacific Northwest study are shown in figure 5.1. The first group to be examined for participation in the Pacific Northwest changes is a sample of 25 Caucasian Americans from the Seattle metropolitan area in the western region of the state. Speakers recorded in the other regions will be treated in the following sections.

METHODS. The metro Seattle Caucasian participants ranged in age from 26 to 93 and were divided into three generations: the oldest ($n = 8$), born between 1900–1950 (including members of the second generation of Caucasians born in the Pacific Northwest); the middle ($n = 12$), born between 1951–70; and the youngest ($n = 5$), born between 1976–86. All speakers were born and raised in predominantly lower-middle-class to middle-class Seattle neighborhoods in central King County (including Ballard, Ravenna,

FIGURE 5.1
Field Sites of the English in the Pacific Northwest Study

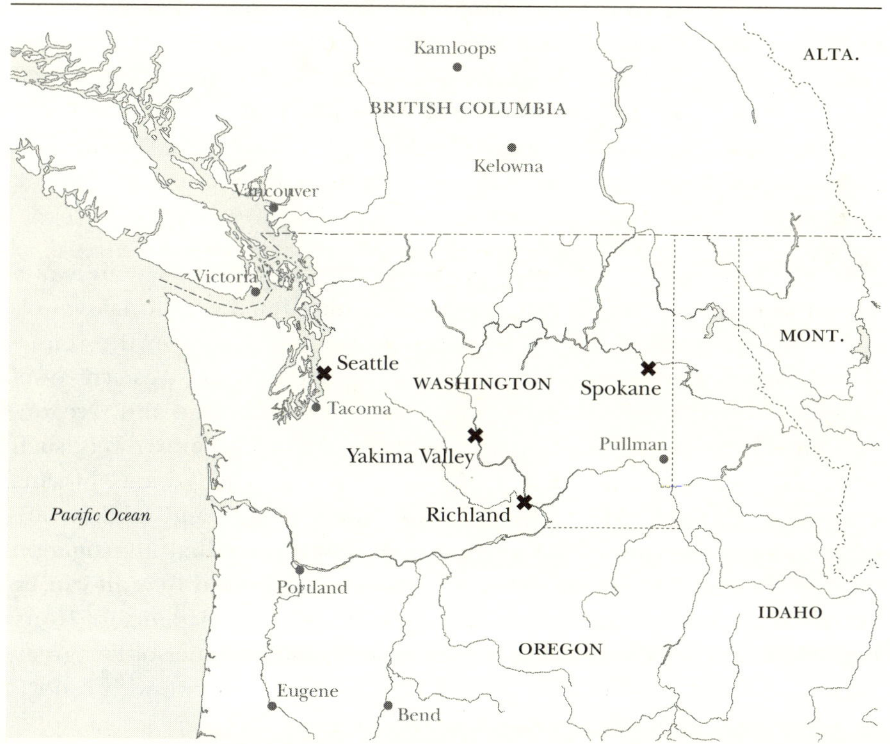

Wedgwood, the University District, Bothell, Sand Point, and Lake Forest Park). None lived outside of the Pacific Northwest at any time from birth to age 13. English was the language of each household represented. All respondents had completed high school. Levels of advanced schooling for those who attained degrees beyond high school varied, from business school to doctoral degrees.

In this section, we focus on data from two tasks, word list and reading passage elicitations. Approximately 930 tokens were analyzed per speaker in the metropolitan Seattle subsample. All phonemes in the vowel system were included (i, ɪ, e, ɛ, æ, ɑ, ɔ, ʌ, o, u, aɪ, aʊ, ɔɪ), though our focus is on a subset of these. Vowels were collected in the carrier frame, "Write —— today" for the word list. The reading passage used was an adaptation of Aesop's fable "The Cat and the Mice."

Recordings were made using M-Audio and Samson H4 Zoom flash recorders at a sampling rate of 44.1 kHz (recordings were subsequently downsampled to 11.025 kHz). The recordings were automatically segmented using the Penn Phonetics Laboratory Forced aligner (P2FA) (Yuan and Liberman 2008). Spectral analysis was accomplished over a 0–5500 Hz range, with a 30 dB dynamic range. F1–F3 were measured at three temporal locations (20%, 50%, 80%) using a Praat script (Boersma and Weenink 2014) and then checked manually. Nearey-2 normalization was used for comparison of vowel data (Watt, Fabricius, and Kendall 2011). Inferential statistical testing was accomplished in R. For vowel summarization and plotting, the R library phonR was used (McCloy 2013). The speaker sample and elicitation methods of the larger study are more fully described in Wassink (2015).

RESULTS. An overall view of the Caucasian Seattleites' vowel system is presented in figure 5.2 (/g, ŋ/ contexts are excluded for the front lax vowels /ɛ, æ/). Most notably, Seattle Caucasians do not participate in the retraction of /æ/ BAT and /ɛ/ BET—the second component of the Western vowel pattern referred to elsewhere in this volume for California and Oregon. Additionally, we do not see lowering of the /ɪ/ BIT and /ɛ/ BET vowels, such as is found in both Canada (Clarke, Elms, and Youssef 1995) and California (Hinton et al. 1987). Mid-front and back vowels /e/ BAIT and /o/ BOAT are quite monophthongal (see Wassink 2015). While a detailed investigation of /o/ BOAT is not within the research questions addressed here, it can be noted on the basis of the figure that /o/ BOAT shows no evidence of fronting. It was typically the vowel in the system with lowest values of F2 (greatest retraction). (r)-insertion is present, but receding. In line with reports by Foster and Hoffman (1966), older Washingtonians insert (r) in words

FIGURE 5.2
Vowel Polygon Showing Normalized Means for Seattle-Area Caucasian Speakers, Pooled by Gender

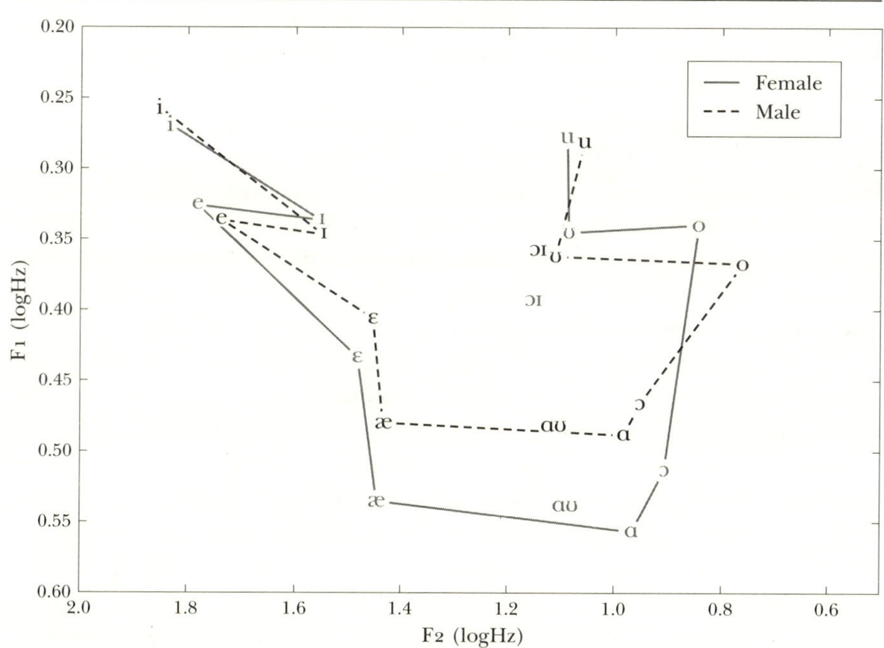

like *Washington, squash,* and *wash,* which emerge as [wɑɹʃɪŋtən], [skwɑɹʃ], and [wɑɹʃ], respectively. Finally, a three-way merger of *Mary, marry,* and *merry* was observed, so that all words are produced [meᵊɹɪ] (Reed 1952), a pattern observed in the United States more broadly. In terms of Western state features, advancement is apparent in the low back merger of /ɑ~ɔ/ BOT ~ BOUGHT and BOOT-fronting. These two patterns are described in further detail, below. Raising of /æ/ and /ɛ/ was found before the voiced velar stop /g/ and nasal /ŋ/. These patterns merit particular attention because they differ from the vowel systems of neighboring speakers along the Western coastal United States (but see Becker et al. 2016 [this volume], who find it for a sample of Oregon speakers).

THE LOW-BACK MERGER. As expected, all three generations in the Seattle subsample are quite advanced in the low-back merger of /ɑ~ɔ/ BOT ~ BOUGHT. Even among the oldest speakers, merger is the predominating pattern. Auditory inspection of the data indicates that the phonetic quality of the target of merger ranges from raised [a̝] to a fairly fronted [ɔ] to [ɑ]. Males and females appear to treat the merger differently. Males produce a merged form that is auditorily between [a̠] ~ [ɔ]; females frequently produce one that is backed and lowered toward [ɑ]. The difference between genders was found to be statistically significant in a series of nonparametric multifactorial ANOVA with GENDER and GENERATION as social factors, and normalized values of F1 or F2 as the continuous outcome variable (table 5.1). A GENDER × GENERATION interaction for F2 signifies that Seattle females reduce the F2 difference between vowels as age decreases. Males of all generations and younger females tend to have an [ɔ] that is proximal in height and fronting to [a], suggesting that the Seattle /ɑ~ɔ/ BOT ~ BOUGHT vowel may be fronting over time. Taken together, these results reveal that the older females were somewhat more conservative. (Some variation may be an artifact of the normalization process, so caution is recommended in interpreting the significance of the between-gender difference [Wassink 2015].) It must be noted that hypercorrection was found in some speakers, particularly younger females. This may help to account for the gender effect. For youngest generation females, BOUGHT class forms were sometimes produced lower in the system than BOT forms. These may be spelling-pronunciations, such as are commonly found in citation tasks. Or it may be that some younger females have a mental representation in which the word-classes are inverted. Confusion about word class memberships, or so-called flip-flop, is not uncommon in cases of (near-) merger (Labov 1994; Hall-Lew 2013). Similar findings have been reported for Oregonian English (Becker, Aden, and Best 2014).

BACK VOWEL FRONTING. Fronting of back vowels /u/ BOOT, /ʊ/ BOOK, and /o/ BOAT has been identified as a feature of the so-called California Vowel

TABLE 5.1
Multifactorial ANOVA Modeling the Influence of Gender and Age on Normalized Midpoint F1 and F2 of Vowels Produced in /ɑ/ BOT vs. /ɔ/ BOUGHT

	Midpoint F1		*Midpoint F2*	
	F	*p*	*F*	*p*
VOWEL	2.21	0.13 (ns)	1.25	0.26 (ns)
GENDER	6.2	0.01**	4.7	0.03*
GENERATION	5.42	0.02*	2.30	0.13 (ns)
VOWEL × GENDER	0.00	0.93 (ns)	0.36	0.54 (ns)
VOWEL × GENERATION	3.4	0.06 (ns)	1.4	0.24 (ns)
GENDER × GENERATION	2.9	0.08 (ns)	3.9	0.05*
VOWEL × GENDER × GENERATION	0.00	0.93 (ns)	0.66	0.42 (ns)

$^*p < .05$; $^{**}p < .01$

Shift (Hagiwara 1997; Eckert 2004; Kennedy and Grama 2012). It is considered a change occurring across other U.S. varieties (Labov, Ash, and Boberg 2006), including nearby Portland (Ward 2003; Becker, Aden, and Best 2014). Labov, Ash, and Boberg (2006) indicate that the West generally shows /u/ BOOT-fronting, but not /o/ BOAT-fronting. Indeed, we find no /o/-fronting for the metro Seattle Caucasian speakers. /o/ appears in plots of normalized F1 × F2 data to have the lowest F2 (i.e., be most retracted) for all speakers, with some speakers showing fronting for both /u/ BOOT and /ʊ/ BOOK relative to /o/ BOAT. For the latter two vowels, figure 5.2 shows (for both genders) that average normalized F2 falls around 1.1 (logHz). This will become important in the analysis of eastern Washington speaker data below.

RAISING OF *BAG* AND *BEG*. The Seattle speakers show widespread raising of /æ/ and /ɛ/, but restricted to voiced prevelar environments, BAG and BEG. While /æg/ BAG is consistently raised, it overlaps acoustically with /ɛ/ BET rather than /e/ BAIT. For most speakers, the areas of the ellipses /ɛg~e/ overlap by over 75%, classified as "complete spectral overlap." (See Wassink 2015 for a discussion of overlap fraction data for this sample.) The auditory qualities of nonvoiced-prevelar forms of these two lax vowels were consistently [æ] BAT and [ɛ] BET, respectively. Notably, prealveolar nasal /n/ raising of /æ/, often found in other dialects (recall discussion of the Midlands above), was not found. For most speakers (both male and female), /æg/ and /æŋ/ targets are extremely raised, and /æg/- and /ɛg/-raising are evident in speakers of all ages in the sample, even the eldest. A typical pattern is one in which BAG tokens fall within the distribution of the larger /ɛ/ class, making *bag* rhyme with *beg* (and auditory analysis suggests that some tokens of /æg/ can sound raised as high as [eᶦ]). Meanwhile, the prevelar subset of the /ɛ/ class itself overlaps the /e/ category, making *beg* rhyme with *bake.* For some speakers of both genders, /ɛg/ targets fall entirely within the distribution of /e/ (Freeman 2014; Wassink 2015). It was quite common for speakers to produce *tag* and *bag* as [tɛːg] and [bɛːg], respectively, while *legs* and *peg* surface as [leːgz] and [peːg] or [lɛ̝ːgz] and [pɛ̝ːg].

IS PREVELAR RAISING LEXICALLY DETERMINED? The history of /ɛg/-raising described above begs the question: might prevelar raising of /ɛ/ and /æ/ simply occur as it does in the rest of the United States—sporadically, in a small set of select words like *egg*? A detailed examination of lexical frequency, phonolexical patterns, or morphological conditioning was not undertaken for this study. However, we may provide a brief descriptive consideration of the lexical distribution of /æ, ɛ/. Tokens of /æ, ɛ/ were elicited in a range of phonological and morphological environments to investigate whether raising might be lexically restricted (table 5.2). Monomorphemic forms with both monosyllabic and polysyllabic shapes were included, such as *drag* and *dragon*. Monomorphemic as well as bimorphemic forms (e.g., *drag* and *dragging*) were included because grammatical conditioning has been found to predict advancement in vowel changes in other dialects of American English and cross-linguistically (in changes that have been found to be lexically diffusing at least in their early stages). For example, Labov found in Philadelphia that tense forms of short-*a* (/æ/ BAT) were more likely when an inflectional suffix closed the syllable: *planning* and *passed* were more advanced than *plan* and *past* (Labov 1994, 507–9). This was particularly interesting, because disyllabic forms such as *hammock, castle* were lax, confirming operation of a morphological, and not a phonological, constraint.

Figure 5.3 provides data for /æ/ and /ɛ/ for one typical younger male speaker. It can be seen in the left panel that both monosyllabic forms (*leg, egg, beg, peg*) and polysyllabic ones (*negative, leggings*) may be raised. Monomorphemic (*leg*) and bimorphemic forms (*legs, leggings*) follow suit. For some speakers, not all monosyllabic forms are raised. *Peg* is sometimes the exception to the raising rule. For /æ/, there is clearer evidence of near-categorical application of prevelar raising: it appears that any monomorphemic word of monosyllabic (*hang, bang, nag*) or polysyllabic shape (*magnet, dragon*) may be raised, as can be any polymorphemic form (*nagging,*

TABLE 5.2
Lexical Forms Targeted in the /æg/ BAG and /ɛg/ BEG Word Classes

	æ	ɛ
__[+lab]	*babble, family, happy, happened*	*web*
__[+cor]	*aunt, bad, began, cat, dad, dance, fast, had, hat, hatch, pan, plan, sat, that*	*best, dead, head, hett, mess, pen, said, set*
__[+vel]		
__k	*actions, actually, back, crack, lack, sack*	*beckon, deck, next*
__g	*bag, brag, crag, drag, dragon, lag, magnet, nag, pragmatic*	*beg, egg, leg, leggings, negative, peg, regular*
__ŋ	*bang, hang*	n/a
__+{*-ing, -ed*}	*bragged, bragging, hanging, hatched, nagging, passed, zagged*	*begging*
__[ɹ, l]	*marry, pal*	*merry, fell, very*

FIGURE 5.3
Prevelar Raising of /æ, ɛ/ for a Typical Male Speaker (Speaker 27, Gen 3)

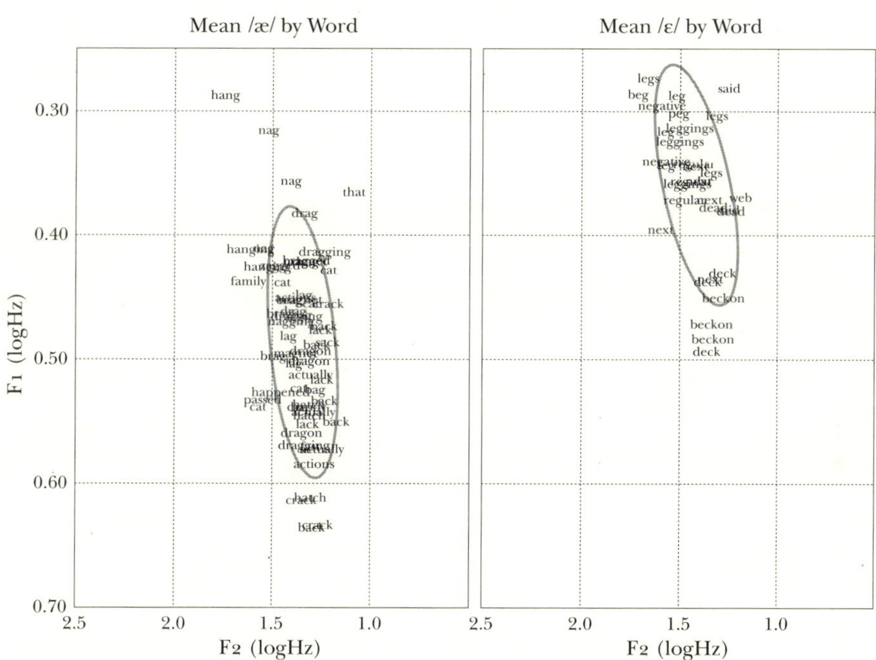

NOTE: Ellipses indicate two standard deviations.

hanging, zagged). For this speaker, the polysyllabic form *dragon* was variably raised.

To summarize the first results section, data for the Seattle-area speakers in the Western part of the state reveal several clear patterns. Merger of /ɑ~ɔ/ BOT ~ BOUGHT is advancing, while not yet complete. Fronting of /u/ BOOT and /ʊ/ BOOK, in contrast, is most advanced in younger speakers. This seems reasonable, given that Labov, Ash, and Boberg (2006) regard this as a newer set of changes. Prevelar raising of lax mid and low front vowels /ɛ, æ/ is widespread. /ɛg/ BEG may be raised in both mono- and polysyllabic environments (whether mono- or polymorphemic) but shows greater lexical restriction than /æg/ BAG. (See Wassink 2015 for discussion of interspeaker variation in the phonetic height of raised /ɛg/ and /æg/.) This seems to signify more widespread voiced prevelar raising than was noted in the 1950s by Reed and would thus be an important pattern to track going forward. We will be particularly interested to see whether speakers of other backgrounds participate in these changes. We turn our attention to this below.

CENTRAL AND EASTERN WASHINGTON

SPEAKERS. We now direct our attention to data for 48 speakers of Yakama, Japanese American, Mexican American, African American, and Caucasian descent. (Brief histories of each group are provided in corresponding sections below.) A Caucasian American subsample from east of the Cascade Mountains was desired for comparison with the metro Seattle Caucasian data for reasons discussed above. With regard to the nonwhite ethnicities, we selected groups that have had an enduring presence in the state since the mid-1800s or earlier and that represent the largest nonwhite groupings in the state. The central and eastern Washington field sites are indicated in the map presented earlier in figure 5.1. An attempt was made to include equal numbers of speakers from each group, sampling into three generation cohorts and two genders, but meeting these quota proved difficult. The breakdown of data analyzed for each group is shown in table 5.3. Because numbers are uneven across cells, generational cohorts were collapsed for analysis. Each group will be treated in a separate section, so that its particular history and any linguistic considerations particular to its community's linguistic repertoire may be treated.

METHODS. For all groups, speakers were recruited using word of mouth, radio announcements, and print advertisements. All speakers were screened to ensure that English was natively spoken and constituted the primary language of the home. Even for the Mexican American and Yakama subsamples, English was spoken as the dominant language. No speakers reported native fluency in a heritage language other than English.

Each group underwent the same procedures described for the metropolitan Seattle subsample above. Field recordings were made in subjects' homes or other quiet public location. Full sociolinguistic interviews were collected (casual conversation in peer dyads, interview, lexical tasks, reading passage, word list). However, the central data to be considered here are

TABLE 5.3
Nonwhite, Central, and Eastern Washington Subsamples ($n = 48$)

	Females	*Males*	*TOTAL*
Caucasians (Spokane Area)	6	2	8
Mexican Americans	9	2	11
Yakama	4	4	8
Japanese Americans	9	6	15
African Americans	5	1	6

FIGURE 5.4
Monophthongal Vowels (Normalized) for Central and Eastern Washington Caucasian, African American, Japanese American, Mexican American, and Yakama Subsamples

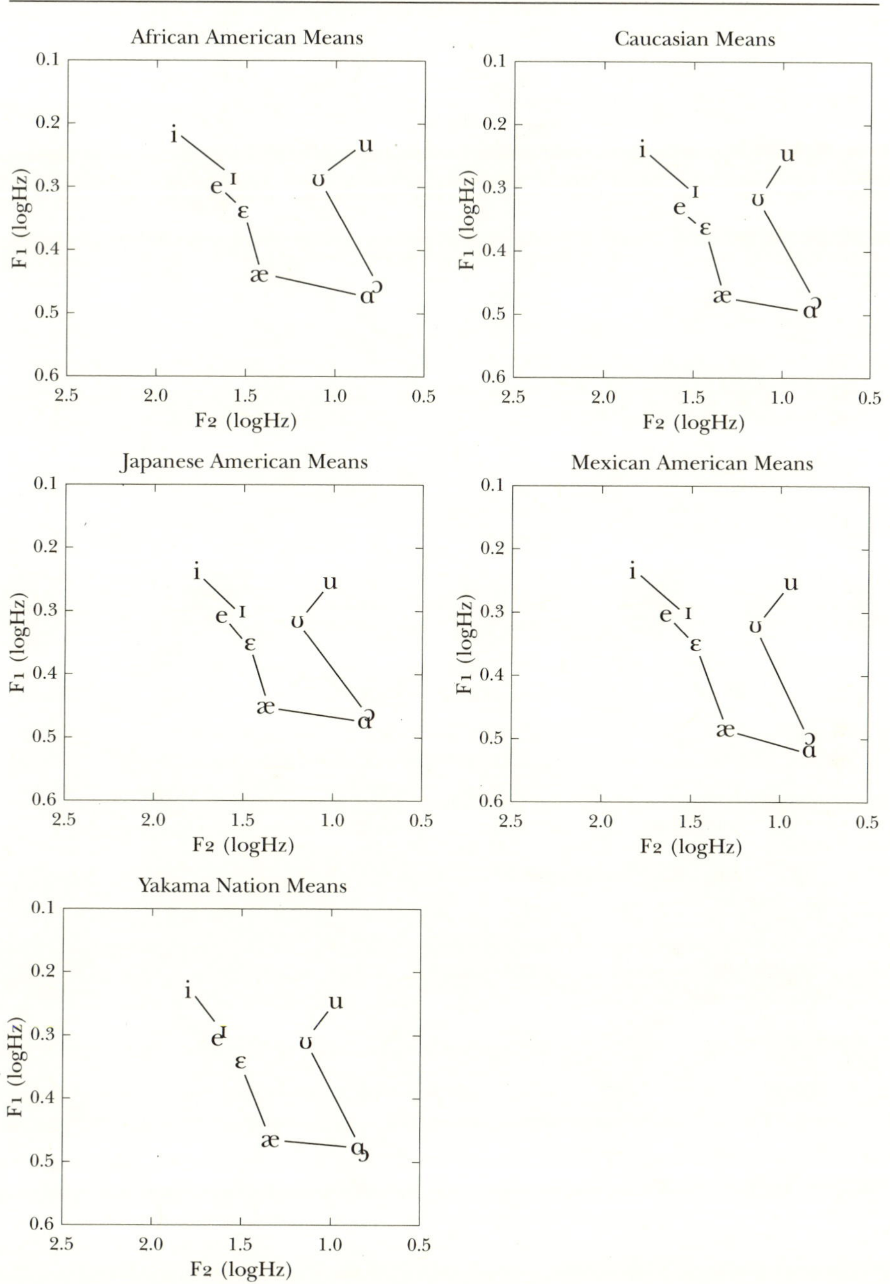

FIGURE 5.5
Prevelar Raising Vowels (Normalized) for Central and Eastern Washington Caucasian, African American, Japanese American, Mexican American, and Yakama Subsamples

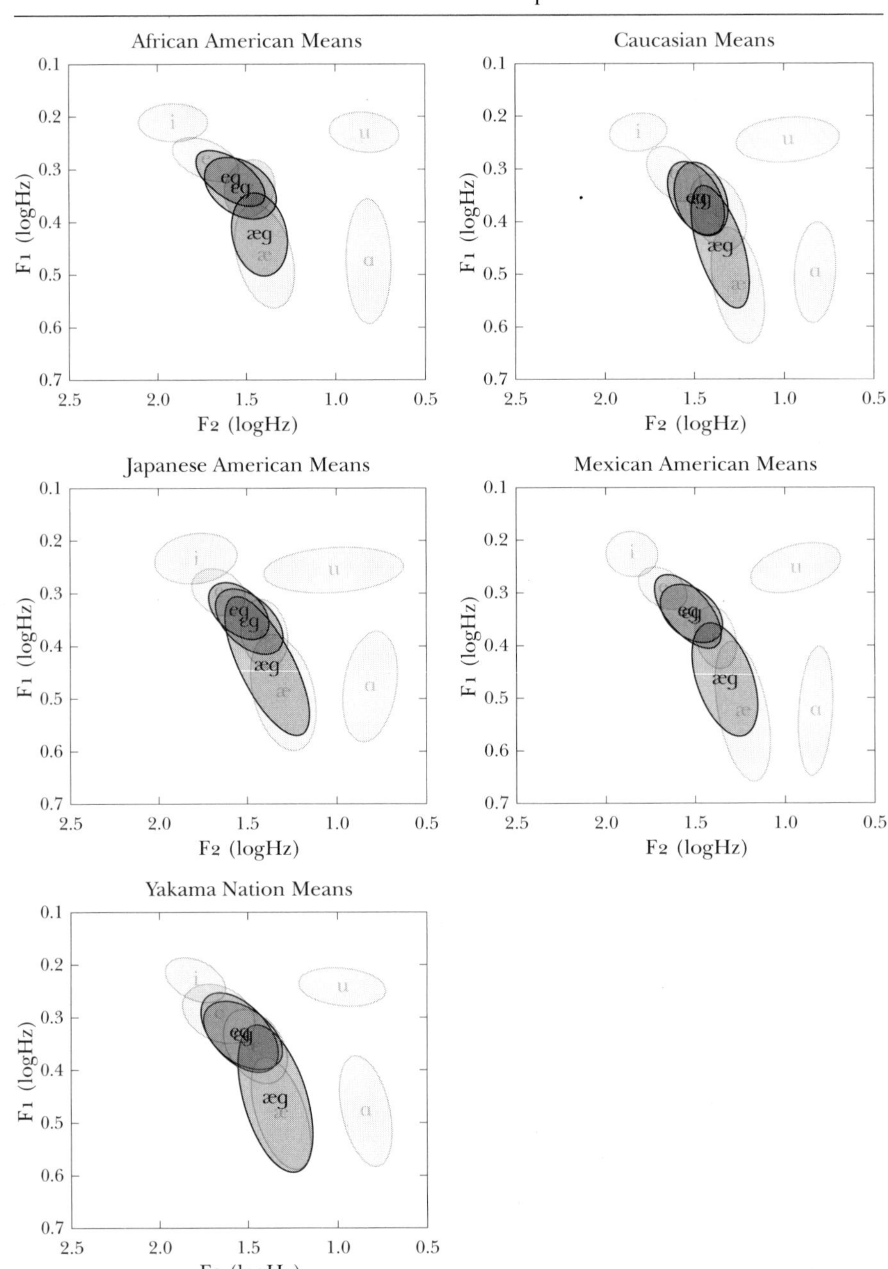

from the word list task. The word list dataset includes about 113 tokens per speaker.

Vowel system charts for each subsample are provided in figure 5.4, with accompanying means in appendix 1. We will first provide a snapshot of each community. Then, for each grouping, we describe findings for the /ɑ~ɔ/ BOT ~ BOUGHT, /u/ BOOT, and prevelar raising vowel changes. Means and plots for the prevelar vowels are presented separately in figure 5.5 and appendix 2. Statistical tests for between-ethnicity differences will be presented at the close of the section.

AFRICAN AMERICANS. The African American subsample includes one male from Spokane in the eastern part of the state and five women from the greater Seattle area. All had ethnically balanced social networks. In all cases, self-reported close friend networks were no more than 60% African American. Interestingly, Washington State's African American population emerged quite early; the first African American settler traveled from Massachusetts to California, from there to Vancouver, B.C., and then arrived in Seattle in 1858, where he was joined by his family shortly thereafter. Others arrived in Seattle in the late 1800s following similar coastal routes or overland with jobs on the railway (e.g., porter positions) (Taylor 1994). In addition to Seattle, African Americans settled in several small towns along the rail line, such as the coal-mining town of Roslyn, which had a 22% black population in 1900 and was the first town in Washington to have an African American mayor. The African American middle class in Seattle thrived in the 1960s as is apparent in the existence of early groups such as the Rhinestone Club, the first debutante society for African Americans in the United States (Beason 2002).

For the African American speakers sampled, /ɑ/ BOT and /ɔ/ BOUGHT appear in figure 5.4 to be nearly merged, but remain more separate than for any other group. By comparison to the Seattle metro male speakers above, whose vowels were 37 Hz (0.05 logHz) apart in F1, these speakers' vowels are 108 Hz (0.10 logHz) apart on average. Both genders separate vowels by height. Females' means for F1 are about 83 Hz (0.04 logHz) apart, which falls above the threshold for perceptual discrimination for reference vowels at this frequency (Flanagan 1955); the male speaker's means are an even greater 133 Hz (0.11 logHz) apart. Females' F2 means result in category separation of around 152 Hz (0.05 logHz); and the male's separation by F2 is similar. The position of the /u/ BOOT vowel shows no fronting. Visual inspection of the graphs and inspection of means data in appendix 1 shows that at 1181 Hz (0.85 logHz) the /u/ BOOT vowel F2 lies further back in the system than for all other groupings. It was interesting to discover that this group does participate in prevelar raising. The mean F1 of both the male and female speakers' /æg/ BAG is actually lower (meaning the vowel is higher in the system on average) than for the central and eastern Washington Caucasian speakers. Thus, this pattern is not only observed for the Seattle females—the Spokane-area male raises, too. On the other hand, we see that these speakers do not appear to separate the /ɛ/ BET and /ɛg/ BEG vowels as the other groups do. The prevelar environment shows no raising relative to the plain environment.

CENTRAL AND EASTERN WASHINGTON CAUCASIANS. Data were collected for eight Caucasian Americans born and raised in rural towns and one small city in central and eastern Washington to allow for comparison with the Caucasians from the metropolitan Seattle area west of the "Cascade curtain." These speakers came from Clayton, Deer Park, Richland, and the Spokane Valley. Clayton is a small town west of Spokane with a population of under 500 (U.S. Census Bureau 2010) and a median household income of under $32,000. Deer Park lies north of Spokane (in Spokane County) and has a population of about 3,650. Both are over 92% Caucasian. Both towns were settled in the late 1880s, with the draw of jobs in the lumber and apple farming industries. Unlike the predominantly liberal political leanings of the Seattle area voting population, these communities strongly tend to be divided between voters who favor independents and those who favor conservative political candidates (Morrill 2013). This provides a sharp picture of the intense east-west polarization of the state. Richland (Benton County) is in the south-central part of the state near Yakima. It is one of the Tri Cities (together with Kennewick and Pasco), with a population of about 48,000 in 2013. Although mainly known today as the site of the infamous Hanford nuclear facility, Richland has had a longer history, somewhat ironically, as an important agricultural area because of its location at the confluence of the Yakima and Columbia Rivers. It tends to be politically conservative and is majority Caucasian (87% in 2010), with a slightly higher Asian population than Deer Park (4% compared to 0.2%). Similar to the demographic patterns reported above, the close-friend networks of the central and eastern Washington Caucasian American subsample were predominantly white. Only one speaker reported three Hispanics in her close friend network.

As may be seen in figure 5.4, /ɑ/ BOT for this subsample is entirely merged with /ɔ/ BOUGHT. F1 means in appendix 1 are less than 30 Hz (0.01 logHz) apart, and F2 differences are negligible. By comparison with the Seattle-area Caucasian speakers, /u/ BOOT shows slightly less fronting (about 100 Hz/0.1 logHz on average). Thus, the Seattle Caucasians show slightly greater advancement than the rural Washington whites in /u/ BOOT-fronting. Both prevelar changes are observed: mean F1 for /æg/ BAG is comparable to the mean for the Seattle subsample; mean F1 for /ɛg/ BEG is quite high—in fact, it overlaps for both males and females with the mean for /eg/ VAGUE, BAGEL (means are within 0–7 Hz/0.001 logHz apart). As has been discussed elsewhere (Freeman 2014; Wassink 2015), /eg/ has a higher F1 than /e/ BAIT in plain consonantal contexts, and therefore, a lower target than might be expected. So /ɛg~eg/ BEG ~ BAGEL appear to be merged for these speakers, similar to what has been found elsewhere for other Washingtonians.

JAPANESE AMERICANS. The third group sampled were Americans of Japanese family background, now representing about 8% of the state's population. Five speakers were born and raised in Spokane in the eastern part of the state; the remaining 10, in the Western region (Seattle, Bainbridge Island, and Kingston). The first Japanese Americans arrived a year after Washington became a state in 1890. In 1910, Seattle had the largest Japan Town in the U.S. West. In 1941, most of the Japanese population was forcibly removed to internment camps for the duration of World War II by Executive Order 9066 (Hirabayashi 1934–2012). All of our subjects reported that their parents were affected by this measure. Most had families that heretofore had lived in ethnically diverse neighborhoods—internment represented the first time their parents lived together with other Japanese. After the war, many returned to ethnically mixed communities. This regional mobility, characterized by interethnic contact, is typical in Japanese American Washington families. All of our Japanese American subsample speakers were themselves born and raised in majority white communities in Seattle and reported friend networks that were either white-dominant or equally divided between Asian and Caucasian Americans. None reported fluency in Japanese.

The first thing that stands out in figure 5.5 is that the Japanese American speakers are very similar to the Caucasians in every respect. /ɑ/ BOT and /ɔ/ BOUGHT are completely merged, and /u/ BOOT is every bit as fronted. The prevelar graphs in figure 5.5 show that /æg/ BAG spans the widest range of any group. The table data show that females' F1 for /æg/ BAG is 47 Hz higher than for /æ/ BAT (at 33 Hz, males' separation of the categories is not as pronounced). Thus, females are clearly leading in the adoption of prevelar raising for this subgroup. /ɛg/ BEG is also raised relative to its prevelar counterpart, though not as dramatically (36 Hz for females, 27 Hz for males).

MEXICAN AMERICANS. The Mexican American subsample was mainly drawn from the Yakima Valley in south-central Washington. Gamboa (1981) dates earliest arrival to the Yakima Valley of Mexicans to 1800. The number of Mexicans in Washington grew in the 1930s and 1940s with systematic recruitment by the U.S. government in programs like the Yakima Valley Food for Victory Program, an emergency wartime measure designed to remedy the farm labor shortage in the Yakima Valley using braceros, Mexican nationals paid to do migrant labor. Two participants in the Mexican American subsample were from Spokane. Close friend networks were very similar for all members of this group: fairly evenly divided between Mexican Americans and Caucasians. One reported three close friends of Yakama descent. While most reported hearing some Spanish in the home growing up, only one had used Spanish and English equally in the home. None of the others considered themselves natively fluent. Two reported learning Spanish in school.

/ɑ~ɔ/ BOT ~ BOUGHT merger is observed for all speakers in this group. Like the African Americans, Mexican Americans do not show widespread /u/ BOOT fronting. Prevelar raising does occur, both for /æg/ BAG and for /ɛg/ BEG. For the former, we see that females' /æg/ BAG lies a full 100 Hz (0.07 logHz) higher than its plain counterpart /æ/, with males showing less raising (by about 33 Hz/0.03 logHz). For /ɛg/, females and males both raise, but again, females lead: prevelar contexts lie about 80 Hz (0.05 logHz) higher in vowel space than their /ɛ/ BET. This is as compared with males' difference in F1 of 23 Hz (0.02 logHz). In this group, then, similarly to the Japanese American subgroup, participation in the prevelar changes appears to be female led.

THE YAKAMA. The final subsample includes members of the Yakama Nation living in traditional reservation lands, constituting 1.3 million acres in the Yakima Valley between the Cascade Mountains and the Columbia River. The population of the Yakama in 2000 was 31,799. The Yakama Nation includes the tribes and bands of the Columbia Plateau, including the Palouse, Klickitat, and Yakama. The Yakama figured centrally in the building of intertribal relations by brokering deals between other tribes. They were responsible for negotiating the 1855 treaty with then-governor Isaac Stevens to end hostilities between the U.S. military and 14 Washington Territory tribes, who then became members of the Confederated Tribes and Bands of the Yakama Nation (Connell-Garretson 1968; Confederated Tribes and Bands of the Yakama Nation 2015). They reside on traditional lands in south-central Washington and comprise 1.8% of the present population of the state. English was the reported primary language of all Yakama subsample speakers, although two reported that their parents used Yakima Sahaptin in addition to English in the home. One younger male speaker teaches Yakama Sahaptin to heritage learners. A middle generation female speaker reported being raised in a mixed Yakama/Shoshone home, with English, Shoshone, and Yakima all home languages. However, she reported that she commanded only English with native fluency.

It may be seen that for these speakers, /ɑ/ BOT is clearly merged with /ɔ/ BOUGHT. Females separate mean F1 for these word classes by approximately 40 Hz (0.02 logHz), but males overlap F1 entirely. F2 means are completely overlapping for both genders. /u/ BOOT shows no fronting whatsoever and falls into the same spectral location as it does for the other nonwhite groupings from the central and eastern part of the state, with the exception of the African American subsample (whose productions were even more retracted). With regard to the prevelar raising vowels, an interesting difference emerges. Although their vowel system looks very much like that of the Japanese, Caucasian, and Mexican American subsamples in other respects, Yakama speakers are not as advanced in the raising of /æg/ BAG. The means data in appendix 2 show clearly that while other participating groups separate mean F1 of /æ/~/æg/ BAT ~ BAG by approximately 80–100 Hz (0.05 logHz), Yakama speakers' means for /æ/ in these two environments are only approximately 40 Hz (0.02 logHz) apart for both male and female speakers.

Four linear mixed effects analyses were conducted to test the relationship between ethnicity and the key vowel variables considered above (for the subgroups in this part of the project only). R (R Core Team 2012) and lme4 (Bates et al. 2014) were used. ETHNICITY was the fixed effect in all models, with random effects for SPEAKER. WORD was additionally included as a random effect in the prevelar raising tests. For /ɑ~ɔ/ BOT ~ BOUGHT, normalized midpoint F1 of /ɔ/ BOUGHT was selected as the dependent variable, as this process seems to involve lowering and merging on /ɑ/. As expected, no significant effects of ETHNICITY were found ($\chi^2(4) = 2.3769$, $p = .667$). Normalized midpoint F1 of /æg/ BAG was selected as the dependent variable to represent raising in the second test. *P*-values were obtained using likelihood ratio tests of the full model against the model with random effects only. No significant effect of ETHNICITY was found, indicating that all groups are participating in prevelar raising of /æg/ BAG on this measure ($\chi^2(4) = 2.62$, $p = .6224$). An inspection of the estimates of each ethnic group intercept shows little variation: Caucasian, 0.03 logHz; JapaneseAm, 0.01 logHz; MexicanAm, 0.04 logHz; Yakama, 0.02 logHz. For raising of /ɛg/ BEG, normalized midpoint F1 was the dependent variable. Here, a *p*-value approaching, but not reaching, significance was attained

($\chi^2(4) = 8.17$, $p = .08555$). For fronting of /u/ BOOT, the dependent variable was normalized midpoint F2. No significant effect of ethnicity was found ($\chi^2(4) = 0.00$, $p > .99$).

In summary, the nonwhite ethnic groups sampled all exhibit the primary Pacific Northwest English feature of interest—prevelar raising of /æg/ BAG—to some extent. From the descriptive data, Japanese and Caucasian Americans appear to be somewhat more raised overall, followed by the Mexican Americans, with members of the Yakama and African American communities following. All groups also exhibit other Western features. /ɑ~ɔ/ BOT ~ BOUGHT merger is observed in all groups (again with African Americans least advanced) and /u/ BOOT-fronting appears primarily to be a metro Seattle phenomenon at this point. We noted with interest that the western Washington Caucasian sample appears to show the greatest advancement in fronting of /u, ʊ/ of all groups—fronting is more extensive, in fact, than the Caucasian speakers interviewed to the east of the Cascade Mountains. It might be that this phenomenon is most advanced in the west (the Puget Sound cosmopolitan area). Future research will be needed to confirm this result over time. However, while they might be more conservative with respect to the newer back-vowel-fronting changes, the nonwhite groups in the central and eastern parts of the state were all participants to some degree in the older changes. While there is insufficient space here to discuss use of ethnolectal forms together with mainstream forms by nonwhite speakers, it is clear that these speakers share vowel system features. It is very clear that these speakers all "sound Washingtonian," and it is highly likely these form part of a rich set of linguistic resources they command.

WASHINGTON AND ITS NEIGHBORS

/æ/ AND REGIONAL DIFFERENTIATION. The above suggests that Washington speech is quintessentially Western but also a little different from other dialects. The raising of /æ/ and /ɛ/ play an important role in regional differentiation. While it may seem that focusing on prevelar raising is making a big deal out of two small phones, one of these, the /æ/ BAG vowel, appears to be doing a great deal of work to regionally subdivide the West. To the north, Sadlier-Brown and Tamminga (2008) find retraction of /æ/ in the variety of Canadian English spoken in Vancouver. To the south, Kennedy and Grama (2012) show that the BAT vowel /æ/ is lowered to [æ̞] or retracted to [a] for a sample of Californian speakers. They use Labov, Ash, and Boberg's (2006) mean for California TELSUR sample speakers as a benchmark for comparison to a contemporary sample. Their speakers' tokens are substantially backed, which they take to indicate retraction by comparison to Labov, Ash, and Boberg's (2006) data, collected a generation earlier, they estimate. So, the raised and fronted vowel used in Washington appears to be moving in an entirely different direction than that of our California cousins.

As for their neighbors in Oregon, Becker et al. (2016 [this volume]) find Oregonians utilize both California Vowel Shift features as well as the raised /æg/ BAG found in Washington. They report that 74% of their speakers retracted /æ/ BAT, with young speakers leading. For /ɛ/ BET, retraction was also found, but for fewer speakers (32%). Young women appear to be leading this change. And /ɑ/ BOT showed backing at similar levels (32%, with women of all ages leading). More generally, they show that this backed /ɑ/ BOT vowel is merged with the /ɔ/ BOUGHT vowel, so that the low-back merger appears to be complete and to have a backed target, near [ɑ]. This is in partial agreement with earlier findings for Oregon reported by Conn (2000), who found /æ/ BAT-lowering in a sample of Oregon speakers. The California pattern of retraction of /æ/ BAT was found in younger speakers. However, Becker and colleagues also find raising of /æg/ BAG and /ɛg/ BEG for some speakers in their sample. They interpret this to indicate that Oregonians show a split regional pattern: Washington voiced-prevelar raising in relevant contexts, but California retraction in others. It appears to be the younger speakers that show the voiced prevelar raising pattern. This might suggest that the Washington pattern is spreading southward across state lines. More research needs to be done to investigate the relative timing of the start of voiced prevelar raising in the Pacific Northwest.

CONCLUSION

In Washington English, we do not find a system entirely comprising regionally unique markers (like the interconnected changes taking place in the Northern Cities Shift), but a complex constellation of features. Taken together, the overall configuration is something apart. Two hundred years after Lewis and Clark's historic voyage to the Pacific Coast, it appears the vowel system of Washington State shows not irregularity without structure, but the emergence of regularity.

APPENDIX 1

Monophthongal Vowel Means, Central and Eastern Washington Speakers

		/i/					/ɪ/				
Ethnicity	*Sex*	*F1*		*F2*		*Duration*	*F1*		*F2*		*Duration*
		(Hz)	*(logHz)*	*(Hz)*	*(logHz)*	*(ms)*	*(Hz)*	*(logHz)*	*(Hz)*	*(logHz)*	*(ms)*
Japanese Am	F	323	0.21	2777	1.87	175	430	0.29	2314	1.56	127
	M	247	0.19	2596	2.04	132	337	0.26	2074	1.63	72
Caucasian	F	359	0.24	2742	1.83	151	461	0.31	2260	1.51	99
	M	291	0.22	2368	1.79	155	401	0.30	1963	1.49	108
Japanese Am	F	361	0.24	2739	1.82	140	456	0.30	2318	1.54	95
	M	306	0.23	2385	1.78	140	411	0.30	2037	1.50	87
Mexican Am	F	346	0.22	2841	1.86	120	467	0.30	2339	1.54	84
	M	279	0.22	2294	1.84	117	368	0.29	1904	1.52	89
Yakama	F	325	0.22	2595	1.81	157	400	0.28	2347	1.64	88
	M	289	0.23	2273	1.79	188	388	0.01	1968	1.56	116

		/ɑ/					/ɔ/				
Ethnicity	*Sex*	*F1*		*F2*		*Duration*	*F1*		*F2*		*Duration*
		(Hz)	*(logHz)*	*(Hz)*	*(logHz)*	*(ms)*	*(Hz)*	*(logHz)*	*(Hz)*	*(logHz)*	*(ms)*
Japanese Am	F	743	0.49	1199	0.81	248	660	0.45	1047	0.71	271
	M	477	0.37	1102	0.86	169	610	0.48	1162	0.91	198
Caucasian	F	740	0.49	1268	0.85	211	711	0.48	1228	0.82	237
	M	665	0.50	1075	0.81	231	649	0.49	1042	0.79	248
Japanese Am	F	715	0.48	1267	0.84	198	715	0.48	1240	0.82	205
	M	650	0.48	1064	0.78	210	626	0.46	1038	0.76	211
Mexican Am	F	811	0.53	1258	0.82	194	791	0.52	1273	0.83	211
	M	626	0.50	1095	0.88	140	579	0.47	1037	0.84	159
Yakama	F	647	0.45	1267	0.89	187	685	0.47	1220	0.84	215
	M	636	0.52	1014	0.80	242	637	0.50	1004	0.79	227

		/ʊ/					/u/				
Ethnicity	*Sex*	*F1*		*F2*		*Duration*	*F1*		*F2*		*Duration*
		(Hz)	*(logHz)*	*(Hz)*	*(logHz)*	*(ms)*	*(Hz)*	*(logHz)*	*(Hz)*	*(logHz)*	*(ms)*
Japanese Am	F	418	0.28	1606	1.08	136	357	0.24	1219	0.82	201
	M	376	0.29	1458	1.14	89	253	0.19	1143	0.89	124
Caucasian	F	478	0.32	1722	1.16	93	366	0.25	1430	0.97	137
	M	415	0.31	1467	1.11	101	321	0.24	1316	1.00	134
Japanese Am	F	481	0.32	1792	1.19	97	390	0.26	1572	1.04	144
	M	433	0.32	1637	1.20	103	341	0.25	1337	0.99	149
Mexican Am	F	502	0.33	1729	1.13	101	388	0.25	1382	0.90	140
	M	399	0.32	1530	1.22	94	311	0.25	1358	1.09	138
Yakama	F	425	0.29	1648	1.16	94	338	0.24	1433	1.00	166
	M	401	0.32	1418	1.12	126	309	0.25	1200	0.94	189

APPENDIX 2

Prevelar Raising Vowel Means, Central and Eastern Washington Speakers

		/æ/					/æg/				
Ethnicity	*Sex*	*F1*		*F2*		*Duration*	*F1*		*F2*		*Duration*
		(Hz)	*(logHz)*	*(Hz)*	*(logHz)*	*(ms)*	*(Hz)*	*(logHz)*	*(Hz)*	*(logHz)*	*(ms)*
Japanese Am	F	676	0.45	2099	1.41	218	629	0.42	2150	1.45	207
	M	628	0.49	1720	1.35	153	538	0.42	1723	1.35	142
Caucasian	F	786	0.52	1845	1.24	177	701	0.47	1995	1.33	156
	M	678	0.51	1699	1.29	191	561	0.43	1830	1.39	165
Japanese Am	F	723	0.48	1953	1.29	176	639	0.42	2124	1.41	164
	M	673	0.49	1754	1.30	176	617	0.45	1848	1.37	174
Mexican Am	F	835	0.55	1851	1.21	163	730	0.48	2029	1.32	167
	M	560	0.45	1666	1.33	147	527	0.42	1749	1.39	152
Yakama	F	673	0.47	1862	1.31	177	635	0.44	1950	1.37	196
	M	625	0.49	1682	1.33	203	595	0.47	1702	1.33	206

		/ɛ/					/ɛg/				
Ethnicity	*Sex*	*F1*		*F2*		*Duration*	*F1*		*F2*		*Duration*
		(Hz)	*(logHz)*	*(Hz)*	*(logHz)*	*(ms)*	*(Hz)*	*(logHz)*	*(Hz)*	*(logHz)*	*(ms)*
Japanese Am	F	513	0.35	2195	1.48	152	512	0.34	2276	1.53	145
	M	394	0.31	1896	1.49	95	390	0.31	1942	1.52	111
Caucasian	F	587	0.39	2025	1.36	115	547	0.37	2191	1.47	127
	M	488	0.37	1829	1.38	126	460	0.35	1931	1.46	139
Japanese Am	F	561	0.37	2121	1.41	115	525	0.35	2277	1.51	131
	M	514	0.38	1886	1.39	124	487	0.36	1977	1.46	128
Mexican Am	F	599	0.39	2111	1.38	116	518	0.34	2339	1.53	133
	M	449	0.36	1761	1.41	102	426	0.34	1862	1.49	127
Yakama	F	479	0.34	2113	1.49	121	460	0.32	2230	1.57	140
	M	477	0.38	1819	1.43	142	437	0.35	1890	1.49	157

		/e/					/eg/				
Ethnicity	*Sex*	*F1*		*F2*		*Duration*	*F1*		*F2*		*Duration*
		(Hz)	*(logHz)*	*(Hz)*	*(logHz)*	*(ms)*	*(Hz)*	*(logHz)*	*(Hz)*	*(logHz)*	*(ms)*
Japanese Am	F	420	0.28	2535	1.70	267	478	0.32	2336	1.57	181
	M	351	0.28	2313	1.82	166	385	0.30	2079	1.63	118
Caucasian	F	466	0.32	2402	1.62	206	540	0.36	2274	1.52	147
	M	400	0.30	2127	1.61	228	460	0.35	1919	1.46	171
Japanese Am	F	442	0.29	2551	1.69	197	503	0.34	2345	1.56	153
	M	404	0.30	2185	1.62	211	447	0.33	2074	1.53	155
Mexican Am	F	440	0.29	2590	1.69	187	515	0.34	2352	1.54	153
	M	379	0.30	2062	1.64	166	411	.033	1942	1.55	132
Yakama	F	402	0.28	2436	1.71	221	447	0.31	2259	1.58	165
	M	385	0.30	2055	1.60	256	437	0.35	1915	1.51	185

NOTE

Research was supported by National Science Foundation grant #BCS-1147678. The author is grateful to John Riebold for analysis of a portion of the data reported here, software support, and feedback.

REFERENCES

Bates, Douglas, Martin Maechler, Ben Bolker, and Steven Walker. 2014. lme4: Linear mixed-effects models using Eigen and S4_. R package. Version 1.1-7. http://CRAN.R-project.org/package=lme4.

Beason, Tyrone. 2002. "Rhinestones Still Glittering: Debutante Ball Emphasizes African-American Education." *Seattle Times*, Dec. 28. http://community.seattletimes.nwsource.com/archive/?date=20021228&slug=rhinestones28.

Becker, Kara, Anna Aden, and Katelyn Best. 2014. "Ideologies of Non-accent: Linking Perception and Production in Oregon English." Paper presented at the Cascadia Workshop in Sociolinguistics (CWSL), Victoria, B.C., Mar. 1–2.

Becker, Kara, Anna Aden, Katelyn Best, and Haley Jacobson. 2016. "Variation in West Coast English: The Case of Oregon." In *Speech in the Western States*, vol. 1, *The Coastal States*, edited by Valerie Fridland, Tyler Kendall, Betsy Evans, and Alicia Beckford Wassink, 107–34. Publication of the American Dialect Society 101. Durham, N.C.: Duke University Press.

Benson, Erica J., Michael J. Fox, and Jared Balkman. 2011. "The Bag That Scott Bought: The Low Vowels in Northwest Wisconsin." *American Speech* 86.3: 271–311. doi:10.1215/00031283-1503910.

Boersma, Paul, and David Weenink. 2014. Praat: Doing Phonetics by Computer. Versions 4.5–5.4. http://www.fon.hum.uva.nl/praat/.

Carver, Craig M. 1987. *American Regional Dialects: A Word Geography*. Ann Arbor: University of Michigan Press.

Clarke, Sandra, Ford Elms, and Amani Youssef. 1995. "The Third Dialect of English: Some Canadian Evidence." *Language Variation and Change* 7.2: 209–28. doi:10.1017/S0954394500000995.

Confederated Tribes and Bands of the Yakama Nation. 2015. Yakama Nation Museum and Cultural Center Website. http://www.yakamamuseum.com/home-history.php (accessed June 15).

Conn, Jeff. 2000. "Portland Dialect Study: The Story of /æ/ in Portland." Master's thesis, Portland State University Department of Applied Linguistics.

Connell-Garretson, Margaret A. 1968. "The Yakima Indians: 1855–1935, Background and Analysis of the Rejection of the Indian Reorganization Act." Master's thesis, University of Washington.

Eckert, Penelope. 2004. "Vowel Shifts in Northern California and the Detroit Suburbs." http://www.stanford.edu/~eckert/vowels.html.

Evans, Betsy. 2011. "'Seattletonian' to 'Faux Hick': Perceptions of English in Washington State." *American Speech* 86.4: 383–413. doi:10.1215/00031283-1587232.

Fant, Gunnar. 1960. *Acoustic Theory of Speech Production, with Calculations Based on X-Ray Studies of Russian Articulations.* The Hague: Mouton.

Flanagan, James L. 1955. "A Difference Limen for Vowel Formant Frequency." *Journal of the Acoustic Society of America* 27.3: 613–17. doi:10.1121/1.1907979.

Freeman, Valerie. 2014. "Bag, Beg, Bagel: Prevelar Raising and Merger in Pacific Northwest English." University of Washington Working Papers in Linguistics, 32. http://depts.washington.edu/uwwpl/vol32/freeman_2014.pdf.

Foster, David William, and Robert J. Hoffman. 1966. "Some Observations on the Vowels of Pacific Northwest English (Seattle Area)." *American Speech* 41.2: 119–22. doi:10.2307/453130.

Gamboa, Ernesto. 1981. "Mexican Migration into Washington State: A History, 1940–1950." *Pacific Northwest Quarterly* 72.3: 121–31.

Gordon, Matthew J. 2004. "The West and Midwest: Phonology." In *Handbook of Varieties of English: A Multimedia Reference Tool,* vol. 1, *Phonology,* edited by Edgar W. Schneider, Kate Burridge, Bernd Kortmann, Rajend Mesthrie, and Clive Upton, 338–50. New York: Mouton de Gruyter. doi:10.1515/9783110208405.1.129.

Hagiwara, Robert. 1997. "Dialect Variation and Formant Frequency: The American English Vowels Revisited." *Journal of the Acoustical Society of America* 102.1: 655–58. doi:10.1121/1.419712.

Hall-Lew, Lauren. 2013. "'Flip-Flop' and Mergers-in-Progress." *English Language and Linguistics* 17.2: 359–90. doi:10.1017/S1360674313000063.

Hinton, Leanne, Birch Moonwomon, Sue Bremner, Herb Luthin, Mary Van Clay, Jean Lerner, and Hazel Corcoran. 1987. "It's Not Just the Valley Girls: A Study of California English." In *Berkeley Linguistics Society: Proceedings of the Thirteenth Annual Meeting, February 14–16, 1987,* edited by Jon Aske, Natasha Beery, Laura Michaelis, and Hana Filip, 117–28. Berkeley, Calif.: Berkeley Linguistics Society. doi:10.3765/bls.v13i0.1811.

Hirabayashi, Gordon K. 1934–2012. Gordon K. Hirabayashi Papers. University of Washington Special Collections, Manuscript Collection Accession Numbers 3159-006 to 009.

Holton, Jim. 2004. *Chinook Jargon: The Hidden Language of the Pacific Northwest.* San Leandro, Calif.: Wawa Press.

Kennedy, Robert, and James Grama. 2012. "Chain Shifting and Centralization in California Vowels: An Acoustic Analysis." *American Speech* 87.1: 39–56. doi:10.1215/00031283-1599950.

Krezschmar, William A., Jr. 2004. "Standard American English Pronunciation." In *Handbook of Varieties of English: A Multimedia Reference Tool,* vol. 1, *Phonology,* edited by Edgar W. Schneider, Kate Burridge, Bernd Kortmann, Rajend Mesthrie, and Clive Upton, 37–51. New York: Mouton de Gruyter. doi:10.1515/9783110208405.1.37.

Labov, William. 1991. "The Three Dialects of English." In *New Ways of Analyzing Sound Change*, edited by Penelope Eckert, 1–44. New York: Academic Press.

———. 1994. *Principles of Linguistic Change*. Vol. 1, *Internal Factors*. Oxford: Blackwell Publishers.

Labov, William, Sharon Ash, and Charles Boberg. 2006. *The Atlas of North American English: Phonetics, Phonology, and Sound Change*. Berlin: Mouton de Gruyter.

McCloy, Daniel. 2013. phonR: R tools for phoneticians and phonologists. R package. Version 0.4-2. https://github.com/drammock/phonR.

Mills, Randall V. 1950. *Oregon Speechways*. New York: Columbia University Press.

Morrill, Richard. 2013. "How Polarization Plays Out in Washington State: Voting for President and the Same-Sex Marriage." *New Geography*, Jan. 15. http://www.newgeography.com/content/003400-how-polarization-plays-out-washington-state-voting-president-and-same-sex-marriage.

Nickels, Greg. 2002. "East, West Parts of State Need to Work in Harmony." *Spokesman-Review* (Tacoma, Wash.), Mar. 28, B7.

R Core Team. 2012. *R: A Language and Environment for Statistical Computing*. R Foundation for Statistical Computing, Vienna, Austria. http://www.R-project.org/.

Reed, Carroll E. 1952. "The Pronunciation of English in the State of Washington." *American Speech* 27.3: 186–89. doi:10.2307/453476.

———. 1961. "The Pronunciation of English in the Pacific Northwest." *Language* 37.4: 559–64. doi:10.2307/411357.

———, dir. 1965. Linguistic Atlas of the Pacific Northwest (LAPNW). Special Collections Repository of the Library, University of Georgia, Athens.

Reiff, Janice L. 1981. "Urbanization and the Social Structure: Seattle, Washington, 1852–1910." Ph.D. diss., University of Washington.

Riebold, John M. 2015. "The Social Distribution of a Regional Change: /æg, ɛg, eg/ in Washington State." Ph.D. diss., University of Washington.

Sadlier-Brown, Emily, and Meredith Tamminga. 2008. "The Canadian Shift: Coast to Coast." Paper presented at the annual conference of the Canadian Linguistic Association, Vancouver, B.C., May 31–June 2. http://homes.chass.utoronto.ca/~cla-acl/actes2008/CLA2008_Sadlier-Brown_Tamminga.pdf.

Sale, Roger. 1976. *Seattle Past to Present: An Interpretation of the History of the Foremost City in the Pacific Northwest*. Seattle: University of Washington Press.

Taylor, Quintard. 1994. *The Forging of a Black Community: Seattle's Central District, from 1870 through the Civil Rights Era*. 3rd ed. Seattle: University of Washington Press.

Thomas, Charles Kenneth. 1958. *An Introduction to the Phonetics of American English*. 2nd ed. New York: Ronald Press.

U.S. Census Bureau. 2010. "Profile of General Population and Housing Characteristics: 2010 Demographic Profile Data." American Fact Finger. http://factfinder.census.gov/bkmk/table/1.0/en/DEC/10_DP/DPDP1/1600000US5312735.

Ward, Michael. 2003. "Portland Dialect Study: The Fronting of /ow, u, uw/ in Portland, Oregon." Master's thesis, Portland State University. http://www.pds.pdx.edu/Publications/Ward.pdf.

Wassink, Alicia Beckford. 2015. "Sociolinguistic Patterns in Seattle English." *Language Variation and Change* 27.1: 31–58. doi:10.1017/S0954394514000234.

Wassink, Alicia Beckford, and John M. Riebold. 2013. "Individual Variation and Linguistic Innovation in the American Pacific Northwest." Paper presented at the Workshop on Sound Change Actuation, University of Chicago, Apr. 18–20. http://washo.uchicago.edu/pub/workshop/wassink.pdf.

Wassink, Alicia, Robert Squizzero, Mike Scanlon, Rachel Schirra, and Jeffrey Conn. 2009. "Effects of Gender and Style on Fronting and Raising of /æ/, /e:/ and /ɛ/ before /g/ in Seattle English." Paper presented at the 38th annual meeting of New Ways of Analyzing Variation (NWAV 38), Ottawa, Oct. 22–25.

Watt, Dominic, Anne Fabricius, and Tyler Kendall. 2011. "More on Vowels: Plotting and Normalization." In *Sociophonetics: A Student's Guide*, edited by Marianna Di Paolo and Malcah Yaeger-Dror, 107–18. London: Routledge.

Wolfram, Walt, and Natalie Schilling-Estes. 2006. *American English: Dialects and Variation*. Malden, Mass.: Blackwell.

Yuan, Jiahong, and Mark Liberman. 2008. "Speaker Identification on the SCOTUS Corpus." *Journal of the Acoustical Society of America* 123.5: 3878–81. doi: 10.1121/1.2935783.

Zeller, Christine. 1997. "The Investigation of a Sound Change in Progress: /æ/ to /e/ in Midwestern American English." *Journal of English Linguistics* 25.2: 142–55. doi:10.1177/007542429702500207.

ALICIA BECKFORD WASSINK is an associate professor in the Department of Linguistics, University of Washington, and director of the Sociolinguistics Laboratory. She has served as principal investigator of the English in the Pacific Northwest study since 2006. She is a former Howard and Frances Nostrand Endowed Professor of Language and Cultural Competence. Wassink's research interests lie in production and perception of the time-varying features of vowel systems, language ideology, social network modeling, dialect contact, development of sociolinguistic competence in children, and creole linguistics. Her work has appeared in books on *Language and Identity* (Edinburgh University Press, 2010), *African-American Women's Language* (Oxford University Press, 2015), *Best Practices in Sociophonetics* (Routledge, 2010), and *Language in the Schools* (Elsevier, 2005). Primary reports of her research have appeared in *Journal of the Acoustical Society of America*, *Journal of Phonetics*, *Language in Society*, *Language Variation and Change*, *Journal of English Linguistics*, and the *International Journal of Speech-Language Pathology*. E-mail: wassink@u.washington.edu.

6. VARIATION IN WEST COAST ENGLISH: THE CASE OF OREGON

KARA BECKER, ANNA ADEN, KATELYN BEST,
and HALEY JACOBSON

THIS CHAPTER DESCRIBES the vowel patterns of residents of Oregon, a state that sits within the immense dialect region referred to as "The West" by Labov, Ash, and Boberg (2006, 280) in *The Atlas of North American English.* They, as well as other early dialectologists (e.g., Carver 1987), found little linguistic evidence of features that mark this region. They cite only two characteristic features of the West: the low back merger of /ɑ/ and /ɔ/ (BOT and BOUGHT) and the fronting of /u/ (BOOT), features found elsewhere in North America. This dialectological view aligns with many Western speakers' folk perceptions of language, which focus on both the homogeneity and standardness of Western speech (Hartley 1999; Evans 2013).

Labov, Ash, and Boberg's (2006) atlas was intended to serve as a departure point for further scholarship that could sample more broadly within a region. Building on their work in the West, this chapter focuses on the western part of Oregon and describes Oregonians who make use of a broad linguistic repertoire of distinctive features that link them to neighboring regions, particularly California to the south and Washington State to the north. Oregon's geographic location, as a transitional area between these two locales, provides a unique opportunity to chart the spread of emerging features of West Coast English. This study, alongside others in this volume, combats a view of "The West" as a monolithic dialect region.

DIALECT DISTINCTION IN THE WEST

In contrast to the monolithic view of the West, scholarship in California and Washington has identified dialect distinction within the region. Work in both locales has verified the presence of the low back merger and the fronting of BOOT (Reed 1952, 1961; Hinton et al. 1987; Fought 1999; Hall-Lew 2011, 2013; Kennedy and Grama 2012; Wassink 2015, 2016 [this volume]). Given the prevalence of these features and their use as a diagnostic of Labov, Ash, and Boberg's (2006) West, we refer to them here as General West Coast features (figure 6.1).

Publication of the American Dialect Society 101 DOI 10.1215/00031283-3772923

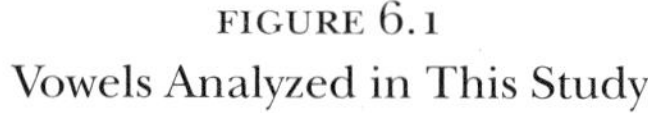
FIGURE 6.1
Vowels Analyzed in This Study

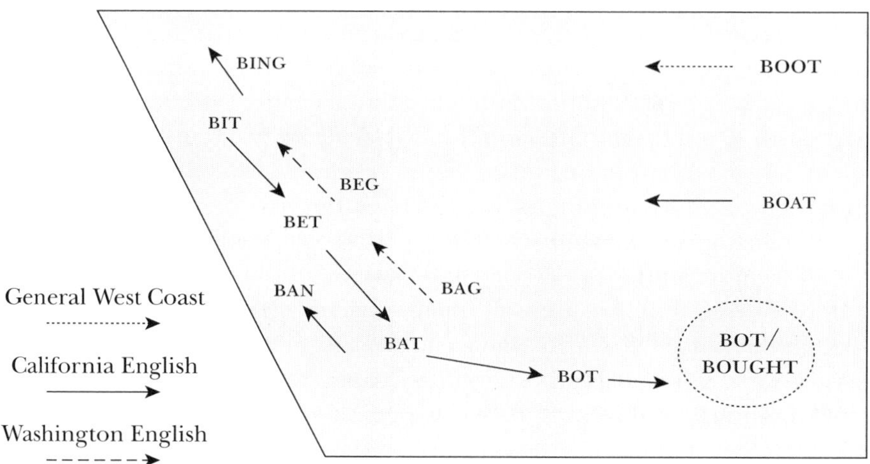

Descriptions of California English focus on the California Vowel Shift (CVS), a rotation of the short vowels /ɪ/ (BIT), /ɛ/ (BET), /æ/ (BAT), and /ɑ/ (BOT), where BIT and BET lower and BAT and BOT retract in the vowel space. This shift has been documented across the state of California, from the urban west (Hinton et al. 1987; Eckert 2008; Podesva 2011) to the more rural inland areas to the east (D'Onofrio et al. 2016 [this volume]), and from Southern California (Kennedy and Grama 2012) north to San Francisco (Cardoso et al. 2016 [this volume]). There is further conditioning of some CVS vowels: /ɪ/ tenses before velar nasals (BING) and /æ/ tenses before all nasals (BAN) (Eckert 2008; Mendoza-Denton 2008; Cardoso et al. 2016 [this volume]). Both Kennedy and Grama (2012) and D'Onofrio et al. (2016 [this volume]) found that young women lead in the retraction of BAT in California, evidence of change in progress. The behavior of BAT in their data suggests this vowel could be the "triggering event" of the CVS, although there is a lack of consensus in the literature. In addition, California English is also characterized by the fronting of the back vowels /o/, /u/, and /ʊ/ (BOAT, BOOT, and BOOK). Although most descriptions of California English treat the CVS short vowel rotation and back vowel fronting as related processes, we distinguish these two aspects of California English. For the CVS, the short vowel chain shift is identical to the Canadian Vowel Shift (Boberg 2005), a rotation that does not include back vowel fronting. Further, both BOOT and BOAT fronting are well documented elsewhere in the United States in locales where the short vowel rotation is not found (Labov, Ash, and Boberg 2006). In the West, both Labov, Ash, and Boberg

(2006) and recent work in Washington State (Wassink 2015, 2016 [this volume]) find that BOAT remains retracted. For this reason, BOAT fronting is treated as a feature of California English for the purposes of analysis (figure 6.1), as its presence in Oregon would indicate a link to California, while its absence would indicate a link to areas like Washington State.

Scholars have argued in recent years for dialect distinction in the Pacific Northwest based on phonological data from Washington State (Freeman 2014; Wassink 2015, 2016 [this volume]). These studies have identified the raising of /ɛg/ (in words like *egg* and *keg*, hereafter BEG tensing) and /æg/ (in words like *bag* and *hag*, hereafter BAG tensing) as characteristic of Pacific Northwest speech. For some speakers, there is complete merger of BEG with the BAIT class, while BAG variably raises to overlap with the two (Freeman 2014; Wassink 2015, 2016 [this volume]). With respect to change, Freeman (2014) finds men aged 37–62 (the older group of the two studied) show the most raised forms of BAG and BEG, the opposite of what is expected for change in progress, while Wassink (2015) argues that BAG raising is spreading in the Seattle area. Despite questions about the direction of change, BEG and BAG tensing is suggested to be the defining feature of a Pacific Northwest variety.

Though considered part of the Pacific Northwest, previous sociolinguistic research on Oregon is limited. One study of Portland (Ward 2003) describes BOAT, BOOT, and BOOK fronting and finds that young, working-class women lead these changes. Hartley (1999) conducted a perceptual study in which Oregon speakers performed a regional map task (Niedzielski and Preston 2003). Oregon and Washington emerged as a perceptually salient dialect region for Oregonians in both the map task and the ranking tasks, and speakers from both states were ranked highest on the correctness and pleasantness scales (Hartley 1999, 322–23). However, no research has examined whether Oregonians produce the features more recently found to be distinct along the West Coast, namely, the CVS and BEG and BAG tensing (though see McLarty, Kendall, and Farrington 2016 [this volume]).

With its proximity to both California and Washington, this study seeks to examine Oregon's relationship to California English and Washington English to establish its participation in West Coast vocalic production. Figure 6.1 summarizes the vowels under investigation in this study. With a chain shift attested to the south in California, we ask if Oregonians produce features of California English. With BAG and BEG tensing attested just to the north in Washington State, we contribute data from Oregon speakers to assess whether a Pacific Northwest variety is motivated on the basis of phonological similarity. Finally, we use the methods of perceptual dialectology to investigate how Oregonians' perceptions of English in their state and in the broader West impact their vowel production.

METHODS

Short sociolinguistic interviews were conducted with 42 native speakers of Oregon English at Portland Community College in Tigard, Oregon, just outside of Portland. Speakers were recruited based on whether they self-identified as "native Oregonians." At the beginning of each interview, speakers were asked for a brief summary of where they had lived throughout their lives. Based on their responses, 7 speakers were deemed to be nonnative Oregonians and were removed from the study. Another speaker was removed during analysis for problems with recording quality. Of the remaining 34, 22 were raised in the Portland metropolitan area, and 12 others grew up elsewhere in Western Oregon. Given this, the sample can be seen as representative of western Oregon, which is largely more urban than the eastern side of the state, and more specifically as representative of the Portland metro area. Figure 6.2 shows the western portion of Oregon and the location of Portland.

Due to the brief nature of the interviews (10–15 minutes), participants were not asked to self-report membership in demographic categories, but were instead grouped after the interview. As table 6.1 shows, 21 participants were categorized as men and 13 as women. Participants were divided into three age categories, designed to distinguish college-aged individuals (the majority of students at Portland Community College) from those older: 18–25 (younger), 26–40 (middle-aged), and over 40 (older). Almost all participants were judged to be white, which reflects the low racial and ethnic diversity of Portland, which was 76.1% white according to the 2010 census (U.S. Census Bureau 2014). Consequently, race/ethnicity is not analyzed in this study.

The interview was designed to elicit production data for acoustic analysis as well as speaker attitudes toward English in the West. The first segment was a casual interview, where participants discussed their lives growing up in Oregon. Speakers were then presented with a reading passage and a word list designed to target vowels of interest. Data from casual speech, the reading passage, and minimal pairs are combined for analysis to maximize the overall number of tokens for each speaker.

Finally, participants completed a map task in which they were asked to indicate on a regional map anywhere they thought people spoke English differently (Niedzielski and Preston 2003). The map showed the state of Oregon with neighboring portions of California, Washington, and Idaho included (figure 6.3). Although some cities, towns, and landmarks were included, labels for the surrounding states were intentionally omitted to allow participants to decide whether to note these divisions themselves. Fol-

FIGURE 6.2
The Area of Study

TABLE 6.1
The Sample of Oregonians

	18–25	*26–40*	*Over 40*	TOTAL
Men	6	8	7	21
Woman	7	4	2	13
TOTAL	13	12	9	34

lowing prior work (Benson 2003; Bucholtz et al. 2007; Evans 2011), the scope of the map was designed to focus on state- and regional-level perceptions. As Evans (2011) notes, map tasks that involve the whole country typically rely heavily on national stereotypes. Upon completion of the map task, participants were asked to elaborate on their comments and for their opinions about accents in Oregon, the Pacific Northwest, and other parts of the United States.

FIGURE 6.3
The Map Task

PRODUCTION ANALYSIS. The interviews were transcribed in Praat and submitted to the online vowel analysis suite FAVE, or Forced Alignment and Vowel Extraction (Rosenfelder et al. 2011). The FAVE process extracted measurements from over 1,500 tokens per speaker. This output was then checked, with mislabeled tokens recategorized, outliers removed using the quartile method, and vowels in good contexts selected for analysis (Thomas 2011), which resulted in an average of 225 tokens per speaker from the full vowel space. The data were then normalized to the Labov Telsur G using the NORM vowel normalization and plotting suite (Thomas and Kendall 2007).

A number of methods were used to analyze the production data. The first was the use of Labov, Ash, and Boberg's (2006) benchmarks, which are the mean Hz values for each vowel class from the large atlas sample. Vowels which cross these cut-off points are considered shifted. Benchmarks are provided for the General West Coast feature of BOOT fronting, with benchmarks for both TOOT (/u/ with coronal onsets) and BOOT (/u/ with noncoronal onsets), as well as BOAT fronting, a feature treated as part of California English in this study. The benchmarks for BET lowering and BAT and BOT retraction come from Labov, Ash, and Boberg's description of the Canadian Vowel Shift, which involves an identical rotation of these vowel classes. Kennedy and Grama (2012) used these benchmarks in their analysis of the California Vowel Shift. By normalizing our Oregon speaker data to the Labov Telsur G, results can be directly compared to these benchmarks, which are given in table 6.2.

For statistical analysis, group-level *t*-tests were performed to assess nasal conditioning in California English (BAT vs. BAN and BIT vs. BING), as well as Washington English BAG and BEG tensing (BAG vs. BAT and BEG vs. BET). For BOT and BOUGHT, *t*-tests were performed for each individual speaker to assess merger. All *t*-tests are two-sample, unpaired, unequal variance, and one-tailed, and use a threshold of $p < .05$ to determine significance.

A further measure of low back merger calculated was the Euclidean distance between BOT and BOUGHT. This measure, as well as all relevant formant data, was modeled in Rbrul (Johnson 2012) to investigate the impact of social predictors on the data. All models are linear regressions with the Euclidean distance or formant values run as a continuous response variable and age and gender included as fixed effects. In addition, some models explore the impact of two additional ideology variables, explained in more detail below. A step-down model of main effects was fit to each response variable.

TABLE 6.2

Labov, Ash, and Boberg's (2006) Benchmarks for Vowel Behavior

Vowel Behavior	*Benchmarks*
TOOT fronting	F2 > 1550 Hz
BOOT fronting	F2 > 1200 Hz
BOAT fronting	F2 > 1278 Hz
BET fronting	F1 > 650 Hz
BAT fronting	F2 < 1825 Hz
BOT fronting	F2 < 1275 Hz

MAP TASK. The maps were analyzed through a content analysis of labels appearing on the maps, which grouped individual labels (a total of 109 across 32 maps) into larger themed categories (Bucholtz et al. 2007; Evans 2011). Because our research questions centered on Oregon's relationship (in production as well as perception) to neighboring states in the West, we sought to operationalize our participants' attitudes toward dialect diversity along the West Coast. After the completion of the content analysis, we chose two categories that emerged from that analysis for quantitative analysis: a IDEOLOGY OF NONACCENT category was used to divide participants based on whether or not they noted a belief in a homogenous, accentless variety (Lippi-Green 1997); a CALIFORNIA category was used to divide participants based on whether or not they noted the boundary between Oregon and California. These binary variables were then added to the regression models investigating the CVS and BAG and BEG tensing, with the goal of linking speaker attitudes toward West Coast English with speaker production of West Coast vocalic features.

RESULTS: PRODUCTION

Figure 6.4 presents the production data for the full sample, with each data point representing a speaker's normalized mean value in F1 and F2 for a vowel class in unconditioned contexts.

GENERAL WEST COAST FEATURES. Oregon English speakers participate in BOOT fronting, a feature of General West Coast English. All speakers have a mean F2 for TOOT that is greater than 1550 Hz (see table 6.2 for benchmarks), and all but four (82%) have a mean F2 for BOOT greater than 1200 Hz,[1] in line with the expectations of conditioning (that postcoronal TOOT will be fronter than BOOT) for this sound change (Labov, Ash, and Boberg 2006). BOOT/TOOT are also front of BOAT for most speakers, consistent with the general pattern that BOOT fronting precedes BOAT fronting in the West and elsewhere (Ward 2003; Labov, Ash, and Boberg 2006; Kennedy and Grama 2012).

In 2003, Ward reported that the low back merger was complete in Portland. Here, *t*-tests were performed for each individual speaker. Tests for 21 speakers (62% of the sample) attained significance at the $p < .05$ level in both F1 and F2 at the vowel onset; that is, these speakers are merged for BOT and BOUGHT. For those speakers who were not fully merged, more maintained a distinction in F1. The greater extent of merger in F2 could be related to BOT retraction, a feature of the CVS (although only 32% of

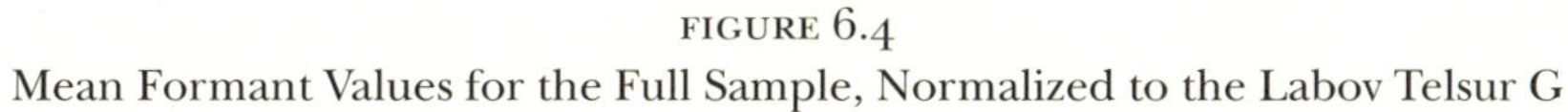

FIGURE 6.4
Mean Formant Values for the Full Sample, Normalized to the Labov Telsur G

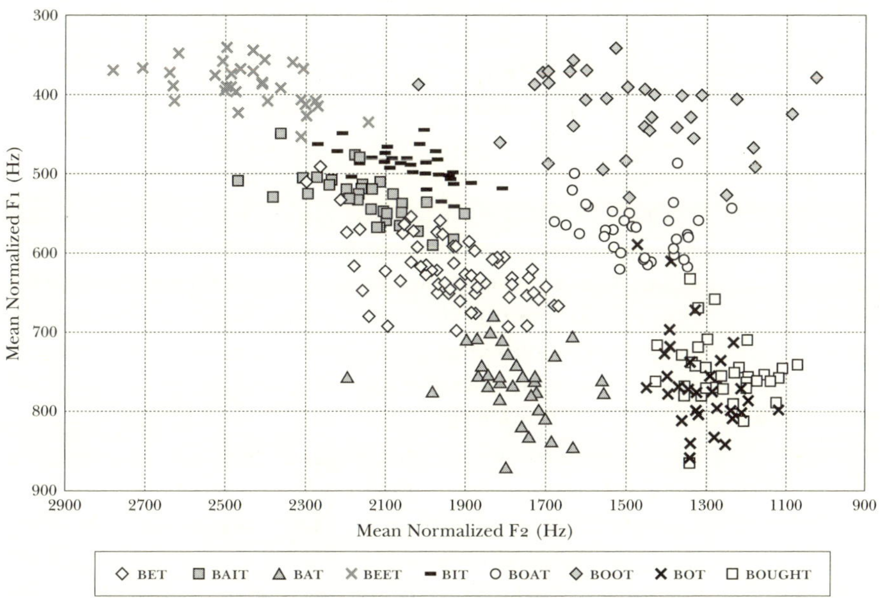

speakers meet Labov, Ash, and Boberg's benchmark for BOT retraction [see below]). Euclidean distances for Oregonians range from 6 to 174, with lower values indicating less distinction between the two vowels. A linear regression fit to the Euclidean distances, with age and gender as fixed predictors (see appendix), found gender, but not age, to be a significant predictor, with women maintaining a greater distinction between the two vowels. This same gender effect was found in Wassink (2015). In sum, while the majority of speakers are merged for BOT and BOUGHT, almost 40% remain distinct. This, combined with no age affect, makes the Oregon data look different from other West Coast studies, which find robust change in progress toward merger (Cardoso et al. 2016; D'Onofrio et al. 2016 [both in this volume]). Further, the longitudinal work of McLarty, Kendall, and Farrington (2016 [this volume]) finds that the low back merger has been well established in Oregon for some time. Because the results here contrast with the dominant view of low back merger in the West, further work is needed to resolve its status in Oregon.

CALIFORNIA ENGLISH FEATURES. Of those features considered distinctive of California English, four have quantitative benchmarks in Labov, Ash, and Boberg (2006): BOAT, BAT, BET, and BOT. A summary of Oregon speakers' vocalic behavior with respect to these benchmarks is presented in table 6.3. Oregon speakers clearly participate in BOAT fronting: 33 of 34 speakers meet the benchmark for a fronted BOAT, with mean F2 values greater than 1278 Hz. A linear regression model fit to the F2 of BOAT, with age and gender as fixed effects (appendix), found both to be significant predictors of BOAT, with younger men leading in BOAT fronting. The findings for age support a picture of a change in progress, although the finding that men lead women is unexpected.

Recall that in the CVS, BET lowers and BAT and BOT retract in the vowel space. As table 6.3 shows, Oregon speakers participate in CVS behavior to varying degrees. There is fairly robust BAT retraction, with almost three quarters (74%) of the sample meeting Labov, Ash, and Boberg's benchmark for a retracted BAT. A linear regression model fit to the F2 of BAT (appendix) found that age, but not gender, was a significant predictor of BAT, with young speakers leading in BAT retraction. This indicates an apparent-time change in progress in our sample for this CVS feature and suggests that the CVS may be making inroads in Oregon.

The results for both BET and BOT are less conclusive, as only some speakers meet the criterion for lowering and retraction, respectively. In both cases, only about a third (32%) of speakers meet Labov, Ash, and Boberg's criteria. However, age and gender are significant predictors for BET lowering (appendix). For gender, women lead in lowering, while for age, the middle-aged group (those aged 26–40) leads in BET lowering, followed by the youngest speakers and then the oldest. Even though the pattern for age is nonlinear, both middle-aged and younger speakers (aged 18 to 40) have positive coefficients in the linear model (and the same mean Hz values), while older speakers have a negative coefficient, suggestive that BET is lowering in apparent time in Oregon. For BOT retraction, age is not selected as a significant predictor, but gender is (appendix), with women producing more retracted BOTs than men.

Table 6.3 is arranged to highlight what looks like an implicational scale for the introduction of California English features into Oregon. All speakers save one front BOAT. Many who front BOAT also retract BAT, and for many speakers both BOAT fronting and BAT retraction must be present for BET lowering and BOT retraction to occur. Only two speakers lower BET (PNW017) or retract BOT (PNW006) without also retracting BAT, and only one speaker rotates all three CVS vowels without fronting BOAT (PNW025). This suggests that the CVS is gaining ground in Oregon with BAT retraction as the triggering event of the chain shift. There is no consensus on the triggering event of the CVS: it may be triggered by the retraction of BOT as it merges with BOUGHT (Clarke, Elms, and Youssef 1995; Boberg

TABLE 6.3
Labov, Ash, and Boberg's (2006) Benchmarks for California Vocalic Behavior

Speaker	*Fronted* BOAT *(F2 > 1278 Hz)*	*Backed* BAT *(F2 < 1825 Hz)*	*Lowered* BET *(F1 > 650 Hz)*	*Backed* BOT *(F2 < 1275)*	BIT *Lower Than* BAIT*?*
PNW011	✔	✔	✔	✔	✔
PNW018	✔	✔	✔	✔	✔
PNW038	✔	✔	✔	✔	
PNW039	✔	✔	✔	✔	
PNW022	✔	✔	✔	✔	
PNW024	✔	✔	✔	✔	
PNW025		✔	✔	✔	
PNW009	✔	✔	✔		✔
PNW016	✔	✔	✔		
PNW034	✔	✔	✔		
PNW023	✔	✔		✔	
PNW035	✔	✔		✔	
PNW041	✔	✔		✔	
PNW001	✔	✔			
PNW003	✔	✔			
PNW004	✔	✔			
PNW005	✔	✔			
PNW007	✔	✔			
PNW010	✔	✔			
PNW012	✔	✔			
PNW019	✔	✔			
PNW020	✔	✔			
PNW026	✔	✔			
PNW027	✔	✔			
PNW037	✔	✔			
PNW017	✔		✔		
PNW006	✔			✔	
PNW002	✔				
PNW013	✔				
PNW015	✔				
PNW028	✔				
PNW030	✔				
PNW031	✔				
PNW036	✔				

2005; Roeder and Jarmasz 2009), the lowering of BIT (Kennedy and Grama 2012), or the retraction of BAT (Kennedy and Grama 2012, 52). Indeed, D'Onofrio et al. (2016 [this volume]) demonstrate that for speakers in Merced and Bakersfield, California, BAT retraction and the movement of BOT to merge with BOUGHT occur in tandem, casting doubt on the necessity for identifying a triggering event. What is clear from prior literature is that there may be different paths for the CVS in real time. The results here lend support to BAT retraction as the triggering event, given the strong evidence for change in apparent time for this feature in Oregon English. The regression findings for BET, which show that women and nonolder speakers lead in lowering, and BOT, which show that women lead in retraction, suggest that there will be further rotation of these vowels as well.

Labov, Ash, and Boberg (2006) do not provide a benchmark for the fourth vowel to rotate in the CVS: BIT, which lowers in the vowel space. Kennedy and Grama (2012) evaluate BIT relationally, by noting whether a speaker's mean for BIT is lower than their mean for BAIT. Only 3 Oregon speakers meet this criterion for a lowered BIT, as shown in table 6.3. Interestingly, all three of these speakers (PNW009, PNW011, and PNW018) are well advanced for other CVS behavior. A linear regression model fit to the F1 of BIT, with age and gender as fixed effects (appendix), found that age is a significant predictor of BIT height, with young people leading in BIT lowering. This is further support of a change in progress in the direction of increased CVS behavior for Oregonians. In addition to the CVS rotation of short vowels in unconditioned environments, there is conditioned tensing of BIT and BAT before nasals. As shown in table 6.4, BAN is significantly higher and fronter than BAT.[2] Although a nasal tensing system is considered the default in American English (Thomas 2001), making it possible that Oregonians have adopted this default, BAN tensing is not found in Washington State (Wassink 2016 [this volume]), and so may be indicative of alignment with California English. In addition, Cardoso et al. (2016 [this volume]) find a change in apparent time toward raising of BAN in nearby San Francisco. For BIT, recall that Californians tense this vowel when it is followed by the velar nasal /ŋ/, or BING (Eckert 2008; Mendoza-Denton 2008). For BING, there is less evidence of California English behavior in Oregonians' speech. While there is a significant difference between BIT and BING, it is not in the expected direction in F1: BING is lower than BIT. However, in F2, BING is significantly fronter than BIT.

Figure 6.5 shows the vowel space of speaker PNW022, who demonstrates robust participation in California English features, including BOAT fronting, rotation of BAT, BET, and BOT, a tensed BING, and a tensed BAN. Notably, this young woman maintains distinct low back vowels.

TABLE 6.4
California English Nasal Conditioning

Vowel	*F1*	*F2*
BAN mean	625 Hz	2096 Hz
BAT mean	765 Hz	1785 Hz
t-value	21.3954	–19.5268
p-value	< .00001	< .00001
Significant at $p < .05$	*	*
BING	518 Hz	2119 Hz
BIT	489 Hz	2042 Hz
t-value	–4.8466	–3.5172
p-value	< .00001	.00028
Significant at $p < .05$	*	*

FIGURE 6.5
Mean Formant Values for Speaker PNW022 (F, 18–25), Who Fronts BOAT, Retracts BAT, Lowers BET, and Retracts BOT

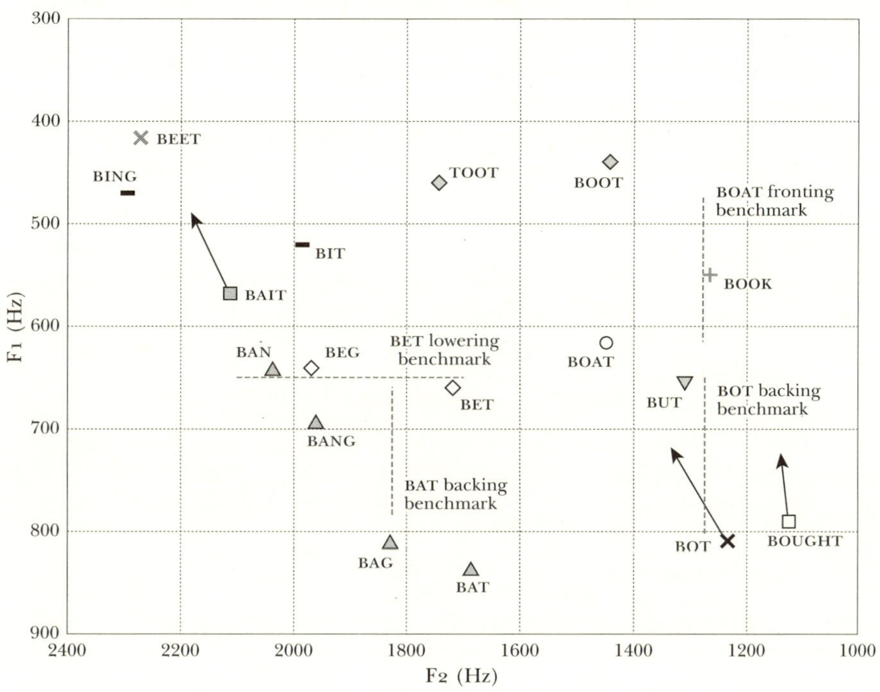

WASHINGTON STATE *BEG* AND *BAG* TENSING. Speakers in Washington State have demonstrated the tensing of BEG and BAG, the merger of BEG with BAIT, and the partial overlap of BAG with these productions (Freeman 2014; Wassink 2015, 2016 [this volume]).[3] Although studies in Washington only analyzed the height of BEG and BAG, the current data confirm the presence of both raising and fronting of BEG and BAG in Oregon. As shown in table 6.5, both BEG and BAG are significantly higher and fronter than BET and BAT.

However, regression analyses conducted on the F1 and F2 of BEG and BAG complicate the picture of tensing as a distinctive Pacific Northwest feature. For BEG in both dimensions, gender but not age is a significant predictor (appendix). In F1, men lead in raising, while in F2, women lead in fronting. For BAG, age but not gender predicts the formant data, but it is older speakers who lead in both raising and fronting. This is the opposite of the expectation for a change in apparent time in the direction of BAG tensing. If anything, this would indicate change in the opposite direction, as young people have lower, more retracted BAG. Further, these results for age mirror those found by Freeman (2014) in Seattle, as well as by McLarty, Kendall, and Farrington (2016 [this volume]), whose younger contemporary speakers do not tense BEG and BAG but whose older contemporary speakers do.

Figure 6.6 shows the vowel space of speaker PNW003, a young female. This speaker tenses both BEG and BAG. While her BOOT and BOAT are fronted, her BOT and BOUGHT remain distinct, and there is little evidence of CVS participation, with BAT just meeting the benchmark for retraction. In summary, Oregon speakers produce the General West Coast feature of BOOT fronting. Although the majority of speakers are merged for BOT and

TABLE 6.5
Washington State BEG and BAG Tensing

Vowel	*F1*	*F2*
BEG mean	609 Hz	2038 Hz
BET mean	629 Hz	1859 Hz
t-value	4.6310	–16.4626
p-value	< .00001	< .00001
Significant at $p < .05$	*	*
BAG	726 Hz	1903 Hz
BAT	765 Hz	1784 Hz
t-value	7.1829	–10.8541
p-value	< .00001	< .00001
Significant at $p < .05$	*	*

FIGURE 6.6
Mean Formant Values for Speaker PNW003 (F, 18–25),
Who Has BEG and BAG Tensing

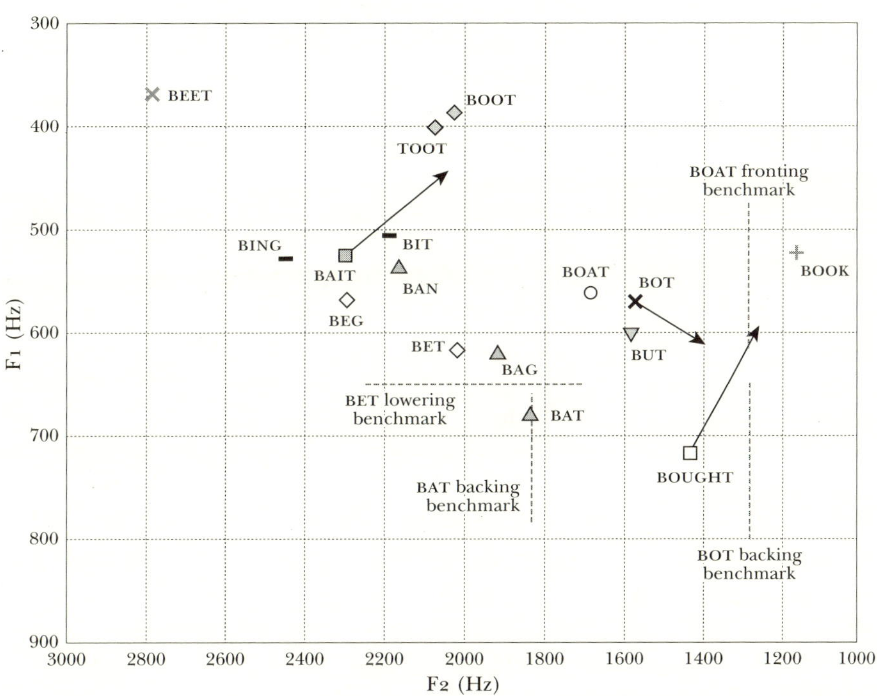

BOUGHT, this is not the complete merger that was expected given the prevalence of the low back merger in the West. Speakers show evidence of California English behavior to varying degrees. Speakers overwhelmingly front BOAT, an established California English feature previously found in Portland (Ward 2003) and verified by McLarty, Kendall, and Farrington (2016 [this volume]) for Oregon, but not present in Seattle (Wassink 2015) or in Labov, Ash, and Boberg (2006). Oregonians appear to be at an early stage of participation in the CVS, with robust BAT retraction and some BET lowering and BOT retraction. Further, there is evidence of change in apparent time, with young speakers leading in BOAT fronting, BAT retraction, and BIT lowering, while women lead in BET lowering and BOT retraction. Oregonians also tense BAN, a feature of California English. Finally, similar to Washington State speakers, Oregonians tense BAG and BEG, but it is older speakers who lead in this behavior.

RESULTS: PERCEPTUAL DIALECTOLOGY

QUALITATIVE ANALYSIS OF MAP DATA. The production results paint a transitional picture for Oregon English, with evidence of vocalic behavior aligned with both California English and Washington English. Here, Oregonians' attitudes toward English along the West Coast are investigated to determine whether and how perceptions of language use align with vowel production. Recall that the map used for the map task (figure 6.3) presented participants with the state of Oregon as well as parts of Washington, California, and Idaho. This section presents an overview of the labels provided during the map task, with a focus on Oregonians' perceptions of dialect distinction within the West as a potential area of insight into the production results.

Table 6.6 presents the six largest categories that emerged from a content analysis of the map task. The most prominent category refers to a belief in a standard U.S. English, a language ideology common to regions whose residents are linguistically secure, like the Midlands and the Inland North, despite the presence of dramatic chain shifts like the Northern Cities Shift (Niedzielski 2002; Campbell-Kibler 2012). Hartley's (1999) work in Oregon also suggested that residents saw the Pacific Northwest as an area where Standard English is spoken. Evans (2013) found that many participants believe English is homogenous in Washington State, prompting the article's title, "Everyone Talks the Same." We adopt the term IDEOLOGY OF NONACCENT from Lippi-Green (1997, 47) to refer to this belief in "a mythical, homogenous standardized spoken language." This language ideology was the most commonly expressed on the map task: many Oregonians rejected the notion that the map area had any distinctive features. Figure 6.7 shows the map of a speaker characterized as having an ideology of nonaccent; this participant essentially declined to participate in the map task and simply wrote "All the same" across the entire region depicted. In table 6.6, the IDEOLOGY OF NONACCENT category includes labels about nonaccent at different geographic levels. Some speakers noted urban centers in the Pacific Northwest like Portland, Salem, Tacoma, and Seattle as distinguished by a lack of dialect distinction, while others circled or labeled the entire map.

The second most common type of label was categorized as COUNTRY, with comments like "farmers and truckers" or "southern accent." The majority of these labels were located on the eastern parts of the map, both in Oregon and in eastern Washington State and in Idaho, and were used to oppose the rural east (seen as "country") to the urban coastal west, where "average, native, normal English" is spoken. This aligns with other work in the West that highlights the importance of an urban/rural divide that

TABLE 6.6
The Six Largest Categories from a Content Analysis of the Map Task

Category	*Frequency*	*Example Label*
Ideology of nonaccent	22 (21%)	"All the same"; "Sounds like TV people"; "average/normal/native/normal English"
Country	17 (16%)	"Country people, farmer + truckers"; "Affected Southern accent"; "Drawl—cowboy accents?"
California	13 (12%)	"Sacramento, hyphy,[a] etc."; "S. Cal—beach talk, succinct"; "Different!"
Pronunciation	12 (11%)	"Warsh = Wash"; "Southern accent—a little bit"
Rate of speech	10 (10%)	"Slower"; "Slightly faster than normal Oregonians, due to fast pace lifestyle in Portland"
Laid back	9 (8%)	"Laid back, casual, fun"; "Relaxed"; "Laid back/hippyish"

a. The term *hyphy* is a slang term that means "hyperactive" and is associated with hip hop culture in Oakland and, by extension, the Bay Area.

FIGURE 6.7
A Participant Who Demonstrates an Ideology of Nonaccent

generally contrasts urban, coastal regions to rural, inland regions, both in production (D'Onofrio et al. 2016 [this volume]) and perception (Evans 2013; Villarreal 2016 [this volume]). Since the speakers in this study represent the western, urban part of Oregon, and metro Portland more specifically, their negative attitudes toward rural areas to the east are evident.

A third category was formed from participants who noted the presence of CALIFORNIA in some way, with labels like "Southern California—beach talk, succinct," "Sacramento—hyphy," or simply "different." Many participants indicated positive attitudes toward California, using labels like "happy, smile more, laugh more" and "laid back, causual [*sic*]—fun" (figure 6.8). The remaining three categories were PRONUNCIATION (for example, many participants pointed out that residents of Washington used an intrusive /r/ when pronouncing their state's name), RATE OF SPEECH (which appears linked to the urban/rural divide, with faster talkers in urban areas and slower talkers in rural areas), and a lifestyle attribution, labeled LAID BACK, which encompass descriptions like "relaxed" and "hippyish."

FIGURE 6.8
A Participant Who Notes California Positively on the Map Task

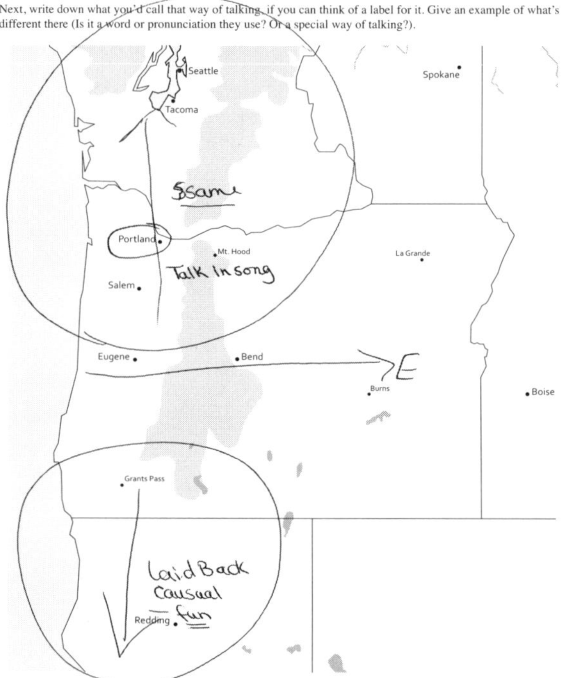

LINKING PERCEPTUAL DIALECTOLOGY TO PRODUCTION

After the content analysis was complete, two categories from table 6.6 were operationalized with the goal of linking speaker attitudes toward English in the West with the production data. We first looked to the CALIFORNIA category, given that the production results found evidence of the introduction of the CVS in Oregon. Participants were divided into those who noted California in some way on the map task ($n = 13$) and those who did not ($n = 21$). We hypothesized that these notations indicated increased awareness of California and California English, which would correlate with greater use of CVS features. Second, we looked to the IDEOLOGY OF NONACCENT category, given its prevalence in the sample. Participants were divided into those who noted an ideology of nonaccent in some way on the map task ($n = 19$) and those who did not ($n = 15$). We hypothesized that a belief in standard speech would correlate with decreased use of marked regional features. While acknowledging that these binary divisions no doubt obscure important distinctions within subgroups, the aim was to begin to explore whether grouping participants according to perceptual responses would predict vowel production. These binary variables were added as predictors in regression models on both the CVS and Washington State vocalic features explored in the production data above: the CVS features of BIT lowering, BET lowering, BAT retraction, and BOT retraction, and the Washington State tensing of BEG and BAG. A summary of these regression models is presented in the appendix.

The CALIFORNIA variable was not a good overall predictor of variation. In eight models, it was selected as a predictor four times: noting California on the map task predicted a fronter BAT, a lower BEG, a fronter BEG, and a fronter BAG. The first result relates to a California English feature, but in the opposite direction of our hypothesis: those who note California on the map task are less likely to back BAT. The other three results relate to Washington State BEG and BAG tensing, and there is no discernible pattern: those participants who noted California on the map task are more likely to front both vowels, but are also more likely to lower BEG. Overall, this measure of speaker perception does not seem to be linked to speaker production in any meaningful way. This might be because the variable is too broad in simply opposing those who note California to those who do not. Noting California most likely indicates a range of attitudes toward the state; conversely, it cannot be known whether those who did not note California on the map task are less aware of the state and its linguistic features. This was a hypothesis that does not appear to be borne out in analysis.

In contrast, the IDEOLOGY OF NONACCENT variable was a significant predictor in seven of eight regression models. As seen in the appendix, participants who note an ideology of nonaccent on their maps lead in three of the four measures of BEG and BAG tensing: they have a higher BEG and a higher and fronter BAG than those who do not note this ideology on the map task. For the CVS rotations, participants who note an ideology of nonaccent are less likely to participate in all four of the CVS shifts: they produce a higher BIT, a higher BET, a fronter BAT, and a fronter BOT than those who do not note this ideology on the map task. In short, participants who hold an ideology of nonaccent are more likely to participate in BEG and BAG tensing (in contrast to our hypothesis), but less likely to rotate CVS vowels.

One interpretation for these results is that participants who hold an ideology of nonaccent are more oriented to the Pacific Northwest, a region that is clearly associated with standard, homogenous speech (Hartley 1999; Evans 2013) and less oriented to California or a broader West Coast variety marked by CVS rotation. Related to this is the notion that the CVS and BEG and BAG tensing have differing statuses with respect to social salience. The CVS is part of California English, a variety that has been referenced in popular culture for decades (Hinton et al. 1987). Those participants who hold an ideology of nonaccent, then, may be aware of California's dialect distinction and are choosing not to participate in the vowel shift associated with their salient dialect neighbor to the south. In contrast, BEG and BAG tensing may lack the salience of the CVS, not a surprise given how recently it has been described by linguists and how little it shows up in popular discourse. Those participants who possess an ideology of nonaccent, then, may not be aware that these productions mark dialect distinction in the West. If anything, it is those participants who express the most uniquely Pacific Northwest ideology—that of "everyone talks the same"—who produce the most uniquely Pacific Northwest features—BEG and BAG tensing.

Further explorations are necessary to argue with any certainty for a link between perception and production for Oregonians, but these results are certainly suggestive of a connection between a view of English in the West—the ideology of nonaccent—and production of West Coast English features—the adoption of BEG and BAG tensing and the nonadoption of CVS vowel rotation.

CONCLUSION

The speech of the Oregonians in the present study reflects their geographic location on the West Coast between California and Washington, suggesting that clean divisions of the West Coast into distinct dialect regions may not capture the fluidity of vocalic behavior in the West. Speakers participate in the General West Coast fronting of BOOT, and many—though not all—are merged in the low back space. The existence of speakers who maintain a distinction between BOT and BOUGHT, combined with a lack of evidence for change in apparent time, is surprising: follow-up research should be done to confirm the status of the low back merger in Oregon. For features of California English, some vowels show robust shift, like BOAT fronting and BAT retraction, while there is more limited BET lowering and BOT retraction. These vowels appear to stand in an implicational relationship, as depicted in table 6.3. The implicational scale, in combination with evidence of change in apparent time—with young people leading in BOAT fronting, BAT retraction, and BIT retraction, and women leading in BET lowering and BOT retraction—suggest that California English features will continue to spread in Oregon. Further, the prevalence of BAT retraction lends support for this vowel to be the triggering event for the CVS.

These results suggest that the term "California Vowel Shift" may in fact be a misnomer if this shift is active and spreading in Oregon and elsewhere. Indeed, the CVS rotation of BIT, BET, BAT, and BOT is identical to another "CVS"—the Canadian Vowel Shift (Clarke, Elms, and Youssef 1995; Boberg 2005; Labov, Ash, and Boberg 2006; Roeder and Jarmasz 2009). Although the current study cannot resolve the issue of whether these two shifts are in fact the same, we would again point to Oregon's geographic location north of California and south of the Pacific Coast of Canada as potential evidence for a broader shift that characterizes the so-called "Third Dialect" of North American English (Labov 1991). As more and more studies identify the CVS outside of California and Canada, a new name for this vowel rotation may be needed. Further, combined work may also lead to more information as to its triggering event, be it low back merger, BAT retraction, or BIT lowering.

Turning northward, Oregonians do participate in the BEG and BAG tensing suggested to be a distinctive feature of a Pacific Northwest English (Wassink 2015, 2016 [this volume]), but they do not appear to be advancing this change. Instead, regression models find that older speakers lead in the tensing of BAG, while there is no age pattern for BEG. These results in apparent time are echoed in the work of Freeman (2014) and McLarty, Kendall, and Farrington (2016 [this volume]). So, while the overall finding of BEG and BAG tensing in these data links Oregon to Washington and lends support for a distinct Pacific Northwest variety, the fact that this variety's only distinctive feature may be in recession suggests caution in assigning a Pacific Northwest dialect moniker. It is possible that dialectologists failed to recognize BEG and BAG tensing as a distinctive feature of the region early on (see the small note in Reed 1961), when its use was active and change was robust. Another possibility, suggested in Wassink (2015), is that speakers may raise BAG through diphthongization rather than at the midpoint or nucleus (52), such that the current analysis fails to look at the correct measure of raising. Further investigation is called for, though the recession of BEG and BAG tensing in apparent time considered in tandem with the evidence for California English behavior in Oregon but not in Washington leaves the status of a unified Pacific Northwest variety in doubt at this time.

Yet Oregonians are linked to Washingtonians in their assertion of an ideology of nonaccent (Evans 2013), a language attitude that is linked to production in these data. Participants with an ideology of nonaccent are more likely to produce BEG and BAG tensing and less likely to produce CVS vowels, suggesting that this language ideology could play an important role in resolving Oregon's status as a transitional area where resources are linked to both California and Washington. Whether the ideology of nonaccent will be maintained in the face of the spread of the CVS in Oregon remains to be seen: perhaps Oregonians will resist sounding like their salient southern neighbor, or perhaps their language attitudes will change as they become more aware of their language use. In continued study of the region, the connections suggested here between perception and production should prove a fruitful area for further research.

The data here and in the rest of the volume stand in contrast to earlier presentations of the West as monolithic (Labov, Ash, and Boberg 2006). The West is full of dialect diversity, active sound change, and changing language ideologies, and the current volume contributes to the increase of contemporary sociolinguistic scholarship that both describes and connects this Western dialect diversity.

APPENDIX

Summary of Linear Regression Models Fit to the Production Data

The response variable for each model is presented in the left-most column, followed by the intercept (given in log-odds). The *p*-value for each factor and its significance at the $p < .05$ level is then reported. Finally, the levels of each significant factor are presented with their accompanying coefficients from the linear model and their mean values.

Model/Factor	*Level*	*Coefficient*	*Mean*
BOT and BOUGHT ED (intercept = 78.18)			
Age (p = .528)[n.s.]			
Gender (p = .0296)*	Women	15.066	93
	Men	–15.066	63
F2 of BOAT (intercept = 1460.984)			
Age (p < .00001)*	Younger	43.146	1504
	Middle	–2.251	1465
	Older	–40.895	1428
Gender (p = .014)*	Women	–19.098	1454
	Men	19.098	1480
F2 of BAT (intercept = 1796.391)			
Age (p < .00001)*	Younger	–36.132	1753
	Middle	–32.323	1765
	Older	68.456	1865
Gender (p = .414)[n.s.]			
California (p = .00005)*	Note Calif.	21.111	1801
	Do not note Calif.	–21.111	1773
Ideology of Nonaccent (p = .0431)*	Note INA	13.027	1804
	Do not note INA	–13.027	1760
F1 of BET (intercept = 628.893)			
Age (p = .0267)*	Younger	2.291	634
	Middle	9.415	634
	Older	–11.706	610
Gender (p = .0122)*	Women	7.291	637
	Men	–7.291	622
California (p = .956)[n.s.]			
Ideology of Nonaccent (p = .0261)*	Note INA	–7.037	622
	Do not note INA	7.037	638
F2 of BOT (intercept = 1322.96)			
Age (p = .342)[n.s.]			
Gender (p = .023)*	Women	–16.414	1307
	Men	16.414	1339
California (p = .723)[n.s.]			
Ideology of Nonaccent (p = .00151)*	Note INA	22.254	1346
	Do not note INA	–22.254	1301
F1 of BIT (intercept = 489.446)			
Age (p = .0328)*	Younger	4.856	494
	Middle	–4.903	485
	Older	0.047	489
Gender (p = .057)[n.s.]			
California (p = .099)[n.s.]			
Ideology of nonaccent (p = .0128)*	Note INA	–4.056	486
	Do not note INA	4.056	494

F1 of BEG (intercept = 614.977)			
Age (p = .594)$^{n.s.}$			
Gender (p < .00001)*	Women	12.77	625
	Men	–12.77	600
California (p = .0169)*	Note Calif.	7.439	618
	Do not note Calif.	–7.439	604
Ideology of nonaccent (p = .0347)*	Note INA	6.47	619
	Do not note INA	–6.47	602
F2 of BEG (intercept = 2052.979)			
Age (p = .25)$^{n.s.}$			
Gender (p < .00001)*	Women	36.652	2081
	Men	–36.652	2013
California (p = .0015)*	Note Calif.	25.074	2064
	Do not note Calif.	–25.074	2022
Ideology of nonaccent (p = .619)$^{n.s.}$			
F1 of BAG (intercept = 727.571)			
Age (p = .009)*	Younger	7.084	737
	Middle	12.253	737
	Older	–19.336	698
Gender (p = .087)$^{n.s.}$			
California (p = .057)$^{n.s.}$			
Ideology of nonaccent (p < .00001)*	Note INA	–19.634	707
	Do not note INA	19.634	752
F2 of BAG (intercept = 1906.184)			
Age (p < .00001)*	Younger	–28.689	1869
	Middle	–35.261	1871
	Older	63.951	1987
Gender (p = .317)$^{n.s.}$			
California (p = .007)*	Note Calif.	22.063	1912
	Do not note Calif.	–22.063	1897
Ideology of nonaccent (p < .00001)*	Note INA	67.624	1963
	Do not note INA	–67.624	1818

NOTES

1. It is worth noting that the token counts for BOOT are quite small, in some cases as low as 1–2 tokens, due to the low frequency of words with /u/ in noncoronal contexts.
2. These tests compare unconditioned BAT to BAN before the front nasals /n/ and /m/ only. The status of BAT followed by a velar nasal (BANG) is important here as it contrasts a California English feature (where BAT tenses before all nasals) with a Washington State one (where BAT may tense before all velars, although only /g/ has been investigated in the literature). In the Oregon data, BANG is

significantly different from BAG in both F1 and F2. It is also significantly different from BAN in F2, but not significantly different in F1. Although it appears to pattern with other nasals and not with BAG (indicating a more "California-like" behavior), because the *t*-test results were not conclusive in both F1 and F2, the velar nasal following environment is excluded from calculations. It is of note that Cardoso et al. (2016 [this volume]) found a robust change in apparent time in the direction of raising of BANG in San Francisco.

3. At the time of data collection, we were not aware of the possibility that BAT and BET before /g/ could be merging with BAIT before /g/. Very few words fit into the BAIT before /g/ category: *bagel, pagan, plague, vague, Reagan.* Unfortunately none of these words were targeted in the reading passage or word list, and none came up in interview speech, so this class cannot be investigated here.

REFERENCES

Boberg, Charles. 2005."The Canadian Shift in Montreal." *Language Variation and Change* 17.2: 133–54. doi:10.1017/S0954394505050064.

Benson, Erica J. 2003. "Folk Linguistic Perceptions and the Mapping of Dialect Boundaries." *American Speech* 78.3: 307–30. doi:10.1215/00031283-78-3-307.

Bucholtz, Mary, Nancy Bermudez, Victor Fung, Lisa Edwards, and Rosalva Vargas. 2007. "Hella Nor Cal or Totally So Cal? The Perceptual Dialectology of California." *Journal of English Linguistics* 35.4: 325–52. doi:10.1177/0075424207307780.

Campbell-Kibler, Kathryn. 2012. "Contestation and Enregisterment in Ohio's Imagined Dialects." *Journal of English Linguistics* 40.3: 281–305. doi:10.1177/0075424211427911.

Cardoso, Amanda, Lauren Hall-Lew, Yova Kementchedjhieva, and Ruaridh Purse. 2016. "Between California and the Pacific Northwest: The Front Lax Vowels in San Francisco English." In Fridland et al. 2016, 33–54. doi:10.1215/00031283-3772890.

Carver, Craig M. 1987. *American Regional Dialects: A Word Geography.* Ann Arbor: University of Michigan Press.

Clarke, Sandra, Ford Elms, and Amani Youssef. 1995. "The Third Dialect of English: Some Canadian Evidence." *Language Variation and Change* 7.2: 209–28. doi:10.1017/S0954394500000995.

D'Onofrio, Annette, Penelope Eckert, Robert J. Podesva, Teresa Pratt, and Janneke Van Hofwegen. 2016. "The Low Vowels in California's Central Valley." In Fridland et al. 2016, 11–32. doi:10.1215/00031283-3772879.

Eckert, Penelope. 2008. "Where Do Ethnolects Stop?" *International Journal of Bilingualism* 12.1–2: 25–42. doi:10.1177/13670069080120010301.

Evans, Betsy. 2011. "'Seattletonian' to 'Faux Hick': Perceptions of English in Washington State." *American Speech* 86.4: 383–413. doi:10.1215/00031283-1587232.

———. 2013. "'Everybody Sounds the Same': Otherwise Overlooked Ideology in Perceptual Dialectology." *American Speech* 88.1: 63–80. doi:10.1215/00031283-2322637.

Fought, Carmen. 1999. "A Majority Sound Change in a Minority Community: /u/-Fronting in Chicano English." *Journal of Sociolinguistics* 3.1: 5–23. doi:10.1111/1467-9481.t01-1-00060.

Freeman, Valerie. 2014. "Bag, Beg, Bagel: Prevelar Raising and Merger in Pacific Northwest English." University of Washington Working Papers in Linguistics, 32. http://depts.washington.edu/uwwpl/vol32/freeman_2014.pdf.

Fridland, Valerie, Tyler Kendall, Betsy Evans, and Alicia Beckford Wassink, eds. 2016. *Speech of the Western States.* Vol. 1, *The Coastal States.* Publication of the American Dialect Society 101. Durham, N.C.: Duke University Press.

Hall-Lew, Lauren. 2011. "The Completion of a Sound Change in California English." In *Proceedings of the 17th International Congress of Phonetic Sciences (ICPhS XVII), 17–21 August 2011, Hong Kong,* edited by Wai-Sum Lee and Eric Zee, 807–10. Hong Kong: City University of Hong Kong. https://www.internationalphoneticassociation.org/icphs-proceedings/ICPhS2011/OnlineProceedings/RegularSession/Hall-Lew/Hall-Lew.pdf.

———. 2013. "'Flip-Flop' and Mergers-in-Progress." *English Language and Linguistics* 17.2: 359–90. doi:10.1017/S1360674313000063.

Hartley, Laura C. 1999. "A View from the West: Perceptions of U.S. Dialects by Oregon Residents." In *Handbook of Perceptual Dialectology,* vol. 1, edited by Dennis R. Preston, 315–32. Amsterdam: Benjamins. doi:10.1075/z.hpd1.27har.

Hinton, Leanne, Birch Moonwomon, Sue Bremner, Herb Luthin, Mary Van Clay, Jean Lerner, and Hazel Corcoran. 1987. "It's Not Just the Valley Girls: A Study of California English." In *Berkeley Linguistics Society: Proceedings of the Thirteenth Annual Meeting, February 14–16, 1987,* edited by Jon Aske, Natasha Beery, Laura Michaelis, and Hana Filip, 117–28. Berkeley, Calif.: Berkeley Linguistics Society. doi:10.3765/bls.v13i0.1811.

Johnson, Daniel Ezra. 2012. Rbrul. Version 2.05. Retrieved from http://www.danielezrajohnson.com/rbrul.html.

Kennedy, Robert, and James Grama. 2012. "Chain Shifting and Centralization in California Vowels: An Acoustic Analysis." *American Speech* 87.1: 39–56. doi:10.1215/00031283-1599950.

Labov, William. 1991. "The Three Dialects of English." In *New Ways of Analyzing Sound Change,* edited by Penelope Eckert, 1–44. San Diego: Academic Press.

Labov, William, Sharon Ash, and Charles Boberg. 2006. *The Atlas of North American English: Phonetics, Phonology, and Sound Change.* Berlin: Mouton de Gruyter.

Lippi-Green, Rosina. 1997. *English with an Accent: Language, Ideology, and Discrimination in the United States.* London: Routledge.

McLarty, Jason, Tyler Kendall, and Charlie Farrington. 2016. "Investigating the Development of the Contemporary Oregonian English Vowel System." In Fridland et al. 2016, 135–57. doi:10.1215/00031283-3772934.

Mendoza-Denton, Norma. 2008. *Homegirls: Language and Cultural Practice among Latina Youth Gangs*. Malden, Mass.: Blackwell.

Niedzielski, Nancy. 2002. "Attitudes toward Midwestern American English." In *Handbook of Perceptual Dialectology*, vol. 2, edited by Daniel Long and Dennis R. Preston, 321–27. Amsterdam: Benjamins. doi:10.1075/z.hpd2.22nie.

Niedzielski, Nancy A., and Dennis R. Preston. 2003. *Folk Linguistics*. Berlin: Mouton de Gruyter.

Podesva, Robert J. 2011. "The California Vowel Shift and Gay Identity." *American Speech* 86.1: 32–51. doi:10.1215/00031283-1277501.

Reed, Carroll E. 1952. "The Pronunciation of English in the State of Washington." *American Speech* 27.3: 186–89. doi:10.2307/453476.

———. 1961. "The Pronunciation of English in the Pacific Northwest." *Language* 37.4: 559–64. doi:10.2307/411357.

Roeder, Rebecca, and Lidia-Gabriela Jarmasz. 2009. "The Lax Vowel Subsystem in Canadian English Revisited." *Toronto Working Papers in Linguistics* 31: 1–12. http://twpl.library.utoronto.ca/index.php/twpl/article/view/6089.

Rosenfelder, Ingrid, Joe Fruehwald, Keelan Evanini, and Jiahong Yuan. 2011. FAVE (Forced Alignment and Vowel Extraction) Program Suite. http://fave.ling.upenn.edu.

Thomas, Erik R. 2001. *An Acoustic Analysis of Vowel Variation in New World English*. Publication of the American Dialect Society 85. Durham, N.C.: Duke University Press. doi:10.1215/-85-1-vii.

———. 2011. *Sociophonetics: An Introduction*. New York: Palgrave MacMillan.

Thomas, Erik R., and Tyler Kendall. 2007. NORM: The Vowel Normalization and Plotting Suite. Retrieved from http://lingtools.uoregon.edu/norm/.

U.S. Census Bureau. 2014. "Portland City, Oregon: 2010 Demographic Profile." American Fact Finder. https://factfinder.census.gov/bkmk/cf/1.0/en/place/Portland%20city,%20Oregon/POPULATION/DECENNIAL_CNT.

Villarreal, Dan. 2016. "'Do I Sound Like a Valley Girl to You?' Perceptual Dialectology and Language Attitudes in California." In Fridland et al. 2016, 55–75. doi:10.1215/00031283-3772901.

Ward, Michael. 2003. "Portland Dialect Study: The Fronting of /ow, u, uw/ in Portland, Oregon." Master's thesis, Portland State University. http://www.pds.pdx.edu/Publications/Ward.pdf.

Wassink, Alicia Beckford. 2015. "Sociolinguistic Patterns in Seattle English." *Language Variation and Change* 27.1: 31–58. doi:10.1017/S0954394514000234.

———. 2016. "The Vowels of Washington State." In Fridland et al. 2016, 77–106. doi:10.1215/00031283-3772912.

KARA BECKER is an assistant professor of linguistics at Reed College. She is a sociolinguist and dialectologist with interests in variation and change, ethnicity, gender and sexuality, and social meaning. E-mail: kbecker@reed.edu.

ANNA ADEN holds a B.A. in linguistics from Reed College. She currently lives in Myanmar, where she works in women's protection and humanitarian aid. E-mail: aaden124@gmail.com.

KATELYN BEST holds a B.A. in linguistics from Reed College. She is currently living in Portland, Oregon, where she works as a freelance journalist. E-mail: okbest20@gmail.com.

HALEY JACOBSON holds a B.A. in linguistics from Reed College. She currently works in China, leading service and language immersion trips in the beautiful Southwest. E-mail: jacobsonhaley@gmail.com.

7. INVESTIGATING THE DEVELOPMENT OF THE CONTEMPORARY OREGONIAN ENGLISH VOWEL SYSTEM

JASON McLARTY, TYLER KENDALL,
and CHARLIE FARRINGTON

As many of the chapters in this volume note, there has been a general lack of research on English in the Western United States and in particular the Pacific Northwest. Recently, we have seen growing interest in expanding our knowledge of the dialects in the Pacific Northwest (Ward 2003; Conn 2006; Labov, Ash, and Boberg 2006; Riebold 2009, 2012; Wassink et al. 2009; Nelson 2011; Becker et al. 2013; Becker, Aden, and Best 2014; Freeman 2014a; Wassink 2015). Recent work examining the sound system of English varieties more generally has also turned attention to investigating the sound systems of speakers available in archival recordings (Hickey, forthcoming). To supplement these growing interests, this chapter focuses on tracking the greater time-course of changes to the vowel space of Oregonians from the end of the nineteenth century to the beginning of the twenty-first century. Becker et al. (2013, 2014, 2016 [this volume]) find that within the Portland metro area, the main urban center in Oregon, speakers exhibit vocalic patterns found in Northern California and in the Seattle, Washington, area. We investigate if other Oregonians, in particular those from the Willamette Valley, the most densely populated part of the state, also display vocalic patterns similar to surrounding regions, namely, Northern California and Washington, and more centrally, when these changes took place. To investigate these questions, our analysis compares contemporary speakers from the Willamette Valley region of Oregon to archival recordings of Oregonians from the *Dictionary of American Regional English* (*DARE* 1985–2013), recorded in 1967, while also examining these findings in light of previous work in surrounding regions.

This chapter is organized into eight parts. In the next section, we provide a description of the settlement history of Oregon. Next we provide background on English in the West in general and Oregonian English in particular. We then describe our project as it relates to previous research

Publication of the American Dialect Society 101 DOI 10.1215/00031283-3772934

and also research in this volume. The data, materials, and methodology are described next, followed by the presentation of aggregate vowel plots of the contemporary and archival data, with these plots connected to what we know about English in the West. We then examine several quantitative measures to further investigate trends we see in the vowel spaces of these Oregonians. Finally, we close with some brief concluding thoughts and future directions.

SETTLEMENT HISTORY

To contextualize our study, we present here a brief historical overview of the settlement patterns in Oregon, as well as a brief overview of the history of English in Oregon. Following the expedition of Lewis and Clark and the subsequent publication of their journals in 1807, pioneer groups began traveling to the Pacific Northwest as early as 1811, most of whom were fur trappers for trading companies. The earliest permanent English-speaking settlers were British and arrived in the Puget Sound area of Washington in 1828. After the United States and Great Britain settled their conflict over the Oregon Territory in 1841, American English-speaking settlers arrived in the region from the Ohio Valley states and Tennessee first, followed by Missouri, Illinois, and Iowa (Schwantes 1989; Wolfram and Schilling-Estes 2006). The Oregon Territory set up its first provisional government in 1843, serving as the main body of government until Oregon's statehood in 1859. Geographically, Oregon is divided by the Cascade Mountain Range, which contributes to the distinct climate zones in the state, which also influenced agricultural practices and settlement patterns. Eastern Oregon is quite arid, and parts of far eastern Oregon are classified desert. Much of the agricultural practices center around raising cattle, sheep, wheat, and grains.

The Willamette Valley, where the majority of the contemporary speakers examined in this study reside, was settled in the 1830s, acting as the end of the Oregon Trail. It is today the most populated region in Oregon (Schwantes 1989; U.S. Census Bureau 2010). The Willamette Valley runs north-south between the Oregon Coastal Mountain Range to the west and the Cascades to the east; it is bound to the south by the Calapooya Mountains, which approach the Klamath Mountain Range, and by the Columbia River to the north. The Columbia River and Willamette River, both of which run through the valley, have acted as cultural and economic centers since the initial settlement of the Oregon Territory. Two-thirds of the population of Oregon resides in the Willamette Valley, which also contains the three most populous cities: Portland, Eugene, and Salem (U.S. Census Bureau

2010). Interstate 5, the main interstate highway along the West Coast, also runs through the Willamette Valley and these major centers. In addition to large metropolitan centers, the Willamette Valley is home to many small towns, primarily farming communities. The Willamette Valley is a fertile basin and is extremely productive agriculturally, with some of the major crops including berries, hazelnuts, grass seed, and hops.

This settlement history provides a backdrop to the description of the vowel systems of Oregonians over time. In comparison to most of the United States, the recency of Western settlement provides a rich area of study for dialectological research. Early settlers in Oregon came from places in the United States that often already had established dialect communities. As these speakers migrated west, they came in contact with speakers of other dialects, and eventually those who settled in Oregon brought with them dialects from varying places in the United States. Recent work on "new" dialects has illustrated that dialect mixing and leveling can occur over just a few generations (Kerswill 2003; Trudgill 2006). Because of the recency of settlement in the region, we have an opportunity through archival and legacy recordings to examine possibly the earliest stages of dialect mixing and leveling in the West (see, e.g., Fridland and Kendall, forthcoming). In addition, by being aware of migration patterns in Oregon, we may be able to get a better sense of what features we might find at given points in time and locations for various regions within Oregon.

BACKGROUND

The Atlas of North American English (Labov, Ash, and Boberg 2006) sets a baseline for phonological patterns in the United States and can act as a springboard for ongoing sociophonetic research in the West. We begin by situating our work in the description of West Coast English by Labov, Ash, and Boberg, who place Oregon within the Western Dialect Region, exhibiting features associated with California, and more broadly West Coast varieties of English, such as the low back merger and back vowel fronting. However, they describe the West as exhibiting "low homogeneity" throughout the region, which is to say there is a great deal of variability within the vowel systems in the Western United States. Specifically, the high and mid back vowels contribute to this lack of homogeneity, where /u/ is generally fronted, but /o/ shows fronting to varying degrees, if at all. In fact, the only speakers in Labov, Ash, and Boberg (2006) who front /o/ to a centralized position (characteristic of more advanced speakers) are located in Southern California; /o/ becomes less advanced along the F2 dimension as one moves further north and east from Southern California.

As noted by several other contributors to this volume, a complicating factor for dialect research in the West is an ongoing tension between viewing the region as one characterized by homogeneity or heterogeneity. Fronting of /u/ and /o/ is described not only as a characteristic feature of English found in Northern California, but also as a pattern of West Coast Englishes, as well as other Englishes, more generally (Luthin 1987; Labov, Ash, and Boberg 2006; Eckert 2008). The fronting of these high and mid back vowels are found in Portland, while in the Seattle metropolitan area, only /u/ is fronted (Becker et al. 2013, 2016 [this volume]; Wassink 2015). The vowel patterns described for Northern California have been referred to in the literature as the California Vowel Shift (CVS) (Eckert 2008; Podesva 2011; Fridland and Kendall 2012). In this chapter, we do not investigate whether or not these described patterns represent a chain shift; rather, we refer to the patterns described for Northern California as the California Vowel Shift for ease of description and to make our work comparable to patterns described in previous work. Other characteristics of West Coast Englishes described as part of the CVS include the low back merger, where the distribution of /ɑ/ and /ɔ/ overlaps along the F1 and F2 dimensions for speakers, as well as the raising and fronting of /æ/ before nasal consonants and /æ/ backing in other environments (Labov, Ash, and Boberg 2006; Eckert 2008). In the CVS, the front lax vowels are generally retracted, such that /ɛ/ lowers toward /æ/ in all consonantal environments, whereas /ɪ/ exhibits a similar pattern as /æ/ in the CVS, with raising before velar nasals and retraction in other environments. In the Seattle area, /æ/ appears to pattern somewhat differently than in Northern California, where research has found that /æ/ raises toward /ɛ/ or /e/ before voiced velar stops (henceforth /æg/-raising), which is not described for the CVS (Eckert 2008; Wassink 2015, 2016 [this volume]). Taken all together, it is not yet clear whether the patterns described for Northern California are indicative of pronunciation patterns of the West Coast more generally or are more subregional.

Very little work has examined the greater time-course of the changes affecting the vowel space of Western speakers. Hinton et al. (1987) found that the fronting of /o/ and /u/ in California seems to have begun for speakers born roughly between 1920 and 1950, with the youngest speakers (born around 1965) being the most advanced in their data, suggesting that this advancement was still progressing at the time of their study. In a recent study examining archival recordings of Californians (from the San Francisco Bay Area) and Nevadans, Fridland and Kendall (forthcoming) found that many features of the CVS, including low back merger, were not yet attested in the speech of the individuals they examined who were born in the late nineteenth century.

OUR PROJECT

As stated previously, our project aims to look backward in time to better understand the current status of the vowel system in Oregonian English. Other chapters in this volume present vocalic patterns for California, Portland, Oregon, and Washington and consider the status of ongoing developments in Western speech. Our aim is to compare our findings for contemporary speakers from the Willamette Valley with the vocalic features of archival recordings of Oregonians born in the late nineteenth and early twentieth century, contextualizing these findings in terms of the vocalic patterns found elsewhere on the West Coast. Through this approach, we hope to shed light on the current status of dialects in the West more generally and in Oregon more specifically. Thus, in this work, we present descriptive views of the vowel spaces of Oregonians born between 1890 and 1993 and utilize a series of quantitative measures for these speakers. We employ these quantitative measures to understand better whether or not Oregonians participate in vowel configurations described for Northern California and Washington.

DATA AND METHODOLOGY

Since our main questions are related to the time-course of the development of the modern vowel system in Oregonian English, we examine recent recordings of contemporary speakers, primarily from the Willamette Valley, and compare them to archival recordings of Oregonians born in the late nineteenth and early twentieth centuries, recorded in 1967 as a part of the *DARE* project (1985–2013). All speakers in these data are European American. Our recordings of contemporary speakers from the Willamette Valley come from several sources. A number of recordings are from a perception/production study conducted by Fridland and Kendall (2012), in which a subset of participants in a panregional vowel identification study were recorded reading a passage and a word list. Here we focus on a subset of the speakers from Oregon: college students born within a few years of 1991. Additional recordings from the Willamette Valley were made in 2012–14 through a combination of student projects in an upper-level sociolinguistics course at the University of Oregon and preliminary fieldwork by the authors in Junction City, a small community in the Willamette Valley (McLarty, Farrington, and Kendall 2014; McLarty and Kendall 2014). As few older contemporary speakers were available in these data, we also include one speaker—a man recorded in 2001—from the Sociolinguistic Archive and Analysis Project (SLAAP) archive (Ocumpaugh, unpublished data; Kendall 2007). Finally, recordings from the *DARE* project were used to obtain data for speakers born around the turn of the twentieth century. The map in figure 7.1 shows where our speakers come from, broken down by sex. The vast majority of our speakers come from the Willamette Valley region of Oregon. In fact, all the speakers in the map who are east of the Cascade Mountain Range are from the archival data. It should be noted that two of the archival speakers are of Basque heritage. One of the *DARE* speakers (#OR18) was heavily accented and was removed from the analysis because Basque clearly influenced the configuration of his vowel space. The other Basque heritage speaker (#OR11) was more assimilated in his accent, illustrated by a similar vowel space to the rest of the archival speakers, and is included in the analyses that follow.

The data examined in this chapter come primarily from reading passages and word lists for all speakers. Because the data come from several different studies, different reading passages and word lists were used. Most

FIGURE 7.1
Map of Oregon Showing the Hometown Location of Speakers

of the contemporary Oregonians read the reading passage used by Fridland and Kendall (2012; available in Kendall 2013, 56–57), while most of the *DARE* speakers read "Arthur the Rat" (http://dare.wisc.edu/audio/arthur-the-rat). It should be noted that since the reading passages between contemporary speakers and archive speakers differ, tokens across groups are not identical. Due to the nature of the archival recordings and difficulty achieving sufficient token counts based on the reading passage alone, measurements for the archival data were also taken from thc conversational portions of the *DARE* interviews, in addition to the "Arthur the Rat" passage. We attempted to gather 5–10 tokens for each vowel category for each speaker, though occasionally, especially in the archival data, we were unable to obtain this many. Altogether, our analysis examines 2,487 vowel tokens. The speakers and materials examined are outlined in table 7.1.

All acoustic measurements were taken in Praat (Boersma and Weenink 2014). Following Fridland and Kendall (2012), F1 and F2 measurements were taken at two points within each vowel's temporal duration, one-third and two-thirds, representing the nucleus and glide of the vowel. In the analysis that follows, we primarily use the one-third point in each vowel's duration as the comparative reference point. All of the data were Lobanov normalized (Lobanov 1971) and plotted using the Vowels package (Kendall and Thomas 2014) in R (R Development Core Team 2012).

VOWEL CONFIGURATIONS OVER TIME

The following vowel plots show the nucleus (one-third measurement point) of all vowels listed, with ellipses indicating one standard deviation from the mean for certain categories of interest. Glides for /u/ and /o/ (two-thirds measurement point) are also included. Following work that has demonstrated that postcoronal /u/ tokens advance more than other phonetic contexts (Labov, Ash, and Boberg 2006; Baranowski 2014), these are presented and examined in two separate classes (/Tu/ and /Ku/, respectively). Several

TABLE 7.1
Speakers and Material

Speakers	*YOB*	*Data Materials*	*Male*	*Female*	TOTAL
DARE	1890–1914	Reading passage ("Arthur the Rat") & conversational interviews	4	1	5
Older	1955–77	Word list & reading passage	3	3	6
Younger	1988–93	Word list & reading passage	7	5	12
TOTAL			14	9	23

vowel classes were excluded for clarity, as they were not of interest for this study. With the exception of prenasal /æ/ (/æN/) and prelateral /u/ and /o/ (/ul/ and /ol/), which are treated separately from the main classes, measurements in prenasal, prelateral, and pre-/r/ positions are not included in the data presented here. /ɛ/ and /æ/ in prevoiced velar stop positions (/ɛg/ and /æg/) are also treated separately from the main classes when available. /ul/ and /ol/ are included as reference points for the back vowels in the contemporary data. For the archival data, both of these pre-/l/ vowel classes are excluded, as tokens were quite limited.

YOUNGER CONTEMPORARY SPEAKERS. The younger speakers in our data, born between 1988 and 1993, show patterns similar to the speakers in the Portland metropolitan area examined by Becker et al. (2016 [this volume]), including characteristics of the CVS. Figure 7.2 presents an aggregate vowel plot for the 12 younger speakers.

The front lax vowels exhibit patterns described in the CVS, such that /ɪ/ is lowered and shares some overlap with /e/. /ɛ/ also exhibits some lowering and backing. Both /u/ and /o/ show degrees of fronting, with /u/ (depicted as /Tu/ and /Ku/), as expected, more advanced than /o/. Visual inspection of the plot indicates that coronal tokens are more advanced than noncoronals,

FIGURE 7.2
Lobanov Normalized Aggregate Vowel Space for Younger Speakers

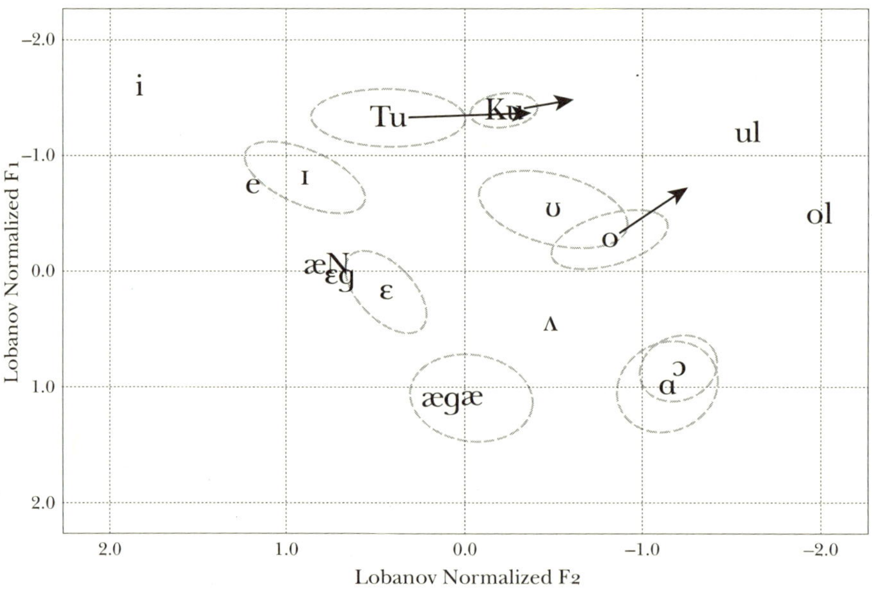

although noncoronals are still quite advanced in these data. We find that /o/ is fronted and falls in line with the description of West Coast Englishes in the CVS (Labov, Ash, and Boberg 2006; Eckert 2008). All of these speakers show a fronting and lowering of /ʊ/ where the vowel is moving toward /ʌ/ as described by the CVS. In fact, the figure shows that the distributions of /ʊ/ and /o/ overlap for these speakers.

With respect to the low back merger, we can see that there is almost complete overlap of F1 and F2 for /ɑ/ and /ɔ/. This is in line with Labov, Ash, and Boberg's (2006) description of the low back merger being widespread in the Western United States; more specifically, we see /ɑ/ and /ɔ/ overlapping in spectral space, similar to previous descriptions of the CVS (Eckert 2008; for more about relative positioning in the Western English low back vowels, see D'Onofrio et al. 2016 [this volume]). Another feature of the CVS relevant to this discussion is the behavior of /æ/, which raises and fronts before nasals, while lowering and backing in other contexts (Eckert 2008). The data here align with what we would expect to see from prior descriptions of West Coast Englishes (Labov, Ash, and Boberg 2006; Eckert 2008) and match up well with what Becker et al. (2016 [this volume]) found in the Portland area. These younger speakers exhibit no /æg/ raising and little-to-no /ɛg/ raising, features that have been found for speakers in the Seattle area (Wassink 2015). Similarly, Becker et al. (2016 [this volume]) found little evidence for /æg/ raising for the younger speakers in their data.

OLDER CONTEMPORARY SPEAKERS. Turning to the older speakers in the contemporary data (born between 1955–77), we see some interesting trends with respect to the patterns described above for the younger speakers. An aggregate vowel plot for these speakers is shown in figure 7.3. First, it is clear that there is similarity between the older and younger contemporary speakers. Both /u/ and /o/ are fronted in these speakers as well, such that /o/ occupies a similar space in the older speakers as it does in the younger speakers. Similarly to the younger speakers, /ʊ/ is fronted and lowered toward /ʌ/, showing overlap with /o/. As with the younger speakers, /u/ is fronted, with the same pattern of postcoronal tokens being more fronted than noncoronals. However, noncoronals show a wider range of variation for the older contemporary speakers than they did for the younger speakers, indicating that some of the older speakers are as front as the younger speakers, while some remain relatively backed. The spread of the data could be, to some degree, a function of simply having fewer tokens for /Ku/ and fewer speakers for the older cohort. Further, similar to the younger speakers, the older speakers also show participation in the low back merger, indicating stability across these two generations.

FIGURE 7.3
Lobanov Normalized Aggregate Vowel Space for Older Speakers

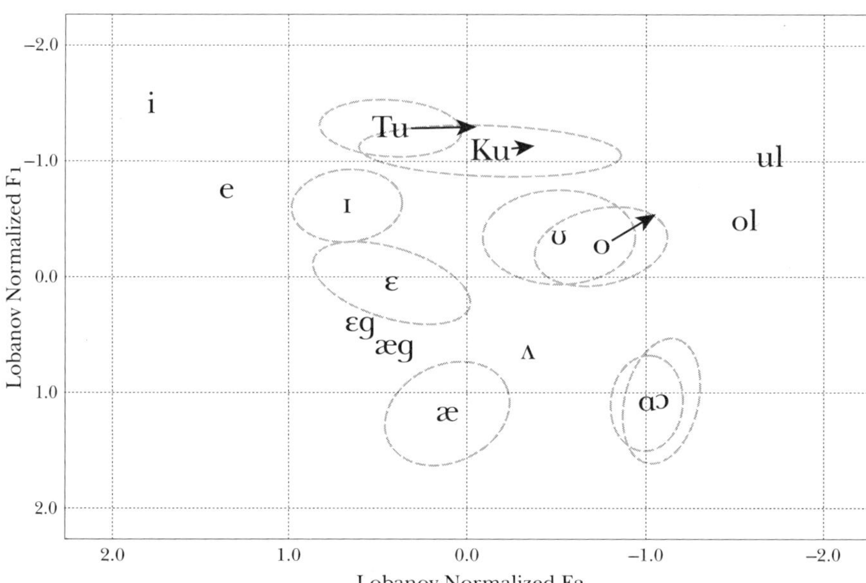

Despite the similarities between these two generations, there are also some noticeable differences. For /æ/, the older speakers' pattern is different from that of the younger speakers. Although there appears to be /æ/ backing for both generations of contemporary speakers, we also see /æ/ fronting and raising before /g/ for these older speakers, which is not evident in our data for the younger speakers. This suggests that /æg/-raising is receding for younger speakers in Oregon, which follows the trends found in both Portland (Becker et al. 2016 [this volume]) and Seattle (Freeman 2014b; Wassink 2015). We cannot say anything about the nasal split with regard to this vowel class, as we did not have enough tokens for these older speakers to examine it fully. Another difference is some /ɪ/ and /ɛ/ retraction among the older speakers, but /ɛ/ does not appear as low as it does for the younger speakers. Finally, there appears to be a shorter glide for /Tu/ in the older speaker data than was seen for the younger speakers, which could be indicative of a current change in progress for Oregonian English.

ARCHIVAL SPEAKERS. We now continue our look backward by turning to the Oregonians born between 1893–1914. Figure 7.4 displays an aggregate vowel space for these speakers, in which we can see vowel configurations that are both similar to and different from those for the contemporary speakers. For /u/ we can make a couple of observations. First, postcoronals

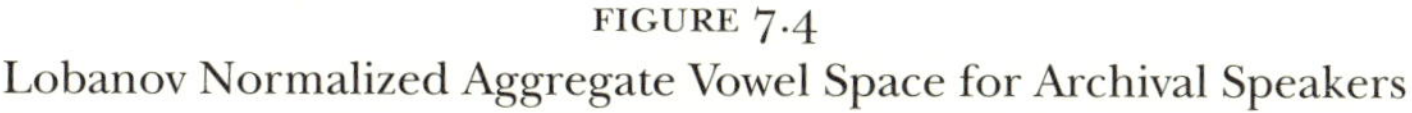

FIGURE 7.4
Lobanov Normalized Aggregate Vowel Space for Archival Speakers

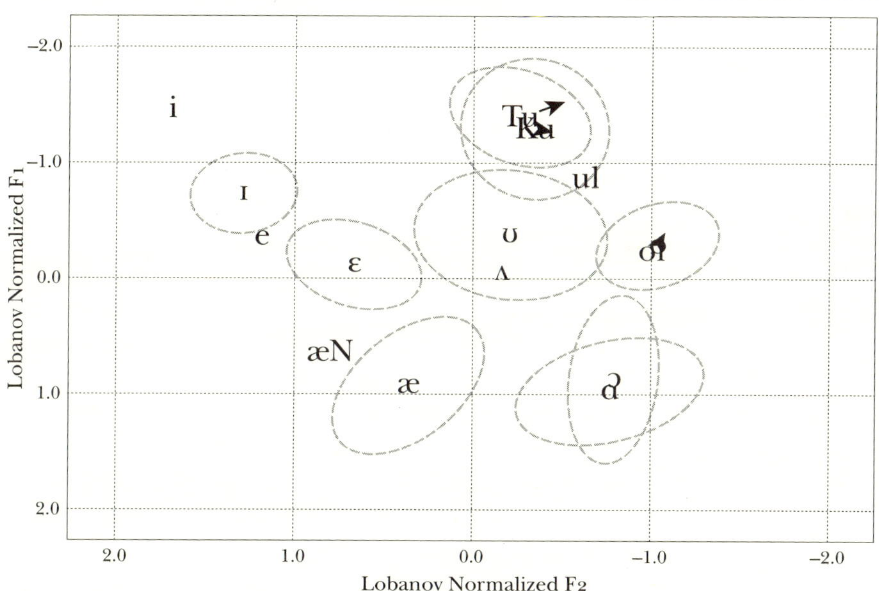

and noncoronals occur in the same space, which we did not see in the contemporary data (where coronals were more advanced than noncoronals). Further, we also see that the /u/ vowel class remains relatively backed. /o/ is also realized in a more backed location. With respect to /ʊ/, we see lowering in these data, with /ʊ/ appearing in front of /o/ but without any overlap in nucleus position between these two classes, in contrast to what we saw for both sets of contemporary speakers. We can also see that, although /ɪ/ appears to be in roughly the same location as it is for the contemporary speakers, /ɛ/ does not appear as low or far back in the vowel space as it is for the contemporary speaker data.

These speakers also show overlap in F1 and F2 for /ɑ/ and /ɔ/, indicating the low back merger was present in the speech of Oregonians at this point in time. The classes distribute slightly differently than they did for the contemporary speakers, but this could be due to noisier data available for this group. We can see that /æ/ is not retracted for the archival speakers as it is for the two contemporary groups. There is some evidence of the nasal split for these speakers, but it appears to be nascent in comparison to the widely split system evidenced by the younger contemporary speakers. Overall, these data from the archival speakers suggest that /æ/-backing was not very advanced at this point in time. While this is necessarily speculative, the slight nasal split could be an immediate precursor to /æ/-backing.

ANALYSIS AND DISCUSSION

These data help us to better understand the development of the current vowel system in English in the Pacific Northwest in general and Oregon in particular. First, we see that, by and large, both generations of contemporary speakers exhibit the Western English patterns described by Labov, Ash, and Boberg (2006). Additionally, the younger contemporary speakers in these data participate almost categorically in the features described as the California Vowel Shift, especially the general retraction of the front lax vowels. For the older contemporary speakers, we see a good bit of the CVS (fronting of the back vowels, /æ/-backing and lowering, the low back merger), but we also see /æg/-raising. As mentioned earlier, this is a feature primarily reported for the Portland and Seattle metropolitan areas among older speakers. In terms of geography, Oregon is situated between Northern California and Washington, so it is reasonable to assume that Oregon would share vocalic features with both of these areas (Becker et al. 2014, 2016 [this volume]). What is of particular interest here is the relationship these contemporary speakers have to the archival speakers. In the archival data, we see almost no evidence of the CVS. Those speakers participate in the low back merger, but realize /u/ and /o/ in fairly back positions and do not show retracted /æ/ or retraction for the other front lax vowels. There is quite a bit of variation in the data for the archival speakers, and we readily admit this could be due to the noisier nature of the archival recordings (both audio quality and the more conversational nature of those recordings) in comparison to the modern recordings. However, taken all together, the contrasts between the archival and contemporary speakers yield insight into the development of speech patterns in the region.

Ultimately, we see some change over time in some vowel categories, but not in others. Archival speaker vowel configurations appear to predate many of the features described for English in the West and the CVS (e.g., front lax vowel retraction), with the primary exception of the low back merger. This suggests that major components of the modern CVS system likely developed in Oregon in speakers born in the early twentieth century, the period between our archival group (born before 1914) and the older contemporary speakers (born after 1955). With such a gap in time in these data, the timing of the instantiation of this system cannot be pinned down further. This finding is in line with other recent work examining the development of the Western dialect region (Fridland and Kendall, forthcoming). At the same time, we also see evidence of some changes still in progress, where the youngest speakers show different patterns than the older and archival speakers.

To further track the time-course of these changes, we generated a series of quantitative measures for each speaker for the vowel classes of interest based on the aggregate vowel plots (all data continue to be assessed in terms of normalized values). These measures include the Euclidean distance between F1 and F2 nuclei positions for /i/ and /ɪ/, /e/ and /ɛ/, /o/ and /ʊ/, and /ʌ/ and /ʊ/ (see Kendall and Fridland 2012, 295, for more on the use of Euclidean distance in this way) and the F2 positions of /o/ and coronal and noncoronal /u/ nuclei (/Tu/ and /Ku/). Additionally, we also looked at the Euclidean distance between /Tu/ and /Ku/, as well as glide lengths and targets for both of these subclasses. Lastly, we also examined /æ/ F1 and F2 and /ɑ/-/ɔ/ Pillai, a measure of distributional overlap useful for characterizing the degree of merger between two vowel categories (see Hay, Warren, and Drager 2006; Nycz and Hall-Lew 2014). We then ran a series of ANOVA tests to assess differences between the groups. In table 7.2, we present the output of these statistical comparisons. We include both the F-value and *p*-value for each ANOVA, as well as *p*-values from Tukey HSD post-hoc tests for ANOVAs that obtain significance. We use a *p*-value level <.05 as a cutoff for Tukey post hoc testing. Since we are running multiple ANOVA tests, we could be stricter by using a Bonferroni corrected, lower *p*-value, but our main focus is uncovering trends over time and not making strict claims about statistical significance, so we proceed with a less strict measure of significance.

TABLE 7.2
Results from ANOVA and Tukey's HSD Tests

Measures	*F-Value*	*p-Value*	*Older-Archival*	*Younger-Archival*	*Younger-Older*
/i/ and /ɪ/ ED	3.930	.054	—	—	—
/e/ and /ɛ/ ED	5.448	.013*	*p* = .022*	*p* = .018*	*p* = .950
/æ/ F1	1.328	.288	—	—	—
/æ/ F2	6.214	.008*	*p* = .118	*p* = .006*	*p* = .454
/ʌ/ and /ʊ/ ED	2.388	.117	—	—	—
/o/ F2	2.520	.131	—	—	—
/ɑ/~/ɔ/ Pillai	0.707	.505	—	—	—
/o/ and /ʊ/ ED	3.761	.044*	*p* = .056	*p* = .063	*p* = .909
/Tu/ and /Ku/ ED	0.792	.467	—	—	—
/Tu/ F2	7.971	.003*	*p* = .011*	*p* = .003*	*p* = .986
/Ku/ F2	0.901	.422	—	—	—
/Tu/ F2 glide target	2.420	.132	—	—	—
/Ku/ F2 glide target	0.861	.438	—	—	—
/Tu/ glide length	10.080	.001*	*p* = .560	*p* = .002*	*p* = .016*
/Ku/ glide length	0.071	.931	—	—	—

Table 7.2 shows interesting trends in the data. We utilize Euclidean distance between /i/ and /ɪ/ and between /e/ and /ɛ/ as a measure to quantify the degree of /ɪ/ and /ɛ/ retraction. This measure has been used by Fridland and Kendall (e.g., 2012) as a way to compare across and within U.S. regional dialects. As indicated by the ANOVA and pairwise comparisons, we see no significant differences for the distance between /i/ and /ɪ/, but a significant difference for /e/ and /ɛ/ for both the older-archival comparison and the younger-archival comparison. Figure 7.5 shows this difference between archival and contemporary speakers rather strikingly. In the figure, and those that follow, we depict each group (archival, older contemporary, and younger contemporary) sorted by the relevant metric. The dashed lines indicate the group mean for the metric. Here, we see that /e/ and /ɛ/ are much more proximate for the archival speakers than for the contemporary groups, and we do not see any substantial difference between the younger and older contemporary speakers.

As shown in table 7.2, we do not see significant differences across groups for /æ/ height (F1), but the difference for /æ/ F2 does reach significance, supporting the notion that /æ/ in Oregonian English has retracted over time. This is illustrated in figure 7.6. The significant difference arises in the younger-archival comparison, but not in the younger-older or older-archival comparison. Figure 7.6 shows that although comparisons with the older contemporary group are not significant, the data overall show a meaningful trend where the older contemporary speakers reflect an inter-

FIGURE 7.5
/e/-/ɛ/ Euclidean Distances

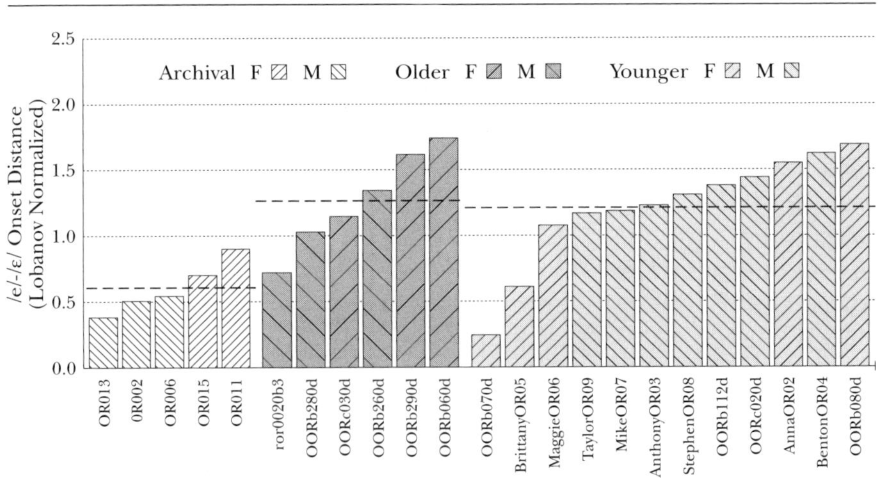

FIGURE 7.6
/æ/ F2

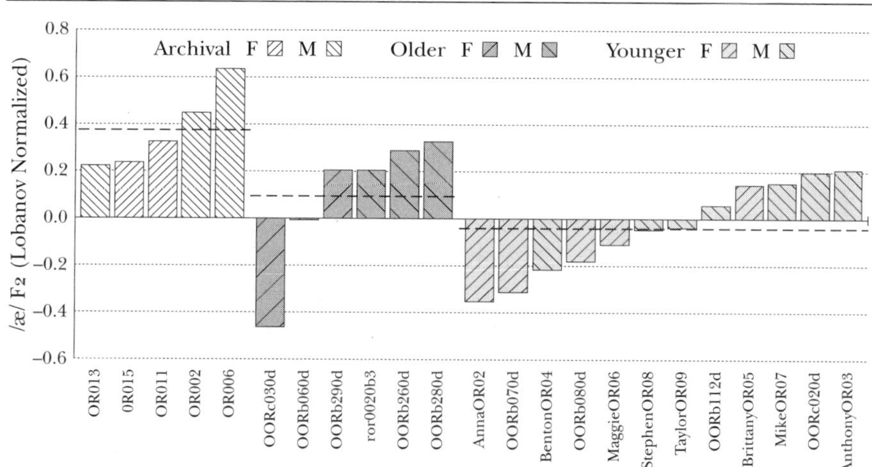

mediate stage between the retracted /æ/ position of the younger speakers and the unretracted position for the archival speakers. We also note that both contemporary groups exhibit a fairly wide range of /æ/ positions, with some speakers being quite retracted while others show /æ/ positions similar to the values for some archival speakers.

Statistical tests on the back vowels yield several outcomes. In table 7.2, we see significant patterns for /o/ and /ʊ/ Euclidean distance, /Tu/ glide length, /Tu/ F2 nucleus, but not for the /Tu/ and /Ku/ Euclidean distance, /Ku/ glide length, /Tu/ and /Ku/ glide targets, or /o/ F2 nucleus. Visual inspection of the vowel plots suggests that the nuclei of /o/ and /ʊ/ do not overlap for the archival data, but do for the contemporary speakers. This suggestion of change over time is supported by the ANOVA ($p < .05$) although the Tukey post-hoc tests indicate the comparisons between groups are not quite significantly different. Figure 7.7 shows the patterns of /o/ and /ʊ/ Euclidean distance. Despite the ambiguous statistics, the figure demonstrates a general trend where both sets of contemporary speakers have less distant /o/ and /ʊ/ classes than the archival speakers. One young contemporary speaker (BrittanyOR05) stands out with an exceptional /o/ and /ʊ/ distance, due to an unusually fronted and raised /ʊ/ and relatively backed /o/ (and /u/), according to our data.

/Tu/ F2 nucleus position shows a similar pattern, as illustrated in figure 7.8. Both the older-archival and younger-archival pairwise comparisons show significance, while the older and younger contemporary speakers are not different. Thus, while /æ/ F2 showed some evidence of incremental

FIGURE 7.7
/o/-/ʊ/ Euclidean Distance

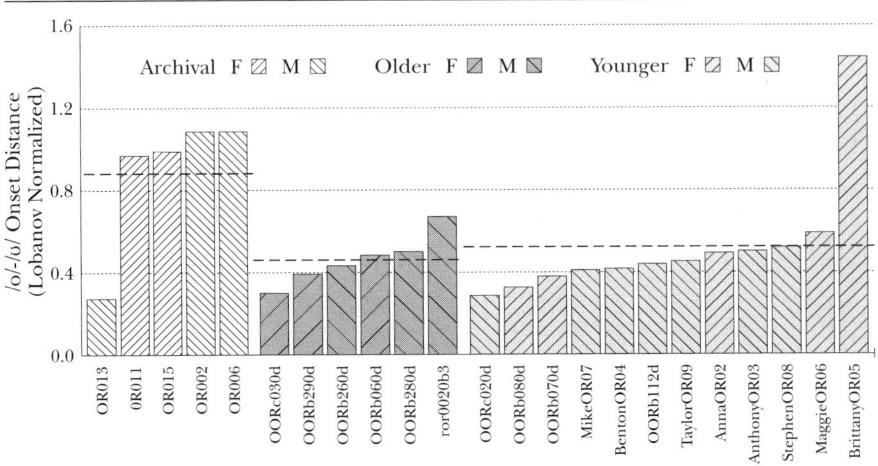

retraction over time, for each of the other comparisons we have examined closely—/e/ and /ɛ/, /o/ and /ʊ/, and /Tu/ F2—the archival speakers are different from the contemporary speakers, but we do not see differences between the two contemporary groups. This supports the observation made earlier that these changes likely began in the generation between the older contemporary speakers and the archival speakers.

FIGURE 7.8
/Tu/ F2

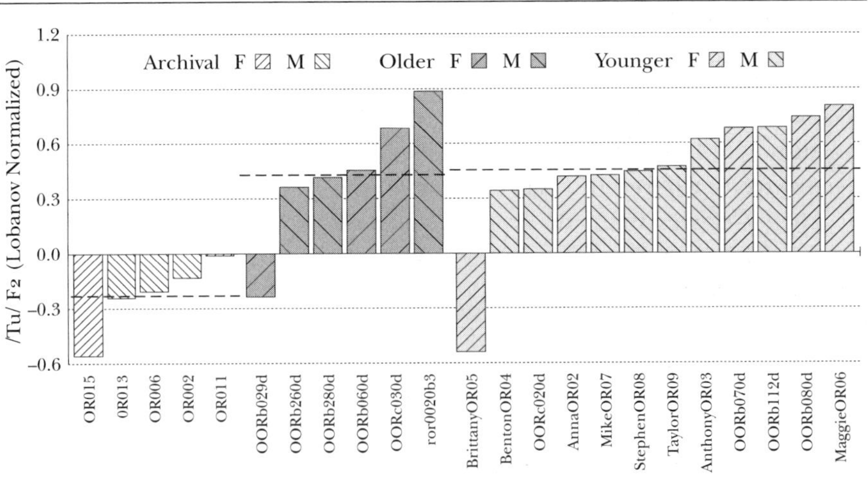

Finally, /Tu/ glide length also shows significant differences in the statistical tests. The primary difference here is in the comparisons between the younger contemporary speakers and each of the older groups. This is shown in figure 7.9. For this metric, we see that there is no significant difference in the older-archival comparison but that there are significant differences between both the younger-archival and younger-older comparisons. Much like with /æ/ F2, /Tu/ glide length appears to follow an incremental change over time, with glides becoming longer over time. Since the younger speakers pattern differently than the older contemporary speakers, we might also posit that this feature remains a current change in progress, although to our knowledge it has not been subject to scrutiny in more general English back vowel fronting studies.

There were several metrics that did not show differences across the three groups' data, but still have implications for this study. /o/ F2, for instance, did not show significant differences. This was somewhat surprising given the evidence that back vowels are fronting over time in other varieties of Oregonian English (Becker et al. 2014, 2016 [this volume]). One possible explanation is due to how noisy the archival data are, both in terms of audio quality and in terms of our relying on conversational tokens more than reading passage or word list elicitations; more speakers and more tokens would allow us to see whether this lack of significant difference is a function of stylistic and data quality differences, or, as the data seem to show, whether there has not in fact been much movement for /o/

FIGURE 7.9
/Tu/ Glide Length

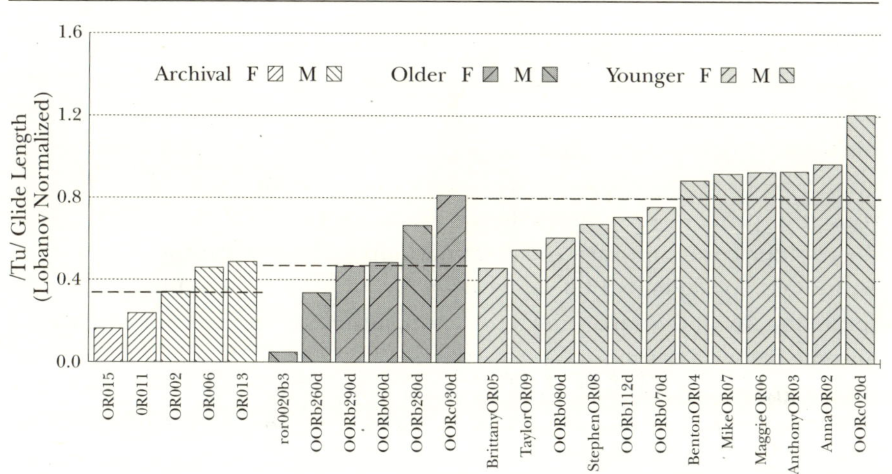

over time for Oregonians. Another set of metrics we examined that did not show any differences over time are for /Ku/. /Tu/ nucleus position (F2 value) does change over time in these data, as well as /Tu/ glide length, but we do not see analogous evidence for /Ku/. We also did not see meaningful differences in the Euclidean distance between the nuclei of /Tu/ and /Ku/, despite an assumption that /Ku/ fronting is generally a later phenomena in English, where /Ku/ targets approach an earlier fronted /Tu/ distribution (e.g., Baranowski 2014). Once again we cannot discount the possibility that this is a function of our data. In our dataset, we have fewer /Ku/ tokens than /Tu/ tokens, especially for the older contemporary speakers as well as the archival speakers. It could be the case that with an increased token count and more speakers we would find significant differences between the generations for these measures. On the other hand, it could also be the case that what we find in Oregon with respect to the relationship between /Tu/ and /Ku/ is different than what, for instance, Baranowski (2014) found for Manchester in the United Kingdom.

Finally, our evidence points to the low back merger being a long-standing feature of Oregonian English, which may predate the archival speakers in these data. We also do not see any meaningful differences in the distance between /i/ and /ɪ/ over time, indicating that /ɪ/ retraction, a feature described as a part of the CVS, may not be a component of Oregonian English. For /æ/, there are significant differences for F2 but not F1, confirming that /æ/ movement has primarily consisted of backing, but not necessarily lowering, over time.

CONCLUSION

The results from our analysis provide important insights into the development of Oregonian English over the course of the late nineteenth and twentieth centuries. For the youngest speakers, we see patterns associated with the California Vowel Shift and no /æg/ raising. As we look backward, we see quite a bit of similarity between the older contemporary speakers and the youngest speakers, save for the length of the glide for /Tu/ and the fact that these older contemporary speakers participate in /æg/ raising. Older contemporary speakers exhibit many aspects of the CVS, including /æ/ and /ɛ/ retraction, /u/ and /o/ fronting, and so on, although they are not as extreme in some respects as the younger speakers. We also note that in both contemporary groups /o/ and /ʊ/ have similar nucleus positions. To our knowledge, this overlapping position of /o/ and /ʊ/ has not been described as part of the

CVS and could perhaps be a vocalic pattern that is unique to Oregon. The archival speakers, born around the turn of the twentieth century, represent a point in time where some of the patterns seen in the contemporary data are not yet in place or appear to be in their inception, with the notable exception of the low back merger, which according to our data may be a long-standing feature of Oregonian English. At the very least, the low back merger is clearly attested in the limited archival speakers available to us at this time. This contrasts with archival recordings for Bay Area Californians and Nevadans examined by Fridland and Kendall (forthcoming), born just a couple of decades before our archival speakers, all of whom show strongly unmerged low back vowel classes.

Perhaps the most important outcome of this investigation is the observation that many relevant changes to the Oregon vowel system must have occurred in speakers born in the time period not represented in our data, the period roughly between the two world wars. In the future, by looking at speakers born in the first half of the twentieth century, we may be able to track the emergence and development of the vocalic patterns seen in present-day Oregon. As discussed above, Oregon has cultural and settlement subregions—in particular differences between eastern and western Oregon—as well as ethnic diversity, all of which have been largely ignored here in our attempt to understand changes over time in the data currently available to us. Future work is needed to add contemporary speakers from more diverse parts of the state and ethnic and cultural groups, as well as to attempt to locate more archival speakers from throughout the state. Despite some limitations in the data examined here, we hope to have shed new light on the state of Oregonian English and its development.

NOTE

We are immensely grateful to the *DARE* project and especially Joan Houston Hall for making the archival tapes available for researchers; without them this project would not have been possible. We would also like to thank Craig Fickle at the University of Oregon for helping with analysis, as well as students in the University of Oregon sociolinguistics course in Winter 2013 and 2014 for help with data collection. Finally, we would like to the thank the National Science Foundation for grants that funded a large portion of the data collection and analysis (BCS-1122950, PI Tyler Kendall, and BCS-1123460, PI Valerie Fridland), as well as a University of Oregon Faculty Research Award for the project Dialect Diversity in Oregon.

REFERENCES

Baranowski, Maciej. 2014. "The Sociolinguistics of Back Vowel Fronting in Manchester English." Paper presented at Methods in Dialectology 15, Groningen, Netherlands, Aug. 11–15.

Becker, Kara, Anna Aden, and Katelyn Best. 2014. "Ideologies of Non-Accent: Linking Perception and Production in Oregon English." Paper presented at the Cascadia Workshop in Sociolinguistics (CWSL), Victoria, B.C., Mar. 1–2.

Becker, Kara, Anna Aden, Katelyn Best, Rena Dimes, Juan Flores, and Haley Jacobson. 2013. "Keep Portland Weird: Vowels in Oregon English." Paper presented at the 42nd annual meeting on New Ways of Analyzing Language Variation (NWAV 42), Pittsburgh, Pa., Oct. 17–20.

Becker, Kara, Anna Aden, Katelyn Best, and Haley Jacobson. 2016. "Variation in West Coast English: The Case of Oregon." In Fridland et al. 2016, 107–34. doi:10.1215/00031283-3772923.

Boersma, Paul, and David Weenink. 2014. Praat: Doing Phonetics by Computer. Version 5.4.04. http://www.praat.org.

Conn, Jeff. 2006. "Dialects in the Mist (Portland, OR)." In *American Voices: How Dialects Differ from Coast to Coast*, edited by Walt Wolfram and Ben Ward, 149–55. Malden, Mass.: Blackwell.

DARE. Dictionary of American Regional English. 1985–2013. Edited by Frederic G. Cassidy and Joan Houston Hall. Cambridge, Mass.: Belknap Press of Harvard University Press.

D'Onofrio, Annette, Penelope Eckert, Robert J. Podesva, Teresa Pratt, and Janneke Van Hofwegen. 2016. "The Low Vowels in California's Central Valley." In Fridland et al. 2016, 11–32. doi:10.1215/00031283-3772879.

Eckert, Penelope. 2008. "Where Do Ethnolects Stop?" *International Journal of Bilingualism* 12.1–2: 25–42. doi:10.1177/13670069080120010301.

Freeman, Valerie. 2014a. "Bag, Beg, Bagel: Prevelar Raising and Merger in Pacific Northwest English." University of Washington Working Papers in Linguistics, 32. http://depts.washington.edu/uwwpl/vol32/freeman_2014.pdf.

———. 2014b. "Social Differentiation of *bag*-Raising in Seattle Caucasians." Paper presented at the Cascadia Workshop in Sociolinguistics (CWSL), Victoria, B.C., Mar. 1–2.

Fridland, Valerie, and Tyler Kendall. 2012. "Exploring the Relationship between Production and Perception in the Mid Front Vowels of U.S. English." *Lingua* 122.7: 779–93. doi:10.1016/j.lingua.2011.12.007.

———. Forthcoming. "English in the Western United States." In Hickey, forthcoming.

Fridland, Valerie, Tyler Kendall, Betsy Evans, and Alicia Beckford Wassink, eds. 2016. *Speech of the Western States.* Vol. 1, *The Coastal States.* Publication of the American Dialect Society 101. Durham, N.C.: Duke University Press.

Hay, Jennifer, Paul Warren, and Katie Drager. 2006. "Factors Influencing Speech Perception in the Context of a Merger-in-Progress." *Journal of Phonetics* 34: 458–84.

Hickey, Raymond, ed. Forthcoming. *Listening to the Past: Audio Records of Accents of English.* Cambridge: Cambridge University Press.

Hinton, Leanne, Birch Moonwomon, Sue Bremner, Herb Luthin, Mary Van Clay, Jean Lerner, and Hazel Corcoran. 1987. "It's Not Just the Valley Girls: A Study of California English." In *Berkeley Linguistics Society: Proceedings of the Thirteenth Annual Meeting, February 14–16, 1987*, edited by Jon Aske, Natasha Beery, Laura Michaelis, and Hana Filip, 117–28. Berkeley, Calif.: Berkeley Linguistics Society. doi:10.3765/bls.v13i0.1811.

Kendall, Tyler. 2007. "Enhancing Sociolinguistic Data Collections: The North Carolina Sociolinguistic Archive and Analysis Project." In "Selected Papers from NWAV 35," edited by Toni Cook and Keelan Evanini. *University of Pennsylvania Working Papers in Linguistics* 13.2: 15–26. http://repository.upenn.edu/pwpl/vol13/iss2/2.

———. 2013. *Speech Rate, Pause, and Sociolinguistic Variation: Studies in Corpus Sociophonetics.* Houndmills, U.K.: Palgrave Macmillan.

Kendall, Tyler, and Valerie Fridland. 2012. "Variation in Perception and Production of Mid Front Vowels in the U.S. Southern Vowel Shift." *Journal of Phonetics* 40.2: 289–306. doi:10.1016/j.wocn.2011.12.002.

Kendall, Tyler, and Erik R. Thomas. 2014. Vowels: Vowel Manipulation, Normalization, and Plotting in R. R Package. Version 1.2. http://cran.r-project.org/web/packages/vowels/.

Kerswill, Paul. 2003. "Dialect Levelling and Geographical Diffusion in British English." In *Social Dialectology: In Honour of Peter Trudgill*, edited by David Britain and Jenny Cheshire, 223–43. Amsterdam: Benjamins.

Labov, William, Sharon Ash, and Charles Boberg. 2006. *The Atlas of North American English: Phonetics, Phonology, and Sound Change.* Berlin: Mouton de Gruyter.

Lobanov, Boris M. 1971. "Classification of Russian Vowels Spoken by Different Speakers." *Journal of the Acoustical Society of America* 49.2B: 606–8. doi:10.1121/1.1912396.

Luthin, Herbert. 1987. "The Story of California (ow): The Coming-of-Age of English in California." In *Variation in Language: NWAV-XV at Stanford; Proceedings of the Fifteenth Annual Conference on New Ways of Analyzing Variation*, edited by Keith M. Denning, Sharon Inkelas, Faye C. McNair-Knox, and John R. Rickford, 312–24. Stanford, Calif.: Dept. of Linguistics, Stanford University.

McLarty, Jason, Charlie Farrington, and Tyler Kendall. 2014. "Perhaps We Used To, but We Don't Anymore: The Habitual Past in Oregonian English." In "Selected Papers from NWAV 42," edited by Duna Gylfadottir. *University of Pennsylvania Working Papers in Linguistics* 20.2. http://repository.upenn.edu/pwpl/vol20/iss2/13.

McLarty, Jason, and Tyler Kendall. 2014. "The Relationship between the High and Mid Back Vowels in Oregonian English." Paper presented at the 43rd annual meeting on New Ways of Analyzing Variation (NWAV 43), Chicago, Ill., Oct. 23–26.

Nelson, Katherine. 2011. "A Cross-Generational Acoustic Study of the Front Vowels of Native Oregonians." Paper presented at the 40th annual conference on New Ways of Analyzing Variation (NWAV 40), Washington, D.C., Oct. 27–30.

Nycz, Jennifer, and Lauren Hall-Lew. 2014. "Best Practices in Measuring Vowel Merger." *Proceedings of Meetings on Acoustics* 20. doi:10.1121/1.4894063.

Podesva, Robert J. 2011. "The California Vowel Shift and Gay Identity." *American Speech* 86.1: 32–51. doi:10.1215/00031283-1277501.

R Development Core Team. 2012. *R: A Language and Environment for Statistical Computing.* Vienna: R Foundation for Statistical Computing. http://r-project.org.

Riebold, John. 2009. "Creak in the Rain: Phonation in Oregon English." Master's thesis, York University.

———. 2012. "There Ain't No Stopping Us Now: Spirantization in the Pacific Northwest." Poster presented at the annual meeting of the Linguistic Society of America, Portland, Ore., Jan. 5–8.

Schwantes, Carlos A. 1989. *The Pacific Northwest: An Interpretive History.* Lincoln: University of Nebraska Press.

Trudgill, Peter. 2006. *New Dialect Formation: The Inevitably of Colonial Englishes.* Edinburgh, U.K.: Edinburgh University Press.

U.S. Census Bureau. 2010. "Census Demographic Profiles." Washington, D.C.: Government. Printing Office. http://www.census.gov.

Ward, Michael. 2003. "Portland Dialect Study: The Fronting of /ow, u, uw/ in Portland, Oregon." Master's thesis, Portland State University. http://www.pds.pdx.edu/Publications/Ward.pdf.

Wassink, Alicia Beckford. 2015. "Sociolinguistic Patterns in Seattle English." *Language Variation and Change* 27.1: 31–58. doi:10.1017/S0954394514000234.

———. 2016. "The Vowels of Washington State." In Fridland et al. 2016, 77–106. doi:10.1215/00031283-3772912.

Wassink, Alicia, Robert Squizzero, Mike Scanlon, Rachel Schirra, and Jeffrey Conn. 2009. "Effects of Gender and Style on Fronting and Raising of /æ/, /eː/ and /ɛ/ before /g/ in Seattle English." Paper presented at the 38th annual meeting of New Ways of Analyzing Variation (NWAV 38), Ottawa, Oct. 22–25.

Wolfram, Walt, and Natalie Schilling-Estes. 2006. *American English: Dialects and Variation.* 2nd ed. Malden, Mass.: Blackwell.

JASON McLARTY is a Ph.D. student in the Linguistics Department at the University of Oregon. His interests are in sociolinguistics, particularly sociophonetics, with a focus on the historical development of different dialects. His primary research involves suprasegmental features of African American English, as well as vowel variation in Oregonian English. With respect to AAE, he looks at intonational differences over time by comparing modern recordings of Southern American English varieties with archival recordings of ex-slaves and ex-Confederates. Currently, McLarty is working with Tyler Kendall and Charlie Farrington in developing the first public corpus of African American English. E-mail: jmclarty@uoregon.edu.

TYLER KENDALL is an associate professor of linguistics at the University of Oregon. Several of his research projects examine language variation and change in Oregon and elsewhere in the United States. In collaboration with Valerie Fridland, he is engaged in a large-scale project investigating the relationship between vowel production and vowel perception in regional varieties of U.S. English. Much of his wider work focuses on corpora in and computational approaches to sociolinguistics. Along these lines, he is the developer of several sociolinguistic software projects, including the Sociolinguistic Archive and Analysis Project (SLAAP) and the Vowels.R package for the R programming language. He is author of the book *Speech Rate, Pause, and Sociolinguistic Variation: Studies in Corpus Sociophonetics* (Palgrave Macmillan, 2013). E-mail: tsk@uoregon.edu.

CHARLIE FARRINGTON is a graduate student in the Department of Linguistics at the University of Oregon. He conducts research on language variation and change, African American English, and vowel variation in American English. The primary focus of his research utilizes a landmark longitudinal study of African American English at the Frank Porter Graham Institute in Chapel Hill, North Carolina, which he helped in archiving and making accessible to researchers with varied interests. Within this corpus, he has looked at word-final neutralization of word final obstruents, and in collaboration with Mary Kohn, analyzed vowel trajectories over the lifespan as they relate to numerous social factors. He is currently working on the development of the first public corpus of African American English with Tyler Kendall and Jason McLarty. E-mail: crf@uoregon.edu.

8. THE COASTAL WEST AND BEYOND: LOOKING FORWARD

THE JOURNEY TO THIS COLLECTION began with the goal of supplementing the dearth of descriptive work on the Western U.S. vowel system. We also hoped to highlight some of the spaces and groups left unexplored by the research conducted in the region in an effort to paint a more detailed picture of the contemporary linguistic landscape and to point toward directions needing further study. The West is a vast region, and there is much more still to do. The research presented here has at least started to fill in some of these gaps in our understanding of what the Coastal states of the continental Western United States sound like and how they fit into the larger picture of U.S. dialect diversity.

With regard to shedding greater light on the nature of Western vowel variation, the chapters presented here certainly do suggest there are some features of Western English shared by speakers in California, Washington, and Oregon. Features such as the low back merger and prevelar raising are often described in the collection, though the degree of participation (and instantiation phonetically) varies by location in ways that suggest a sense of place is not simply delimited by state or regional affiliation. However, we also find differences, involving both nonparticipation in features occurring in other Coastal states, such as /æ/ retraction and /o/ fronting that are occurring in California but not in Washington State, and in terms of how features are realized within different speaker sets, such as the contrast in how the low back merger is achieved in inland California communities. In other words, not surprisingly, the research in this collection complicates our previous understanding of the Western vowel system by adding a breadth of description and comparison of features not previously available. While we do find a number of what were earlier envisioned as localized features shared across several diverse sites, only the low back vowel merger could rightfully be called a fully instantiated Western speech feature in terms of characterizing the speech in all three of the states studied here.

All the chapters indeed report evidence of the low back vowel (/ɑ/-/ɔ/) merger in each group studied. However, the chapters indicate that the merger is not acoustically uniform—the process precipitating merger and the position of the merged vowel varies across communities. For example,

Publication of the American Dialect Society 101 DOI 10.1215/00031283-3772945

D'Onofrio et al. (2016 [this volume]) indicate that the low back vowel merger, present in all three inland California communities studied, is achieved primarily by /ɑ/ raising toward /ɔ/ in phonetic space. In contrast, previous work (Eckert 2010; Hall-Lew 2013) finds /ɔ/ lowering rather than /ɑ/ raising in coastal California, and Wassink (2016 [this volume]) notes a fronter/lower merged position in Seattle. D'Onofrio et al. also find that the three inland communities they studied, though similar to larger coastal California norms, vary in the degree to which they participate, with Merced, the community nearest San Francisco, participating the least.

Echoing the variability in the inland California communities, a present but somewhat less consistent pattern of low back vowel merger exists in Oregon. McLarty, Kendall, and Farrington (2016 [this volume]) report that results from their sample of contemporary speakers, and to some degree even their archival speakers, suggest the /ɑ/-/ɔ/ merger that characterizes the speech of their Oregonians is one where /ɔ/ appears to move toward /ɑ/ to achieve the merger. On the other hand, Becker et al.'s (2016 [this volume]) work suggests that some Portlanders do not participate in the merger, though it is prevalent in their sample as well. In Washington State, Wassink (2016 [this volume]) also confirms the presence of the merger in her Seattle speakers, both in older and younger age groups, and finds the merged vowel fronting in apparent time. So, while the research reported here overall supports the claim of convergence toward a merged low back system in younger speakers across the Coastal West, how these features are implemented is, it seems, informed by a local sense of social and geographic space that resists clean regional demarcation. In general, though, the low back vowel merger was by far the most unified feature across the dialect subregions examined here, though we still find, echoing Labov, Ash, and Boberg (2006), heterogeneity within this homogeneity.

Perhaps the finding of shared participation in the low back merger is not surprising, given that the feature has previously been described as widely occurring and expanding throughout a number of speech regions (e.g., Labov, Ash, and Boberg 2006). A less expected development, however, are features previously described as belonging to California that are also evidenced elsewhere in the Coastal West, though not as uniformly. Short front vowel retraction (often referred to as a feature of the California Vowel Shift) was attested to different degrees in both the California and Oregon speaker samples. Both Oregon and inland California communities showed less retraction than urban California communities, as discussed in chapters by Cardoso et al. (2016 [this volume]) and D'Onofrio et al. (2016 [this volume]), but even among Becker et al.'s (2016 [this volume]) Oregonian speakers, backing and/or lowering was present and, at least for

/æ/ and /ɛ/, was shown to be increasing among younger speakers. Likewise, where gender differences emerge, it is mostly female speakers in the lead, often a hallmark of change in progress (Labov 2001). In contrast, McLarty et al.'s (2016 [this volume]) archival data for Oregon suggest little in the way of short vowel retraction—a hint, perhaps, that we are observing an early move toward a potential new norm. Washington State remains an outlier to a pattern of short front vowel retraction, with Wassink (2016 [this volume]) reporting no evidence of retraction or lowering in her speaker groups. Thus, this new California norm may be expanding beyond its borders, but it is not yet entirely clear how far beyond California it can or will be found.

The higher concentration of these features found in urban California speech also supports an earlier California origin to these features and an order of advancement led by /æ/. The less consistent presence in Oregon and the lack of evidence in Washington and archival Oregon data indicate that short vowel retraction is spreading from a California focal point outward. Preliminary evidence (Fridland, Kendall, and Fickle 2015) also suggests short front vowel retraction exists among young Nevadans, suggesting that these vowel features are diffusing first to states bordering California and may well be present much farther from California than previously suspected, something to be addressed further in our forthcoming volume 2, *The Inland West.*

While we need more work with archival data to firmly establish short front /æ/ retraction as an incoming new norm for the West Coast, the young females' lead in contemporary data and the lack of retraction in archival work by McLarty et al. (2016 [this volume])—as well as work in Nevada by Fridland and Kendall (forthcoming)—suggest that short front vowels are engaged in a shift process that began (judging from early reports by Hinton et al. 1987) only in the latter part of the last century and likely in California. However, since these features appear to be present in several Western U.S. states, they can no longer be defined by state boundaries.

Though on the rise, short front vowel retraction still cannot be called a singular new norm for the Coastal West, as several chapters also note some differences in instantiation. For example, though their younger speakers showed some evidence of /ɛ/ retraction, McLarty et al. (2016 [this volume]) showed no evidence of /ɪ/ retraction such as that found in California. As mentioned previously, Wassink (2016 [this volume]) found that speakers in Washington State do not participate at all in front lax retraction in either /æ/ or /ɛ/, suggesting either that these features have not yet spread beyond California and Oregon or that they are simply not features that index being a Washingtonian.

We can well imagine that, at some level, these features are serving a sociolinguistic function, but little work has been done on how Western vowel features are perceived by the speakers that use them. Villarreal (2016 [this volume]) and Becker et al. (2016 [this volume]), however, begin to fill in that gap in their perceptual dialectological studies of how these features are identified by speakers. In Villarreal's chapter, we see that these features do seem to matter to what it means, for example, to be a Californian. Sentences that differ only by vowel F1/F2 in line with the vowel norms described in earlier chapters affect how speakers are regionally identified as in- or out-group members and also how they are rated on personal attributes. On the other hand, as Becker et al. discovered, identifying California on map tasks did not really affect Oregon speaker participation in California vowel features, while believing in an "ideology of nonaccent" did. In their study, speakers who felt Oregon/Western speech was "accentless" were less likely to have California vowel features and more likely to use Pacific Northwest vowel features. So, while these chapters have only begun to tease out the complex relationship between identity and vowel position, it is clear that these vowel features do mean something to the speakers that use and hear them.

Washington State is, it seems, the least similar state in terms of its vowel system, with no apparent short front /æ/ retraction or /o/ fronting, features that were found, at least to some degree, in the other sites studied here. However, a recently noted feature of Washington State English, the raising of short lax vowels preceding voiced velars, appears to be more geographically distributed than anticipated, with all chapters reporting some (often fledgling) evidence of raising, particularly for the /æg/ BAG context. However, it would be premature to suggest this prevelar raising is necessarily the diffusion of a shared feature across these Western states. What we find instead reported here is that there is, for a number of Western speakers, conditioned behavior of /æg/ BAG and /ɛg/ BEG tokens, but that its form is variable by place and social group.

For example, Wassink (2016 [this volume]) finds that BEG and BAG raising is widespread, particularly among Caucasian speakers, and is found among all age groups, with BEG and BAG tokens overlapping the /e/ class. Like Wassink, Becker et al. (2016 [this volume]) found prevelar conditioning of BEG and BAG in mainly their older speakers from Portland, with both vowels higher and fronter before /g/ than before other nonvoiced velar oral contexts. Likewise, McLarty et al. (2016 [this volume]) only found evidence of prevelar raising in their older, but not younger, contemporary sample. So, while prevelar raising is attested, it appears to be receding in the Oregon population. Finally, Cardoso et al. (2016 [this volume]) report that

BEG is mainly fronted (not raised) and BAG is mainly raised (not fronted) in their San Francisco sample, with raising before nasal tokens much more pronounced than for velar tokens. Women in San Francisco are the most advanced in BAG raising, with an interaction between year of birth and gender that suggests young males moving in the direction of this female-led feature. Though not expressly part of the vowel features they examined, D'Onofrio et al. (2016 [this volume]) note that Redding, the community closest geographically and culturally to Oregon, shows some evidence of prevelar raising. In other words, these results may suggest prevelar raising, at least for BAG, is emerging in California. However, the phonetic targets for these prevelar tokens, at least in San Francisco, appear to differ from those in Washington State, suggesting that as the raising is found more widely, we might expect to find differences in how it is realized such that the differences distinguish various local vowel systems. Speakers in Oregon, situated in the middle of these varied dialect influences, appear to be incorporating some vowel features of California and some of Washington, though it may be that the California features are winning out among younger speakers.

In addition to illuminating similarities and differences among Western states, we also hoped to begin to address another much understudied area in vowel variation both in and beyond the West—that of minority group participation. Chapters here begin to add to that conversation by examining how widespread across speaker groups the features of California, Oregon, and Washington English are. Though only two chapters in the current volume take up this discussion, their findings are important points of departure for further study and provide some initial sense of what kind of identity work vowel features might be doing. Wassink (2016 [this volume]) examined four different minority speaker groups in Washington: African Americans, Japanese Americans, Mexican American, and the Yakima. She also compared her Caucasian Seattle speakers to a more rurally based eastern Washington Caucasian sample. Interestingly, her findings showed no statistically significant differences among the speaker groups in terms of participation in the low back merger, prevelar raising, or /u/ fronting. In other words, nonwhite ethnic groups (as well as her more rural speakers) share a similar system to her Seattle Caucasians. However, though not strongly differentiated, a close look at her descriptive data shows that ethnic group participation is a bit more multifaceted: while Japanese Americans showed the least distinction from the Seattle Caucasian speakers, both the Yakima and the African American speakers are less advanced in prevelar raising and show little back vowel fronting compared to the Caucasian group. The overall lack of strong contrast in the vowel system of white and nonwhite groups is echoed in Cardoso et al.'s (2016 [this volume]) work in

San Francisco, where they studied Chinese Americans alongside their Caucasian sample. Again, while their Chinese American participants showed the same pattern of short front vowel retraction as their Caucasians, they tended to show less advancement. It seems, based on these findings, that the vowel features we find in our featured states are panethnic features, though the pattern of advancement suggests a predominately Caucasian origin. Such findings suggest these features are doing place-based identity work that attracts these speakers in ways that may not draw on ethnicity.

In surveying the research presented here, we come away with a sense of a region still in the process of dialect formation—a process that is creating both similarity (e.g., the low back vowel merger) and difference (e.g., prevelar raising) within the region—but it also seems clear that the West, at least along the coast, is not a unitary dialect region as often reported, but one characterized by features that have arisen only within the last 50–100 years, features that have already begun to display the local character of the people that live within its boundaries. We are struck by the evidence of ethnic and rural participation in many of the features found here, and the recurring young and predominately female lead found in many of the communities studied. Such evidence suggests that these features will likely continue to characterize the speech of the Coast, and perhaps even the larger West. Volume 2, looking at vowels in the Inland West, will speak more to this question of how extensively the features noted here are found beyond the Coast. Regardless of what we uncover as we move forward, it is clear that speech in the West is dynamic and changing, and there will be plenty to keep dialectologists busy in the coming years.

REFERENCES

Becker, Kara, Anna Aden, Katelyn Best, and Haley Jacobson. 2016. "Variation in West Coast English: The Case of Oregon." In Fridland et al. 2016, 107–34. doi:10.1215/00031283-3772923.

Cardoso, Amanda, Lauren Hall-Lew, Yova Kementchedjhieva, and Ruaridh Purse. 2016. "Between California and the Pacific Northwest: The Front Lax Vowels in San Francisco English." In Fridland et al. 2016, 33–54. doi:10.1215/00031283-3772890.

D'Onofrio, Annette, Penelope Eckert, Robert J. Podesva, Teresa Pratt, and Janneke Van Hofwegen. 2016. "The Low Vowels in California's Central Valley." In Fridland et al. 2016, 11–32. doi:10.1215/00031283-3772879.

Eckert, Penelope. 2010. "Affect, Sound Symbolism, and Variation." In "Selected Papers from NWAV 37," edited by Kyle Gorman and Laurel MacKenzie. *Univer-*

sity of Pennsylvania Working Papers in Linguistics 15.2: 70–80. http://repository.upenn.edu/pwpl/vol15/iss2/9/.

Fridland, Valerie, Tyler Kendall, and Craig Fickle. 2015. "It's Nev-ae-da, Not Nev-ah-da!" Paper presented at the annual meeting of the American Dialect Society, Portland, Ore., Jan. 8–11.

Fridland, Valerie, and Tyler Kendall. Forthcoming. "English in the Western United States." In *Listening to the Past: Audio Records of Accents of English*, edited by Raymond Hickey. Cambridge: Cambridge University Press.

Fridland, Valerie, Tyler Kendall, Betsy Evans, and Alicia Beckford Wassink, eds. 2016. *Speech of the Western States.* Vol. 1, *The Coastal States.* Publication of the American Dialect Society 101. Durham, N.C.: Duke University Press.

Hall-Lew, Lauren. 2013. "'Flip-Flop' and Mergers-in-Progress." *English Language and Linguistics* 17.2: 359–90. doi:10.1017/S1360674313000063.

Hinton, Leanne, Birch Moonwomon, Sue Bremner, Herb Luthin, Mary Van Clay, Jean Lerner, and Hazel Corcoran. 1987. "It's Not Just the Valley Girls: A Study of California English." In *Berkeley Linguistics Society: Proceedings of the Thirteenth Annual Meeting, February 14–16, 1987*, edited by Jon Aske, Natasha Beery, Laura Michaelis, and Hana Filip, 117–28. Berkeley, Calif.: Berkeley Linguistics Society. doi:10.3765/bls.v13i0.1811.

Labov, William. 2001. *Principles of Linguistic Change.* Vol. 2, *Social Factors.* Oxford: Blackwell.

Labov, William, Sharon Ash, and Charles Boberg. 2006. *The Atlas of North American English: Phonetics, Phonology, and Sound Change.* Berlin: Mouton de Gruyter.

McLarty, Jason, Tyler Kendall, and Charlie Farrington. 2016. "Investigating the Development of the Contemporary Oregonian English Vowel System." In Fridland et al. 2016, 135–57. doi:10.1215/00031283-3772934.

Villarreal, Dan. 2016. "'Do I Sound Like a Valley Girl to You?' Perceptual Dialectology and Language Attitudes in California." In Fridland et al. 2016, 55–75. doi:10.1215/00031283-3772901.

Wassink, Alicia Beckford. 2016. "The Vowels of Washington State." In Fridland et al. 2016, 77–106. doi:10.1215/00031283-3772912.

ABOUT THE EDITORS

VALERIE FRIDLAND is a professor of linguistics in the Department of English at the University of Nevada, Reno. As a sociolinguist, her main focus is on varieties of American English. Most of her research investigates variation in vowel production and vowel perception across the Northern, Southern, and Western regions of the United States. This work explores links between social factors and speech processing. Her teaching areas include general linguistics, sociolinguistics, syntax, and language and gender. She also has a video lecture series entitled "Language and Society" released by The Great Courses (http://www.thegreatcourses.com/courses/language-and-society.html). E-mail: fridland@unr.edu.

TYLER KENDALL is an associate professor of linguistics at the University of Oregon. Several of his research projects examine language variation and change in Oregon and elsewhere in the United States. In collaboration with Valerie Fridland, he is engaged in a large-scale project investigating the relationship between vowel production and vowel perception in regional varieties of U.S. English. Much of his wider work focuses on corpora in and computational approaches to sociolinguistics. Along these lines, he is the developer of several sociolinguistic software projects, including the Sociolinguistic Archive and Analysis Project (SLAAP) and the Vowels.R package for the R programming language. He is author of the book *Speech Rate, Pause, and Sociolinguistic Variation: Studies in Corpus Sociophonetics* (Palgrave Macmillan, 2013). E-mail: tsk@uoregon.edu.

BETSY E. EVANS is an associate professor in the Department of Linguistics at the University of Washington. Her research interests focus on the attitudes and perceptions of language variation and the perceptions of spatial distribution of variation in language. She is the coauthor of the fourth edition of *Language, Society and Power: An Introduction* (with Annabelle Mooney; Routledge, 2015). E-mail: evansbe@uw.edu.

ALICIA BECKFORD WASSINK is an associate professor in the Department of Linguistics, University of Washington, and director of the Sociolinguistics Laboratory. She has served as principal investigator of the English in the

Publication of the American Dialect Society 101 DOI 10.1215/00031283-3836087

Pacific Northwest study since 2006. She is a former Howard and Frances Nostrand Endowed Professor of Language and Cultural Competence. Wassink's research interests lie in production and perception of the time-varying features of vowel systems, language ideology, social network modeling, dialect contact, development of sociolinguistic competence in children, and creole linguistics. Her work has appeared in books on *Language and Identity* (Edinburgh University Press, 2010), *African-American Women's Language* (Oxford University Press, 2015), *Best Practices in Sociophonetics* (Routledge, 2010), and *Language in the Schools* (Elsevier, 2005). Primary reports of her research have appeared in *Journal of the Acoustical Society of America*, *Journal of Phonetics*, *Language in Society*, *Language Variation and Change*, *Journal of English Linguistics*, and the *International Journal of Speech-Language Pathology*. E-mail: wassink@u.washington.edu.

INDEX

Publication of the American Dialect Society 101 DOI 10.1215/00031283-3772956